W9-DBD-013

Shakespeare at the Maddermarket
Nugent Monck and the Norwich Players

Theater and Dramatic Studies, No. 41

Oscar G. Brockett, Series Editor

Leslie Waggener Professor of Fine Arts
and Professor of Drama
The University of Texas at Austin

Other Titles in This Series

Shakespeare at the Maddermarket
Nugent Monck and the Norwich Players

by
Franklin J. Hildy

U·M·I Research Press

Ann Arbor, Michigan

Produced and distributed by
UMI Research Press
an imprint of
University Microfilms, Inc.
Ann Arbor, Michigan 48106

Library of Congress Cataloging in Publication Data

Hildy, Franklin J. (Franklin Joseph), 1953-
Shakespeare at the Maddermarket.

(Theater and dramatic studies ; no. 41)
Revision of the author's thesis (Ph.D.)—
Northwestern University, 1980.
Bibliography: p.
Includes index.
1. Monck, Walter Nugent Bligh, 1878-1958.
2. Norwich Players (Norfolk) 3. Shakespeare,
William, 1564-1616—Stage history—1800-1950.
4. Theatrical producers and directors—England
Biography. I. Title. II. Series.
PN2598.M593H5 1986   792'.0232'0924   86-16155
ISBN 0-8357-1775-5 (alk. paper)

*To Andrew and Betty Stephenson
and to my parents Clyde and Charlotte Hildy*

Walter Nugent Bligh Monck, C.B.E., F.R.A.M., ca. 1936
(Courtesy of the Maddermarket Theatre Trust, Ltd.)

Contents

Figures

Preface

It is hardly possible to find a book dealing with the British theatre during the first half of this century which does not refer to the important work done by Nugent Monck at his Maddermarket Theatre in Norwich, Norfolk. Yet the most detailed account of Monck's work to be readily available has been a brief, five-page description by Norman Marshall in his book *The Other Theatre*. The brevity of this account, I believe, has not been due to any lack of merit in the subject but rather to a lack of available information.

It is the purpose of this study to provide the most complete account now feasible of the career of W. Nugent Monck, with particular emphasis on his work in Shakespearean production, the area in which he exerted the greatest influence. The approach has been historical, attempting to document Monck's achievements, associations, ideas, and influence through his entire fifty-eight-year career. This seems the most valuable approach for reference by other scholars and it has provided the opportunity of preserving a great deal of information that might otherwise have been lost in the very near future.

The original study for this book was carried out over two years, thirteen months of which were spent in Norwich and London. During that period I was able to discuss Monck and his work with a large number of his former associates and was also able to see a number of plays staged in the Maddermarket Theatre, Monck's great legacy to the city of Norwich. The research went beyond London and Norwich to York, Leeds, Stratford-upon-Avon, Chester and Dublin, but the foundation of the study remains the Nugent Monck Collection now in the Norfolk Record Office of the Central Library, Norwich.

The Nugent Monck Collection is a compilation of four previously scattered collections. The County Local Studies Library in Norwich has held its own collection of articles, playbills, programs and photographs relating to the Maddermarket Theatre. Its most valuable holding, however, was its carefully compiled collection of newscuttings, which was begun in 1921 and has been kept current. The Maddermarket Theatre itself maintained its own archives. Of special interest in this collection were the theatre's balance sheets; minutes books for both the Guild of the Norwich Players and the Maddermarket Theatre Trust, Ltd.; a nearly complete collection of programs, many of which were signed by the original cast members; an incomplete collection of Monck's plays and pageants; and a scattered collection of newscuttings. Monck's literary executor, the late Hilary Gardner, meanwhile held a large mumber of Monck's lecture manuscripts and an additional set of his published plays and pageants. Finally, Jack Hall, Nugent Monck's heir, held all of Monck's personal letters, manuscripts, playscripts, miscellaneous legal documents and the majority of articles Monck had received from the newscutting service to which he subscribed.

During my stay in Norwich I was allowed complete freedom in examining all these materials. In this regard, I would like to thank Mr. Frank Sayer and his staff at the County Local Studies Library in Norwich, especially Mr. W. Beattie. I would also like to thank Miss Sally Brecknell, house manager for the Maddermarket Theatre, whose office routine was disturbed for several months by my research. And I must give special thanks to Mrs. Jack Hall for her trouble in making Monck's papers always available to me. With the permission of Mr. Hall, Mr. Gardner and the Maddermarket Theatre Trust, I was allowed to combine their individual holdings into a single collection. This combined collection was generously donated by them to the County Local Studies Library which transferred the complete collection to the Norfolk Record Office in 1983.

Besides Monck's personal writings, which are listed in the bibliography, the primary sources for this study have been personal interviews and about 3,000 newscuttings which are contained in the County Local Studies Library scrapbooks and in the scrapbooks I compiled from Monck's personal collection of newscuttings. The newscuttings proved to be an invaluable source for verifying and providing exact dates for information I collected during my interviews and discussions with Monck's former associates. By the same token, the oral information I collected often helped to make sense out of otherwise confusing information provided by many articles.

Memories are often deceptive and newspaper and periodical articles vary greatly in quality. A further complication in this study has been that Monck himself was careless with dates, enjoyed making exaggerated statements for the effect they had on his hearers and often embellished the stories he told about his life with fictitious additions to make them more entertaining. These are qualities that have at times been emulated by his followers and by those who have previously written about his work. Little of what was written about Monck and the Maddermarket was ever intended to be scholarly. Much of it makes entertaining reading but is often contradictory, inaccurate or misleading. I have tried as much as possible to allow for these factors in preparing this book. Besides the use of contemporary evidence to verify oral accounts I have tried always to compare the writings of local critics and authors with those of critics and authors from outside the Norwich area. The possibilities for error remain uncomfortably large, however, and I can only hope my lengthy concentrated exposure to the subject has allowed me to make sufficiently knowledgeable judgments on the evidence so that any gross errors have been avoided.

It should be noted that I have used the word "producer" throughout this book as it was used in England during most of Monck's career; that is, as the equivalent of the modern term "director." It should also be noted that for obvious reasons I have not provided page numbers for newspaper articles contained in the scrapbooks of the Monck collection. I have, however, provided page and column designations for those newspaper articles not found in that collection because most such articles are available only on microfilm.

Acknowledgments

Over the course of this study I have become indebted to a large number of people whose generous assistance has gone well beyond what was required by the positions they occupied. The members of my original dissertation committee, the staffs of the various libraries to which my research has taken me, the members of the Guild of the Norwich Players, my students and colleagues at Berry College, and my family are among those who I hope will accept my deepest gratitude without individual recognition.

Of those whose efforts on my behalf cannot be acknowledged with so general an expression of appreciation, first and foremost must come Andrew and Betty Stephenson. Mr. Stephenson has chronicled the activities of the Norwich Players for over 55 years. His generosity in providing me with all his personal manuscripts and numerous interviews and his assistance in proofreading much of my original dissertation were equalled only by the hospitality both he and his wife Betty extended to me during my stay in Norwich. Equally generous with their time and hospitality were Professor and Mrs. J. L. Styan. Though engaged in his own research in London, Professor Styan was unfailingly thorough in his corrections of my original text, most generous in his encouragement and, with his wife Connie, always kind and supportive.

I would like to thank Mr. and Mrs. Jack Hall, the late Mr. Hilary Gardner, Mr. Jimmy Livac, Mr. Roy Dehn, Mr. and Mrs. H. J. Starling, Mr. William Hewett and especially Miss Barbara Wilkes for their time and cooperation in discussing Nugent Monck with me and in making available the materials on Monck's career in their possession. I would like to thank Mr. Michael Holroyd, Mr. Hugh Hunt, Mr. Paul Scofield, Mr. Christopher Fry and Sir John Gielgud for taking time from their own important projects to answer my inquiries. The late Professor William P. Halstead, Miss M. J. Harington and Dr. Gary J. Williams have also taken considerable time to provide me with information for this study, and I am ever grateful for their assistance.

It is also my pleasure to thank Jim Smith and Margaret Vandiver who have been extremely conscientious and thorough in their assistance with the proofreading; Mr. William Brainard who has taken great care in developing the prints and in executing numerous architectual drawings used in my original research; my department head, Dr. Mack Smith, for allowing me time to prepare this book for publication and the administration of Berry College for providing assistance in the preparation of the manuscript.

My deepest appreciation and admiration go to Marylee Vandiver for her extreme patience and care in preparing much of the original study, and to Lucy Bredeson-Smith for her unfailing professionalism and dedication in preparing this manuscript for publication. Her enthusiasm and commitment have helped enormously in pushing this project forward in the most difficult of circumstances.

Most importantly of all I want to thank my wife Elizabeth Vandiver. Her intellectual, practical and emotional contributions to this study have been immeasurable. Her excellence in languages and the liberal arts has done much to set a standard for my own efforts and she has enriched my life in more ways than I can say.

Introduction

On October 15, 1953, the following letter appeared in *The Times*:

Sir,
  Many of your readers may recall that Nugent Monck retired as director of the Norwich
Players and the Maddermarket Theatre, Norwich, at the end of 1952.... The work of the
Norwich Players at the Maddermarket Theatre is of international repute, it has done much
to spread the ideas of William Poel, and it has had a notable influence on modern methods
of Shakespearian production in the professional theatre. *The Times,* in a leading article on
Dec. 9 last year, referred to it as "one of the most remarkable theatrical experiments of our
time." The fate of the Maddermarket is not just a matter of local concern, and it is because
of this theatre's international fame and continuing influence that we appeal to lovers of the
theatre everywhere to assist the Norwich Players to carry on their work unencumbered by a
heavy debt.

The letter was signed by Ivor Brown, E. Martin Browne, Lewis Casson, T. S. Eliot, Edith Evans, Christopher Fry, John Gielgud, Hugh Hunt, Barry Jackson, Paul Scofield, Sybil Thorndike and Donald Wolfit.

This remarkable theatrical experiment was the creation of one man, W. Nugent Monck. It was his exceptional abilities as a producer that gave the Norwich Players and the Maddermarket Theatre their international reputation and it was his artistic adaptation of Poel's theories that had such a notable influence on modern methods of Shakespearean staging. "There is nothing in British theatrical history more extraordinary than your creation of the Maddermarket Theatre,"[1] George Bernard Shaw once wrote to Monck; it is the purpose of this study to document this very influential man's career and his extraordinary achievement at the Maddermarket Theatre.

Monck's career spanned 58 years of one of the most innovative periods in the history of Western theatre. During this period Monck exerted considerable influence on many of the early movements that helped to shape the British theatre of today.

The Victorian age, in which Monck grew up, was an age of great actor-managers and a time when scenic spectacle had come to dominate the stage.

With the beginning of the Edwardian age a new spirit began to enter the theatre in Britain, a spirit which decried the restrictions of the old system and began to demand both literary and artistic excellence from drama. Those imbued with the new spirit looked with scorn on commercialism in theatre, equating commercial success with total artistic failure.[2] They began a wide variety of noncommercial ventures to bring their ideals of theatre before the public. These numerous noncommercial experiments were styled by the producer and critic Norman Marshall "the other theatre,"[3] and it was in this other theatre that Monck became a leading figure.

Monck's first exposure to the ideas of the modern theatre came through his contact with William Poel, who was attempting to establish modern principles of staging through the exploration of Elizabethan methods. Monck adopted Poel's basic tenets and began his own experiments in reviving Shakespeare's stagecraft, experiments which not only influenced those who signed the letter to *The Times* quoted above, but also such important producers as Tyrone Guthrie, Harcourt Williams, Robert Atkins and W. Bridges-Adams.

During the course of his work in this Elizabethan revival, Monck became influential in other movements. His early work took him to the old mystery plays of England's great religious cycles and his beautiful staging of these old dramas made him one of the most significant influences on the movement to revive religious drama in that country.[4] Closely allied with this movement and with the Elizabethan revival were the various efforts to revive poetic drama as a modern dramatic form. W. B. Yeats was one of the primary proponents of this goal and Monck became an important part of the effort when Yeats invited him to work at the Abbey Theatre during the seasons of 1911, 1912 and 1913. Meanwhile, to support his noncommercial activities, Monck took jobs producing civic pageants. Pageantry experienced a great renaissance over the first 40 years of this century and during that time Monck established himself as the most successful pageant producer in England.[5]

Monck's desire to explore thoroughly his ideas on Shakespearean production eventually led him to establish the Guild of the Norwich Players and to build the Maddermarket Theatre. In establishing the Norwich Players he created one of the very earliest of those groups which constituted the Little Theatre Movement, as it was later known, and in building the Maddermarket he created the first theatre in modern England to be free of the proscenium arch. With his Shakespearean productions and his staging of over 225 other important literary dramas Monck established his Norwich Players as the most famous of these Little Theatre groups and the Maddermarket as one of the most successful experimental theatres in the country, setting a standard of production that was often considered superior to all but the best professional companies.[6]

But all of these achievements in one way or another centered around Monck's primary interest in exploring what methods of production might have been employed in the theatres of Shakespeare's day and which of these methods could be used to give a greater vitality to the production of plays today. In reviving Shakespeare's stagecraft Monck became a significant influence on the shaping of modern British theatre.

1

Finding a Career: 1878–1913

When Nugent Monck retired in 1952 at the age of seventy-four, he announced that he intended to write his autobiography. But the living theatre was Monck's passion and even in retirement he could not stay away from it long enough to give an account of his own place in its history. On his eightieth birthday he would say of the project, "I have lived the life, and I find it dull." Had Monck finished the project he would undoubtedly be far better remembered today than he now is, but he would probably be remembered more for his entertaining writing style than for his real achievements. Monck was an excellent storyteller (although one not always concerned with historical accuracy), but he had a self-effacing character which caused him to belittle his own considerable accomplishments.

Walter Nugent Bligh Monck was born in the village of Welshampton in Shropshire on February 4, 1878. His parents moved to Liverpool just after Walter's eighth birthday and it was there that he first developed an interest in theatre. Liverpool was the major port for transatlantic crossings during Monck's boyhood and the best London actors and companies came there regularly to give their shows one last run before embarking on tours of North America. The young Monck became an avid theatregoer and was able to see much of what was generally recognized as the best in Victorian theatre.

The great attraction of theatre for Monck was the visual beauty he found there, a beauty which contrasted sharply with the drabness of the deteriorating neighborhood in which he lived. The scenic grandeur of productions by the Carl Rosa Opera Company moved him greatly and he was fascinated by Victorian spectacles such as the Hengler's Circus *Cinderella*. The latter production was done in a circus ring with great circular gauze scenery stretched to a 40-foot height by heavy steel cables. The audience looked through the gauze into a deep wood, a vast Gothic kitchen or a baroque fantasy palace, while the audience sitting opposite disappeared from view.[1]

Regular theatre too was being produced with a flair for the spectacular during this time. When the great actor-manager Henry Irving brought his Lyceum Company to Liverpool with a production of *Faust*, the performance young Monck saw gave him nightmares for weeks. "It was particularly the apes who lost a hand or a foot or even a head and whose limbs then seemed to come together again quite naturally which was so terrifying for a small boy,"[2] he later explained. This adaptation of Goethe's epic drama was prepared in 1885 by the Lyceum's regular playwright, William G. Wills. In keeping with the times Wills ignored the literary power of the original work and restructured it emphasizing only its pictorial possibilities.[3]

But in 1892 a new play by the then little-known playwright J. M. Barrie came to Liverpool. It was called *Walker, London* and Monck recalled that "the whole action took place on and in a house-boat on the Thames, so making it quite different to any play I'd ever seen. It had a quiet realism that was new to the drama."[4] Significant changes were occurring in British theatre and the superficial spectacle which had characterized the work of Wills at the Lyceum would gradually give way to new demands for drama that was less ornately staged but more intellectually satisfying. As Monck grew older he became increasingly attracted to this new movement, but he never lost his love for the visual beauty of the Victorian stage.

At the age of sixteen Monck was sent to London to study at the Royal Academy of Music. By 1897 he was hard at work in a singing career but he was also becoming active in theatre, appearing as Sir Toby Belch in scenes from *Twelfth Night* performed at St. George's Hall.[5] In 1899 Monck changed his principal course of study to drama and began classes in elocution under the distinguished actor William Farren, through whom he was introduced to the great traditions of nineteenth-century acting. Monck later rejected these traditions, but he learned them well before starting in new directions.[6] Monck's goal at this point in his career was to become a playwright in the tradition of J. M. Barrie; acting was intended to be only the first step in understanding the complexities of the playwright's craft. But although several of his plays were produced by minor companies in the first decade of this century, it was not as a playwright that Nugent Monck was destined to have an impact on the world of theatre.

Mrs. Patrick Campbell and William Poel

Monck's first venture into professional theatre came in November 1901 when he appeared as Pastor Janson in Mrs. Patrick Campbell's production of Bjørnstjerne Bjørnson's drama *Beyond Human Power*. Mrs. Campbell was one of the greatest actresses of her day and her performance in this play was long considered one of her best. She was a romantic producer who brought great visual beauty to her productions, both in her own movements and in the stage pictures she created. Such visual beauty had first attracted Monck to the stage and though he now found much of what he saw in the commercial theatre merely gaudy and tasteless, he had a deep respect for Mrs. Campbell's art. Beyond this, Monck found in Mrs. Campbell a professional who had strong ideas about what theatre as an art should be and one who was making a strenuous effort as manager of the Royalty Theatre to bring these ideas before the public.

"The Royalty Theatre has prospered in Mrs. Campbell's hands," wrote the leading critic Max Beerbohm in his review of *Beyond Human Power.* "Yet Mrs. Campbell makes no effort to give the public what it wants. Her policy is simply to give the public what she herself likes."[7] After the First World War a similar statement was made about so many producers that it seemed almost to be the motto of the modern movement in theatre. Such statements were often made about Monck himself. But this was not merely an expression of artistic snobbery; any new movement must educate a following. The adherents of the modern movement in theatre had to demonstrate to the public that the literary power of drama was ultimately more satisfying than the visual spectacle audiences had come to expect.

This education of the public took time and in the commercial theatre it cost a great deal of money. Beerbohm had continued his comments on Mrs. Campbell's policy by saying, "A thoughtless person might wonder how it is that such a policy has not spelt ruin. . . . For her it has spelt the more difficult word, success." Actually the policy had put Mrs. Campbell over £6,000 in debt.[8] This served as a warning to those with less ability than Mrs. Campbell to recoup such losses that the education of an audience in the commercial theatre of London was a risky undertaking at best.

In the spring of 1902 Monck was cast in William Poel's highly acclaimed production of the medieval morality play *Everyman.* Poel revived *Everyman* after four centuries of neglect and put it on stage at the Charterhouse, London, in July 1901. It was a splendid success, the first and only of Poel's efforts to earn him a good deal of money. Monck took over the role of Fellowship for the 1902 run and this was his first direct contact with the man whose theories he would champion for the next fifty-six years.

Like Mrs. Campbell, William Poel had compelling ideas about what theatre as an art should be and like her, he made considerable sacrifices to bring those ideas before the public.[9] Poel was the first producer in England to take a definite stand against the ever-increasing scenic realism of the nineteenth-century stage. His particular concern was that the techniques and conventions of the proscenium arch, picture-frame stage were so antipathetic to the stagecraft of Shakespeare's day that much of Shakespeare's method had become incomprehensible. Shakespeare's stagecraft had been completely perverted by the introduction in England of scene changes behind a closed "act curtain." The technique of the act curtain system involved writing scenes which ended with the closing of the curtain at some climactic point, leaving the audience in suspense until the curtain rose again to reveal how the situation had been resolved in the interim. Shakespeare, Poel pointed out, did not write for such a technique. He wrote episodes which had to be resolved in full view of the audience with the characters given reasons to make their exits.[10]

Realism worsened the situation in regard to Shakespeare's plays. Too often, Poel complained, the pursuit of realism led to enormous amounts of money being spent on the reconstruction of the most minute historic or geographic details in Shakespeare's texts.[11] But it was quite likely, Poel said, that Shakespeare himself knew nothing about such details. The life Shakespeare created on the stage was the life he saw around him in England and detailed representations of life in other countries or in other periods were extraneous. What was worse, Poel continued, was that such extraneous detail was then used to justify the rearrangement of scenes in the plays, the inclusion of large numbers of supernumeraries who merely cluttered the stage, the addition of a seemingly endless number of songs and dances, the most inappropriate costuming and the total misinterpretation of many of the most important roles.

Herbert Beerbohm Tree's productions at His Majesty's Theatre epitomized everything about which Poel was protesting. In 1900 Tree staged a production of *A Midsummer Night's Dream* with three-dimensional trees, real grass, live rabbits and the most elaborate flying equipment then available for the fairies' entrances and exits.[12] It was a great success and set the standard for Shakespearean productions in the commercial theatres, but it is unlikely that those who saw this spectacular display came away with any very clear idea of what the playwright Shakespeare had intended. Poel had seen long before anyone else that both the structure of Shakespeare's plays and the impending economic realities of the theatre were working against any continued long-term success for an approach that emphasized the visual over the dramatic in theatrical production.

Poel started his experiments to change the methods of staging Shakespeare with an unheralded production of *Hamlet* in 1881. In 1894 he founded the Elizabethan Stage Society and embarked on a regular program of staging Elizabethan plays "after the manner of the seventeenth century."[13] When Monck joined Poel, Poel was fifty years old and at the height of his career.

Nugent Monck was twenty-four and in Poel he, like many others, found a great source of inspiration. Through research and staging experiments Poel developed a set of principles which he believed were inherent in seventeenth-century English drama. One of his more distinguished pupils, Lewis Casson, once summarized these principles. Poel taught, Casson said, that Shakespeare's plays should be presented with:

1. The full text in its proper order without interpolation or rearrangement.
2. Continuity of speech from scene to scene without breaks between "acts."
3. A permanent architectural set with at least two levels, and an inner stage covered by traverse curtains.
4. A wide platform stage projecting into the audience.
5. Elizabethan dress (with a few period modifications).
6. Rapid, highly coloured musical speech of great range and flexibility.[14]

These principles can be, and were, widely debated and there is no doubt that Poel himself failed to practice them consistently in his own productions. But in Poel's Elizabethan revival Monck found an alternative to the preoccupation with scenic realism which had come to dominate the commercial theatres.

Poel and Mrs. Patrick Campbell were the two great influences in Monck's professional life, he later said, because of the plays they produced and the very serious ideas they had on what theatre should be. From Mrs. Campbell he learned to refine his sense of beauty. Her production of Maeterlinck's *Pelleas and Melisande,* he would say at the end of his long career, "remained in my mind perhaps even more than the simplicity of Poel's Shakespeare."[15] But if Poel's productions did not have the visual effectiveness of Mrs. Campbell's work, Monck saw in Poel's efforts the possibility of developing a new, simplified scenic art for the theatre.

The English Drama Society

William Poel's Elizabethan Stage Society was disbanded for financial reasons in May 1905. Immediately Nugent Monck formed the English Drama Society, incorporating many of the actors who had worked for Poel.[16] For their inaugural production Monck produced Robert Browning's poetic drama *In a Balcony*. It was a distinct departure from the work Monck had been doing with Poel but the play allowed him to explore the application of Poel's theories to modern scripts. The English Drama Society's second production was *The Dialogue of D'Alcarmo* by the Pre-Raphaelite poet Dante Gabriel Rossetti; it was a significant choice for Monck.

The Pre-Raphaelites were a brotherhood of painters and poets who organized themselves in the mid-nineteenth century to protest against what they saw as the materialistic art of the Industrial Revolution. They advocated a return to the comparative simplicity of the symbolic and stylized art of medieval times before the age of Raphael. The materialism against which these artists had protested in the mid-1800s had by the latter part of that century come to dominate the stage. Poel's *Everyman* production had suggested to Monck the value a movement equivalent to the Pre-Raphaelites could have for the theatre. For the next four years he produced for the English Drama Society a series of medieval plays, early plays by Shakespeare, and modern plays (including several of his own) which had the same stylized simplicity of medieval art. His hope was that "we might work as the Pre-Raphaelites did in painting and evolve a new outlet for dramatic sense which would not be hampered by stock traditions, scenery, curtains, footlights, paint, and the other things that make for technique."[17]

From the very start Monck's work with the English Drama Society demonstrated that he was a gifted producer with an artistic sensibility that allowed him to create strikingly beautiful scenes from practically nothing. During his first years with this group, however, the reviews show that he was struggling with the same problems of unclear diction and a lack of vocal expressiveness which had plagued Poel's work. Poel's sixth principle advocated "rapid, highly coloured, musical speech," but the customary complaint of critics about all Poel's productions for the Elizabethan Stage Society was that the verse was spoken too slowly, often with monotonous rhythm and inaudible diction. By contrast Monck's early productions were criticized for overly rapid delivery of lines, though complaints of a lack of energy in the voices and a lack of flexibility in expression remained. These were problems that Monck, unlike Poel, eventually solved.

When Monck was not producing plays for his own drama society he continued to do productions with Poel. By 1908 Monck, by then aged thirty, was a well-established name in what would today be called the fringe theatre. As Poel's most regular stage manager he was readily identified with what was a rather avant-garde movement, his work in religious drama was inspiring some imitators, and his playwriting was considered to have as yet unfulfilled promise. But such work did not pay any better then than it does now, nor did it attract a larger audience. Monck's work as a producer for the English Drama Society and as an actor for various other performing groups was his sole source of income. With no personal fortune, Monck had to find a way to increase this income in order to survive.

Monck's first opportunity to get a reasonable salary for a production came in January 1909. In the provincial city of Norwich, the county town of Norfolk, a local group had secured the patronage of the Prince of Wales for three evenings of one of those patently Victorian entertainments, the *Historic Tableaux,* to be given as a charity benefit. Monck's former classmate, the Reverend R. F. Rynd, was precentor for Norwich Cathedral and recommended Monck for the job of producer.

The production was a triumph for Monck. The reviews pinpoint the aspects of production for which all Monck's later work was so widely known:

the style with which he selected his material; the artistry with which he staged, dressed, and lit the show; his careful attention to historic detail; his selection of period music; and finally, the precision with which everything was organized to move with a swift clarity. Many of these things he had learned from Poel, but by this time the pupil had surpassed the master. "Poel was a poor executant," wrote Robert Speaight. "When it came to illustrating what he had picked up from a page of Marlowe or Shakespeare the result was a poor recording."[18] Monck may not have "picked up" as much from a script; certainly he never demonstrated the powers of original thought that Poel showed in his writing, but what Monck did pick up was never illustrated crudely.

A seemingly unimportant event occurred during the run of this show. A wealthy and rather eccentric woman, Mrs. M. E. Pym, had seen the tableaux and thought that a man of Monck's artistic taste and historic interests might like to live in a fine Tudor house that stood for sale just round the corner from her home. As Monck told the story: "A note was on my breakfast table that morning saying that she would buy the house, do it up, and let it to me at a rent that would cover the interest."[19]

At the time Monck had no plans to live in his newly acquired home. It was intended to be merely an economical place to store furniture and it offered a perfect retreat when he found himself unemployed in London. But in a few short months events in London would make him despair of ever being able to do worthwhile work there, and Monck would choose Norwich in which to make his important contributions to the history of British theatre.

Upon his return to London Monck began work on a production of five plays from the fifteenth-century *Ludus Coventriae*. The production, which he financed himself, had a cast of 32 and lavish, expensive costuming. On the night of dress rehearsal, however, the police arrived to close the show for violation of the blasphemy laws (it was not legal to portray Christ on stage) and for performing in an unlicensed theatre. It was a strange turn of events as neither law had been enforced for years and the new severity came without warning.

Monck hastily formed a "private society" and staged his *Passion Play* the following week but this could hardly have recouped the money he had spent. For four years he had struggled to produce the kind of theatre he believed was important, but as had happened to Poel in 1905, it became financially impossible to continue. Monck's English Drama Society was disbanded. Monck returned to freelance producing and playwriting after this event but his next significant involvement in a production was his appearance as Poel's stage manager and the Innkeeper in a production of *The Two Gentlemen of Verona* during April 1910. This production was one of Poel's most important contributions to the Elizabethan revival.

Poel had been invited to stage the play as part of a Shakespeare festival at His Majesty's Theatre. The invitation came from Beerbohm Tree, whose own production of Shakespeare represented everything to which Poel had long objected. Poel's production took place on April 20 of the festival week. Tree was not converted to Poel's austere methods of staging by this event, but there were two aspects of Poel's work that Tree later copied and which had a significant influence on staging in London theatres. Besides using his usual methods of staging, which employed minimal scenery and worked for an unbroken continuity in the action, Poel had an apron built onto the stage, extending it over the orchestra pit, thereby bringing the actors closer to the audience. A "direct lighting" system was also installed and it was these two elements of the production which were most influential.

In the theatres of the nineteenth and early twentieth centuries, all light for the stage came from sources which were behind the proscenium arch. Footlights, top lights, side lights, and backlights provided all the illumination which could be given to the actors. It was necessary, therefore, that the actors stay behind the plane of the proscenium arch, for if they moved in front of it all light would be behind them and their faces would be dark. Such a system was unworkable when an apron was built over the orchestra pit as Poel had done.

Direct lighting was a new development which placed some lights in the auditorium and directed them back toward the stage. This made the lighting of actors possible, regardless of how far the stage extended beyond the proscenium. In 1910 the most influential theorist of this new development, Adolphe Appia, was only beginning to experiment with its application in a theatre at Hellerau, near Dresden, Germany. Poel does not seem to have employed such an arrangement before this production of *Two Gentlemen of Verona* and his first writing on the subject of direct lighting did not appear until two months later.[20] Monck, however, had used direct lighting for his *Historical Tableaux* at Norwich in January 1909, a full 16 months before Poel's use of it at His Majesty's Theatre. It was common practice in the Edwardian theatre for the stage manager and electrician to be given responsibility for lighting the stage,[21] and it would therefore seem likely that the direct lighting innovation was one of Monck's contributions to this important production. Certainly Monck had long since proved his ability to use this system effectively, and if its application in this instance was not Monck's idea, Poel could not have found a better stage manager to execute it for him.

Monck had a young assistant just down from Oxford for this production. His name was W. Bridges-Adams and he was to be the first of a number of influential producers who, while they were exponents of the theories and ideas of William Poel, got their visual inspiration and practical training in the application of these theories from W. Nugent Monck.

The production of *The Two Gentlemen of Verona* transferred to the Manchester Gaiety Theatre where it was produced in repertory with *Everyman* from April 25 to 30, 1910. On this successful note, Monck left London, never to reside there again. He gave up his flat in Paxton Street and moved all his possessions to Norwich.

The Norwich Players

By this time Monck had clearly absorbed Poel's theories and developed from them his own approach to production. Poel and Monck had a great deal in common. Both were high-minded Victorians with a deep sense of the social value of drama and a total commitment to its furtherance. They were men of wide culture who brought considerable knowledge of many arts to their work. And both men shared the same dissatisfaction with the popular theatre of their day and had basically the same notions of how to correct it. Their respective approaches to producing were quite similar, but there were some significant differences.

Poel, though he was a competent cellist, was trained primarily as an architect. Oddly, he concentrated on the musicality of dramatic production while Monck, who had been trained primarily as a musician, was for the most part visually oriented. Poel cast his plays for vocal quality, as one might do an opera, and carefully worked out the rhythm, stress, and phrasing of every line as if the script were a musical score. For three weeks of a four-week rehearsal period his actors sat round a table learning their "tunes" from him by endless repetition. He worked for a delivery of poetic lines which was modern in being not strictly tied to the meter, but which at the same time was not an attempt to deny the poetic quality of the lines. Context, meaning, and rhythmical and poetic values were all taken into account.

But Poel's work usually suffered from two major failings. First, he was not very successful at communicating his ideas to the average performer. With Poel an actor "had to hear through . . . to what he imagined that Poel himself had heard, and then render it as best he could on his own instrument."[22] For actors of great natural talent who could manage this feat on their own abilities Poel's training was of tremendous value. The less talented, with whom Poel normally worked, however, were often merely frustrated by what they saw as an eccentric rehearsal technique. The fact that "Poel, for all his concern for accurate and musical speech, had little ear for metrical values or their reinforcement of dramatic meaning" did not make an unskilled performer's job any easier.[23] This problem was compounded by Poel's lack of sensitivity to his actors. Speaight relates in his biography of Poel an incident recalled by Granville-Barker. It seems that during a rehearsal of *Richard II*, Poel, lying back on a deck chair, eyes closed, hands across chest, was calling out "more

Figure 1.   Nugent Monck When He Arrived at Norwich in 1909, Age 31
(Courtesy of the Maddermarket Theatre Trust, Ltd.)

hysteria, more hysteria" to an actress attempting a difficult scene. Finally he said, "That's the tone, keep it up," but Barker had to point out to him that the actress's hysteria was by that point real.[24] This is something of which Monck, as will be seen, would never have been guilty. He could, and at times did, drive performers into hysterics, but never because he had failed even for a moment to be aware of what was happening on his stage.

Poel's second failing was in the area of the visual effectiveness of his productions. *Everyman* was a brilliant exception to this deficiency, which may partly account for its great success. There were several other exceptions during his career, but Poel was not consistent. For the most part Poel's productions were marred from the start by his rehearsal method, which, by denying his actors the stage until the final week, left them unsure of themselves and gave his productions the air of being rather tentative attempts.[25] This problem was emphasized by what was essentially a defective pictorial sense. Speaight provides an example of this when he describes how Poel had a Roman centurion standing guard over a production of a Greek play. This was odd in itself, but becomes even odder when it is noted that only the lower half of this figure could be seen from the audience.[26] Another example involved Monck, who was told to strike a certain kneeling pose, holding a candle, in a scene. "This pose made no kind of pictorial or dramatic sense," Speaight writes, "until it was discovered long afterwards that Poel had taken it from a design in an ancient Missal." [27] Speaight intended this as a compliment to Poel's wide culture but Monck at least would not have chosen a stage picture which required research before it made dramatic sense. Monck's pictures were always effective and appropriate.

William Archer's criticism of Poel, which is quoted by Speaight, is an appropriate summation. In 1913, Archer wrote in *The Nation* concerning Poel:

> He had the root of the matter in him; of that there can be no doubt; but both his theories and his practice as Director of the Elizabethan Stage Society were marred by such eccentricities as to deprive them of all persuasiveness either to managers or to the public. In these latter days, no doubt, he has had some influence on such managers as Mr. Granville-Barker and Mr. Martin Harvey, but the movement they represent would certainly have come without him, and it may be questioned whether, in detail, his influence has been altogether for good.[28]

Unfortunately, Poel became more eccentric as he grew older; it was perhaps the natural result of his difficult and lonely struggle. But despite his failings and Archer's contention that the movement toward simplified staging was inevitable, there can be no doubt that without Poel's fanatical dedication our modern approach to Shakespeare would not have come so soon. The recognition Poel has received is completely justified.

It did, however, remain for others to eliminate the eccentricities and to make Poel's theories persuasive by demonstrating that they could be extraordinarily effective when properly applied. Monck used Poel's theories more effectively than any other producer, and Speaight was certainly right in saying that Poel "had no more faithful disciple than Nugent Monck."[29]

For Monck, the beautiful simplicity and clear effectiveness of Poel's *Everyman* was the ideal toward which all productions should aim. In that production Poel had achieved a balance of the visual and the aural. But during his London struggles Monck had come to realize that audiences were not quite ready for this new, austere stagecraft. At Norwich he set about the difficult and laborious task of training both his actors and an audience to appreciate it fully.

Monck arrived at his new home at 6 Ninham's Court, Bethal Street, which he called the "Crypt" because of the large, brick-groined cellar it contained, and set to work establishing himself as a producer. By August he had secured an engagement as the producer for another benefit entertainment. The production was called *Narcissus: A Water Frolic in One Act.* It was written and directed by Monck with sets by W. Bridges-Adams. That production was followed by a highly successful outdoor performance of *A Midsummer Night's Dream* in the grounds of St. Andrew's rectory in the village of Thorpe near Norwich. Over 100 people took part. The Elizabethan music and the perfect elocution of the performers were only occasionally disturbed by the anachronistic sound of a passing train, according to the contemporary reports. Twenty-seven years after this production, Andrew Stephenson could still write, "Here, with the fairies flitting and dancing down a wooded hillside, he obtained lighting effects that people still recall with wonder."[30] This was the first Shakespearean play Monck ever produced in Norfolk; forty-three years later, an outdoor production of this same play would be his last Shakespeare there.

Monck enjoyed such pageantlike productions but it was not his ambition to do that work indefinitely. He wanted to continue the experiments he had started with the English Drama Society. The stated purpose of that Society had been to produce plays of literary merit in the simplest, most direct way possible, paying careful attention to details but maintaining a balance between all the various elements of production so that none would dominate. This was still the kind of work Monck wished to do. But by then he had had eight years of experience in London by which to assess the professional theatre. He found the financial pressures too stifling. Artistic quality was consistently sacrificed to economics. To be a financial success one had to squander one's talent on what was to him insipid trash. Those like Mrs. Patrick Campbell and William Poel, who had tried to stage good plays, were overworked to such an extent that they could not achieve the artistic standards at which they aimed and had found themselves bankrupt in the bargain. Monck chose to give up struggling with the increasingly frustrating economics of the professional stage and was now determined to carry on his experiment with amateurs while remaining a professional himself. It was a brilliant and original notion, and in the years after the first great war when the amateur theatre movement in England experienced a phenomenal growth it became an inspiration to many others.

During the course of his work in the Norfolk area, Monck had attracted to himself a group of eight young men who met regularly at his home to read plays and discuss all aspects of art and culture. Monck soon persuaded this group to supplement their literary studies by giving productions of plays that would be "an expression of life in all ages,"[31] and for their first performance they did *The World and the Child* in Monck's first floor living room on the afternoon and evening of November 3, 1910.

This was essentially the first production by the Guild of the Norwich Players, which was destined to become one of the foremost amateur organizations in Britain by 1920. They did not formally establish their aims or conditions of membership until the following spring, which accounts for the considerable confusion that exists over the exact date of their founding, but when they did establish themselves as an autonomous group in May of 1911, the guild title had a real meaning for them. The term guild implied that acting was a craft learned after long apprenticeship. As a consequence membership, which was exclusively male until 1919, was to be decided by unanimous selection after an associate performer had done significant work for the Guild. Nugent Monck was to be their producer, but he himself was not elected as a Player until after the First World War. Their stated purpose was "to produce plays of literary and artistic merit in the best and most vital manner possible," and "to bring such within the level of the democracy," though what this latter phrase meant was never made quite clear.[32]

The first official production of the Norwich Players took place on May 24 and 25, 1911, at Monck's home, the Crypt. They performed Monck's own adaptation of *St. George and the Dragon* and an adaptation of medieval carols he had done with one of the Players, Martin Kinder, called *The Holly and the Ivy*. The group continued to be known as Nugent Monck's Players until September 2, 1912, however, when the *Eastern Daily Press* finally began referring to them by their official title, "The Norwich Players."

Between productions with the Norwich Players Monck continued his freelance producing for other groups. In February he was asked by a local organization to produce W. B. Yeats's *The Countess Cathleen,* a play never seen before in England. Knowing that Yeats himself was then in England touring with the Irish Players, Monck wrote to him inviting him to attend. To nearly everyone's surprise, Yeats did. This production proved to have a far-reaching effect on Monck's career.

The Abbey Theatre School of Acting

In the history of the Abbey Theatre, 1911 was a year of major importance. After a long and at times bitter struggle, W. B. Yeats and Lady Gregory had won complete control of the enterprise. For the first time it was possible for them to pursue freely the principles they believed should guide the modern theatre. The first of these principles, the supremacy of the dramatist over the actors, was already well established at the Abbey. But their desire to reintroduce verse drama as a popular form had yet to be realized. The Abbey Theatre's acting company, the Irish Players, was outstanding in realistic performances but since the loss of the Fay brothers, Willie and Frank, there had been no really satisfactory verse productions.[33] The Fay brothers were early casualties of the struggle for power and they had left the Abbey on less than friendly terms in 1908. Late in 1910 this struggle had caused a more serious loss, that of the theatre's sole benefactor, Miss A. E. F. Horniman. With considerable animosity Miss Horniman had withdrawn her support from the Abbey organization and in 1911 was expending all her energies on her other remarkable theatrical venture, the Gaiety Theatre, Manchester. This left Yeats and Lady Gregory in control of an organization without funds or legal title to the theatre in which it worked. To secure money for support of the company and the purchase of the deed of title to the theatre, Yeats embarked on a lecture tour followed by a performance tour with the Irish Players in the winter and spring of 1910–11.

Yeats was in the middle of these difficult financial problems when he received a letter from Monck inquiring about the original promptbook and music for *The Countess Cathleen* and outlining his own ideas for production of the play. It was February 9 before Yeats could find time to respond; "I am delighted that they have chosen you to produce *The Countess Cathleen*," he wrote to Monck, "and if you will tell me the date, I will try to come down and see it."[34] Monck had suggested doing the play in English Saxon costume and Yeats fully approved: "I care nothing for historic accuracy writing as I do of the vague period which comes into the folk tales ... It is any period you please in which it is possible to believe in demons and not to be too far from the old gods, while living in the midst of Christian fervour." Yeats went on to say that the original production was not very good and that the production book would be of little use to Monck. He concluded, "I remember your Chester Mystery Plays very well, and found them a delight. I hardly like even to make suggestions to you, for I should like to see what you will do with things yourself ... I wrote it before I knew my business." Monck sent the performance dates as requested and Yeats made the trip to Norwich to see what Monck had done with the play. He was much impressed by Monck's work.

In March Yeats returned to Norwich to see Monck's production of *Job*. The success of the production prompted him to invite Monck to produce *King Argimenes and the Unknown Warrior* by Lord Dunsany,[35] and *The Well of the Saints* by J. M. Synge for the Irish Players' three-week summer engagement at the Court Theatre, London. The season began on June 5, but Monck's productions did not appear until near the end, June 26 through 28. His work was well received, though the reviews were not outstanding. Monck never did exceptional work when he was restricted to a proscenium stage. But overall, this engagement was the Irish Players' most successful venture up to that time and it proved to be a major turning point in their fortunes. On the strength of their Court Theatre performances they were offered a four month tour of the United States, with all expenses guaranteed and thirty-five percent of the profits. The offer could hardly have come at a better time.

This first United States tour by the Irish Players is now famous. The riots and attacks which plagued their production of *The Playboy of the Western World* did more to publicize the work of the Abbey Theatre than any other event in their history. It was also a major financial success at a time when one was desperately needed. But while the main company was embattled in America winning fame and fortune, Yeats was hard at work in Dublin trying to lay the foundations which would insure the continuation of the Abbey after the money and notoriety from this first tour had faded away.

As early as March 14, 1911, Yeats had proposed in a letter to Lady Gregory that a school of acting be created at the Abbey under the direction of one of the company's leading actresses, Sara Allgood. Initially this school was intended only to provide a source of new talent for the main company. But the offer of the United States tour gave the project even greater importance. The Irish Players were going on this tour during the autumn when they would normally be in residence at the Abbey. If the tour was a success, it was bound to be repeated. There was therefore the grave risk that, with nothing going on at the Abbey during these periods, its audience would get out of the habit of going there and the Irish Players would become a visiting company in their own hometown. But with a school training local talent and giving public performances, the Abbey would remain in the public eye and maintain its identity. As none of the company's leading performers could be spared from the main company to run such a school, Yeats offered the job to Monck.

September of 1911, the month before Monck arrived to take up his new duties, proved to be an exceedingly eventful month for the Abbey management. On September 7, Marie O'Neill, sister of Sara Allgood and the actress who played Pegeen Mike in the Abbey production of *The Playboy of the Western World,* dropped out of the proposed American tour. Yeats had to take the company on without her and it was suddenly necessary for Lady Gregory to follow, training another actress for this all-important role during the eight day ocean voyage. Yeats wrote to Monck on September 10, telling him he would have to start off at the Abbey on his own and instructing him on what to do until Yeats could get back from America.

On the fifteenth of the month Monck received his first letter from Lady Gregory:

> Dear Mr. Monck,
>   Your wire is a great relief. The very day before the Company started for America I had a wire saying Marie Tempest offered 40 per week for my *Workhouse Ward* if we could produce and put it on with scenery and cast.

After explaining that she had hurriedly secured W. G. Fay, a Mr. Powers, and a Miss Welldon for the cast, she continued:

> What makes the matter important is, that we have for some time been talking of forming a small company to play at music halls and do our curtain raisers, as a sort of Nursery ground from which we could supplement our ordinary company at times, and which would also help not only to pay for themselves but to fill the Abbey exchequer. This seems too good a chance of starting it to be missed . . . We don't want one actor to star the company, we want the Abbey itself to be the star, and to send out a company that will keep up its reputation. Fay had done a good deal of production but I didn't want him to do this.

She explained that Fay had always scoffed at the play and could not be trusted to produce it exactly as it had been done that summer at the Court Theatre. She went on:

> Then we don't want him to get control in any way again, he is a genius as a comedian, and what ruined him before was being made manager which he was not well fitted for. Then also it is an Abbey and not a Fay company we want to start with. So I was worried until I thought of you.[36]

The project came to nothing; Lady Gregory believed she had secured Fay's services but when he realized he was not to be the producer, he refused to be involved. Still, the letter did outline the goals and aspirations Yeats and Lady Gregory had for a second company and since Monck had become associated with the plan, it became a logical step to make the formation of this company one of the goals of the new school of acting which Monck was to head.

Monck went to Dublin to open the Abbey School of Acting on October 10, 1911.[37] Yeats arrived about six days later and they immediately began to screen possible candidates for the school. Years afterwards one of these candidates described this event:

When the day of the audition arrived my anticipation about the order was correct ... I was the only "W." There were no "X, Y, or Z's." ...

The procession started. One after the other they went at it.... "To be or not to be." ... "Now is the Winter of our discontent." ... "Is this a dagger." ... All of them tempting fate with Shakespearean fragments of the most hackneyed type.

My heart sank lower and lower. I felt convinced that long before it came to be my turn, Yeats and Monck would either have fallen asleep, or stolen silently out of the stalls and gone home.

At last the secretary called my name and I sallied on to the stage. I spoke my piece. I half expected to be pulled up but, no, I was allowed to finish it. Then there was a pause. I was sure they were asleep. Then Monck came up to the footlights. "Mr. Wilson, is it?"

"Yes!"

"Would you mind saying that over again?"

I spoke my piece all over again, and stood and waited while Monck and Yeats had a short argument in the stalls. Then Yeats came up to the footlights.

"It is Carlyle, isn't it, Wilson?"

I agreed that it was.

"Is it *Sartor Resartus*?" asked Monck.

"Yes, a bit towards the end."

Monck turned to Yeats gleefully. "I knew it!"[38]

Andrew Wilson won a place in the school and went on to become a member of the main company.

The school began with an enrollment of 57 which swelled to 60 by the end of the month. Yeats was quite pleased to write to Lady Gregory on October 28 that as each student had paid £1, Monck's salary was more than covered. It was soon obvious, however, that with so many students Monck could only give each one about five minutes instruction per day and even this left him teaching for seven hours before he could start on his production work. "He doesn't complain," Yeats wrote to Lady Gregory on November 3, "but the situation is impossible," and he explained that he told Monck to hire Elizabeth Young to teach voice production. This did not prove to be a solution to the problem, though; a few weeks later Yeats had to report: "The trouble is that the pupils will not go to Miss Young's lesson & demand Monck."[39]

Monck struggled on and by November 16 the school was ready for its first semipublic performance; they did *The Interlude of Youth, The Marriage,* and *The Shadow of the Glen* for four nights. At the opening performance Yeats officially announced his intention of forming a second company from the school to provide his audience with regular performances while the main company was on tour, and to take Abbey plays to the provinces when the main company was at home. What Yeats did not announce was that a further goal of this second company was to provide competition for the main company's leading actors. Arthur Sinclair especially was causing problems for Yeats, who wanted to strengthen his own position by having "such a stock of players to draw from that we can defy rebels."[40] A great deal of the Abbey's future was resting on Monck's ability to train such players.

The medieval morality play Monck chose to do at this performance, Yeats noted, had special advantages for young actors. In such plays pupils could not attempt poor imitations of great actors, for no one ever saw Irving or Beerbohm Tree in a morality play.[41] But this was not the only advantage Yeats saw in Monck's taste for religious drama. On the morning of November 18, he wrote to Lady Gregory, "I am going to see Edward Martyn[42] & ask his advice about working the religious drama through the Church as I judge by the success of our invitation show that it would take here." That afternoon Yeats reported that he asked Martyn "if our second company were to specialize in religious drama would the priests take it up as they are doing in Paris?" Martyn thought not; the Abbey, he said, was considered not simply anti-Catholic but anti-Christian, so the Church was unlikely to support anything it did. It was an uphill struggle.

But winning over the Church was not all Yeats hoped to gain from Monck's special talents. "I'm finding out what can be done with the religious drama because I would like to get a verse company," he had told Lady Gregory on November 18, and at this Monck proved a great success. The first public performance by the Abbey Theatre School of Acting was given on November 23 through 25. They did *The Interlude of Youth* and *The Second Shepherd's Play*. The *Freeman's Journal* said of the production, "If there is one feature more than another calling for praise it was that Chaucerian and Shakespearian language was spoken so intelligently and distinctly that it could be followed by the audience."[43]

Of the other features, several were new to the Abbey Theatre. For the first time direct lighting was employed there. A little sentry-box-like structure was built in the balcony, from which the electricians could operate a limelight. Monck had proven the value of this new lighting method so completely that Yeats let him use it in spite of the high cost, which ran as much as £10 per show.[44] In January a carbon arc lamp was purchased; this reduced costs but was quite noisy until the electricians learned to maintain the proper gap between the carbons. Also for the first time a trilevel acting area was employed, with the main stage backed by a brilliantly curtained raised stage and fronted by steps on both sides leading down to the audience where part of the action occurred.

The following week, November 30 through December 2, four one-act pieces were given to provide more of the students with chances to perform. Yeats wrote of Monck's work:

Monck's rehearsals are overpowering things—today even I whose part was small feel worn out. On Sunday we rehearsed from 5:30 until about eleven. Monday & last night we had the first & second of our three dress rehearsals—all actors had to start rehearsing at 6:30 & Monday we got away at 11:15--& last night at 11:30. He is very severe & yet is a great favourite. . . . Tremendous as the rehearsals are I doubt we have enough—the play is very difficult—but I have great faith in Monck.[45]

By the following Monday, December 4, Yeats had completed his plans for the new company. Nine men and ten women from the school seemed very promising and they were to form a self-supporting company that would specialize in religious and dialect plays, thus appealing both to the Church and to the nationalists.

Before Christmas there was to be a final public performance which would feature those selected for the new company in the leading roles. Yeats's newest version of *The Countess Cathleen* had been worked on almost since the school's opening and was finally given, along with *The Interlude of Youth*, on December 14 through 16. For the occasion the stage carpenter provided Monck with a six-foot deep apron in front of the main stage, another first for the Abbey. Yeats had hired a young manuscript illustrator to help Monck paint a wood scene with golden outlined fruit trees against a golden sky, as from a medieval missal. And to make it possible to run the show without an interval of any kind, special music was written into certain scenes, so while these scenes were performed on the apron, the sound of the set being changed behind the curtain would not be heard.[46] On December 15 Yeats wrote to Lady Gregory: "*The Countess Cathleen* was a series of the most lovely pictures . . . Costumes and lighting were lovely—indeed I have seen nothing like them since the early Craig's." And in a note added the next day he said: "A most lovely performance of *Countess Cathleen* last night—the best verse performance given in this theatre." Monck's morality plays may not have converted the Catholic Church, but he had finally given Yeats the actors who could perform the verse drama he had always hoped to make popular. The press was equally impressed with Monck's contribution. "What interested us most . . . was the all round excellence of the performance," wrote the critic Jacques for the *Irish Independent*.[47]

Several weeks afterwards Yeats sent a copy of the new script to Lady Gregory with an outline of his idea for producing it using some special screens that the influential designer and theorist E. Gordon Craig had devised. He added:

> I don't want any performance of it, of course, this tour. It would be most dangerous to my reputation. I must wait on Craig and Monck. I have come to realize from that performance of *Cathleen* in Dublin how much it depends for its effect on the beauty of the picture. It held people probably more as a picture that was beautiful every moment than as something to listen to. They listened as I think I have never heard them listen in the Abbey . . . but it was their eyes that kept them listening.[48]

This points to what was undoubtedly one of Monck's most important discoveries. Pictorial realism tends to stifle imagination and thus works against most drama, verse drama in particular. Much of the language in a poetic play is intended to evoke images in the listener's mind and act as its own illustration. If the visual picture conflicts with this or simply provides an adequate substitute, such language becomes almost superfluous and does not hold the audience's attention. But with tapestry curtains, medieval stylization in the painting of the sets, brilliant costumes and mood lighting, Monck had found a way to stimulate the imagination rather than hinder it. His pictures were beautiful and intended to be filled out by the audience with the poetic imagery of the dramatist. Monck was a Pre-Raphaelite in design, but his stage lighting was more reminiscent of the work of the artist Turner. The combination made a striking impression which complemented poetic language and encouraged the audience to concentrate on the verse. Most critics would say that the actors spoke so well that not a word was missed. It took the poet Yeats to notice that it was not only the training Monck gave the company which accounted for this; of equal importance was the way Monck's visual artistry made the audience listen.

In America Lady Gregory and the company were beginning to win recognition; *The Playboy of the Western World* was still causing considerable controversy, but by now this was doing more to increase profits than to harm the company's reputation. As a consequence, the tour which was to have ended in late December was extended for three more months. Yeats persuaded Monck to return to the Abbey after Christmas and continue his work with the school until the first company's return.

The Abbey Theatre's Second Company

The school must have opened for its second term immediately after Christmas, as the first production of 1912 was staged on January 4 through 6. Monck had his students perform the nativity group from *The Wakefield Mystery Cycle* and a play by Douglas Hyde called *The Nativity Play*. The *Freeman's Journal* welcomed Monck's return, saying, "The success of the school during the last term exceeded the most sanguine expectations."[49] But when reviewing this first production, the same critic said, "It is doubtful if the revival of these plays and the production of them on the modern stage is exactly the sort of work for which the Abbey Theatre School of Acting is best fitted. . . . The public do not go to the theatre to pray, least of all to the Abbey Theatre."[50] This was precisely the criticism leveled at Monck's early revival of *The Interlude of Youth* in London. And, as usual, besides those who did not go to the theatre to pray, there were those who thought the idea of plays on religious subjects was blasphemous. Yeats wrote to Lady Gregory in America:

> I cannot make out whether we have done ourselves good or harm with the mystery plays, we had very poor houses indeed last week, but we had the Opera against us . . . there is no doubt about the enthusiasm of a good many people, on the other hand I hear of people . . . being shocked at the staging of religious subjects, there have been a good many priests but on Saturday a little group of priests left after the first act.[51]

It was obvious that mystery plays neither pleased the Abbey's audience nor won for the Abbey any significant religious support; Yeats soon gave up the attempt.

But the production had been good experience for the students, and as always Monck's work was most impressive. In his letter to Lady Gregory dated January 7, Yeats gave some special praise to Monck's acting abilities:

> The four mystery plays yesterday were lovely things to look at and Monck's own acting as St. Joseph was really very fine. It was like Frank Fay in *The Interior.* He came to play by an accident, he had cast one of the school for the part but found him shortly before the curtain was to go up making a joke of the part or the play to some of those about him. Monck insists on the work being taken very seriously and especially so in the case of these religious plays, he put the man out of the part and took it himself without rehearsal. It was much the best piece of acting he has done.

The school continued on its already established routine of giving performances each Wednesday through Friday. Their second bill was of four one-act Irish plays, all of which had been performed the previous term and only one of which, *Red Turf,* received any special notice. The following week's bill introduced two new plays to the school's repertory, William Boyle's *The Building Fund* and Lady Gregory's *The Rising of the Moon,* which were performed with a revival of her play *Dervorgilla.* These were a remarkable success. The *Freeman's Journal* commented that the quality of the acting was at times even better than that of the first company.[52]

The *Irish Times* was especially impressed:

> It is encouraging to find that while the star artists are sparkling in the American firmament, other luminaries have appeared in the heavens at home. . . . Mr. Nugent Monck has certainly wrought wonders in a short time, and it is only by a combination of efficient tuition and capable material . . . that the results we have seen attained are possible. Ever since the new dramatic school was instituted the improvement in the acting of the students has been so rapid that the student stage has been left behind.[53]

Yeats, in his almost daily letters to Lady Gregory, provided some invaluable insights into how Monck was able to achieve these remarkable results in such a short period. Of Monck's rehearsals he wrote, on January 18, "We are doing as you will see a great mass of work, our rehearsals are so long and thorough that we get up a play in about a week and really they know it better on the average than our main company knows its work on a first night," and on February 15 he added:

> I am amazed at the rapidity of the rehearsals of the School. The reason is that everybody learns his part at home, if they don't they get no more parts from Monck. The result seems to be that 4 or 5 rehearsals does [*sic*] the work that we take a dozen or more to, and most of these people have the work they live by as well.

Monck's ability to get remarkable results from amateur performers would later make his Norwich Players one of the most highly respected amateur groups in England, and Yeats revealed the secret of Monck's success when he said:

> Monck is a genius, an organizing genius, and he has what's even more important, a gift for awakening devotion....Monck has the gift of speaking sternly to people without putting them against him, the man he put out of a part in the Mystery play for making a joke about it in the wings, is as obedient and friendly as possible.[54]

The work of the Abbey Theatre School of Acting excited such favorable comment that the critic J. P. M. of the Dublin *Evening Telegraph* decided to discuss the subject of acting with the man responsible for the School's great success. His article "The School of Acting, Talk with Mr. Monck" appeared in that paper on January 20, and in it Monck gave the clearest explanation of what he was hoping to achieve by his work with medieval drama. The interviewer summarized Monck's comments:

> At present in scenery and dress we overburden the play itself and the actors; it is absolutely necessary to go back to early times in order to counteract this growing tendency. He does not want pre-Elizabethan drama without any adjuncts in the way of scenery to be the predominant feature of our stage. But as the pre-Raphaelite school went back to nature, he wants us to go back to the foundations of drama, and then as the pendulum always swings and then stops, we shall arrive at a happy medium.

After the great acclaim of this third production, Monck had to return to Norwich for a week to organize preparations for a major pageant he was to produce there in June. While he was away the Abbey was leased to the Independent Theatre Company. Meanwhile the School began work on George Fitzmaurice's *The Country Dressmaker* and Lady Gregory's *The Gaol Gate*. When Monck returned he had a severe cold and could not run rehearsals. Dress rehearsal was a disaster and Yeats was deeply disappointed. "It shows how completely they are his puppets," he wrote to Lady Gregory on the morning of February 3. But the students seemed to have pulled themselves together sufficiently by that evening to give *The Gaol Gate,* at least, the most beautiful production Yeats had ever seen of it.

On February 7 through 9 *The Countess Cathleen* was produced again, along with *Spreading the News* by Lady Gregory. Yeats was not happy with the performance. He had failed to hire sufficient technical staff, and as a result the lights were not operated correctly and sound cues were missed. In his description of the event to Lady Gregory on February 12 he wrote, "Beautiful as Monck's production is there are places where I long for Craig's more original pictoral [*sic*] sense. Monck has a great sense of beauty but I sometimes feel I want more phantasy of costume." Yeats got what he wanted the following week when Monck produced Lady Gregory's *The Canavans,* the first full-length play using Craig's specially designed screens, and Douglas Hyde's *An Tincéar agus an tSídheóg* (*The Tinker and the Fairy*), the Abbey Theatre's first attempt at a play in Gaelic.

Gordon Craig's screens were the culmination of his innovative theories on stage design, theories which called for architectural rather than pictorial scenery. The screens were made from varying numbers of wooden frames covered with canvas. These were of uniform height, but of different widths. By varying the location of these screens and folding them either backward or forward at different angles to one another, almost infinite variety in the shape of the stage space could be achieved.[55] This system was not yet fully developed when Craig donated a model of it to the Abbey Theatre and gave Yeats permission to use the system there.[56] But during the two years before Monck's arrival, Yeats had had little opportunity to employ Craig's screens because, above all, the effectiveness of the system depended on a careful use of the most modern techniques in stage lighting. In Monck, Yeats had perhaps the most experienced practitioner of these modern methods in Great Britain, and *The Canavans* was produced with the most elaborate lighting ever seen at the Abbey Theatre.

Craig had designed his system of screens to be moved into various shapes, in full view of the audience, during the course of the performance. This had a great appeal to Monck, who was searching for a method of achieving unbroken continuity in his productions. But the screens proved too cumbersome for such manipulation. Craig himself had experienced a near disaster with them only six weeks earlier when, just before the opening of his production of *Hamlet* at the Moscow Arts Theatre, one screen had fallen, knocking many of the others over like so many dominoes. Monck elected to play for safety and alter the shapes only between scenes, but still this production was one of the few effective experiments ever made in the use of Craig's screens.[57]

Yeats was delighted with Monck's use of the screens, with the beautiful lighting, and with the fantastic *commedia dell'arte* costuming that Monck's London designer, Miss Jennie Moore, had done. But the local critics, though they admired Monck's staging and the acting, were less than enthusiastic about Craig's screens. The *Daily Express* stated, "It is like the Japanese Theatre, all bluster and nothing for the eye," to which Yeats appended the comment, "the Japanese Theatre being the most elaborate in its art in the whole world."[58]

Yeats was by this time convinced that the new second company was better at verse drama than the first company was, though the second company did not have as much comic poise. He decided to test their skills with his poetic play *The Land of Heart's Desire* and he gave Monck complete control in producing it. It proved to be a wise decision. The play was produced along with two other one-act plays on February 22 through 24. The *Evening Telegraph* reflected the consensus of opinion when it printed:

> *The Land of Heart's Desire* has always given many people the idea that it was more fitted for the study than the stage, and that it lost most of its poetic charm when produced. However, its wonderful setting last evening (the credit of which is due to Mr. Nugent Monck) preserved the proper atmosphere.... Mr. Monck himself took the part of Father Hart and delivered his lines with a quiet dignity and clearness of enunciation that charmed the house.[59]

The music Monck had composed for this play was also much admired.

Monck followed this personal success with another one the following week, February 29 through March 2. He produced *The World and the Child,* in which he also took the leading role as Manhood, along with three other one-acts which had been previously produced. "Beautifully staged and impressively acted... Breadth of effect was the note of the staging, with its large and striking unities of colour, and its careful lighting, aided by thoughtful grouping of the players," wrote the critic for an unidentified newspaper.[60] "He has a rare sense of the beauty of words," added the *Freeman's Journal* on March 1. "It speaks volumes for the thoroughness of Mr. Monck's training that all the parts, both great and small, were splendidly filled," concluded the *Evening Telegraph* the same day. It was the most successful religious drama ever staged at the Abbey. It was also the last performance for the Abbey Theatre School of Acting. Monck had to return home to begin work on his upcoming pageant and he left Dublin on March 2. The second company was by now officially formed. They played a bill of four one-acts on March 7 through 9, then performed roughly each Wednesday from the first company's return on March 13 to the close of the season on April 27. From then until the following December they were sent out on tours to Belfast, Galway, Longford, Doneraile, and other cities. The Abbey School of Acting was never revived. Sara Allgood taught voice production classes on Sunday afternoons for a time but nothing like a school was attempted again.

In four months the School had given 44 performances of 22 plays and 9 of these were first productions for the Abbey.[61] During this period Monck had introduced direct lighting, an apron stage, multiple staging, and a host of other staging techniques to Dublin. To the majority of critics Monck's productions were visually superior to any that had been staged at the Abbey.[62] Monck's successors did not maintain his high standards, however, and most of the advances Monck had made for the Abbey were lost in a very short time. But several members of the second company he had trained went on to greater success. A. P. Wilson and Harry Hutchinson joined the main company of the Irish Players a few years later, Una O'Connor went on to a long career in New

York and Hollywood, and Cathleen Nesbitt found a career on the London stage.[63] Those who followed the fortunes of the Abbey were sorry to see Monck go.

The Irish Players' Second American Tour

It was not only the Abbey followers who regretted Monck's departure from Dublin in March of 1912. In a postscript to a letter to Lady Gregory dated March 18, 1912, Yeats wrote:

> I noticed in the part of your letter which you crossed out, you suggested No. Two [company] doing *Kincora*. I think if Monck comes back in the Autumn he should be put to do it. He will get much more out of them than I could or than Robinson could . . . Kerrigan said to me last night, "The new Company have had great good fortune in being rehearsed for six months by a man who knows every part of his business, I wish we could get the same."

But it was in April, when the second company got its chance to do *The Workhouse Ward* and *Hyacinth Halvey* at the Prince of Wales Theatre in London, that Monck was most sorely missed. *The Workhouse Ward* opened as a curtain warmer to *At the Barn* on April 15. It was a disaster. Yeats detailed the entire affair in a letter to Lady Gregory dated April 14, but more likely written April 19. After the second performance, the theatre manager said to Yeats simply, "Worst show I ever saw in a London theatre." The problem was that Monck had trained the cast to act with a subtlety that was not suitable for a large London theatre. Yeats had no idea how to correct the problem. Meanwhile, to the absolute horror of Yeats, the stage manager for the theatre attempted to "put things right," and the description Yeats gave of what he did epitomizes the difference between Monck's methods and those in common use on the professional stage. In this letter, Yeats wrote:

> He said to me on Tuesday 'I have given them a lecture on Dramatic Art, the first thing is to act so that every word will reach the audience, and to use such pantomime that a Frenchman who didn't know what was being said would understand the play. It is only when this has been done, and last in importance, that they should try to be old men.' The very first day he wanted me to tell them to have neither accent nor dialect during the first few minutes of the Play. Now our art is the reverse of all this. We say first of all be old men and do not expect to please everybody. We begin with expression as in the other arts and not with the public.

Yeats could only solve the problem by a drastic recasting of the play with professionals who had experience in London. But he readily conceded, "If Monck had been with us now he could have come over and rehearsed them and stood between them and the Stage Manager here, and on the very first day would have known if changes were necessary." Understandably, Yeats was anxious for Monck's return to the Abbey Theatre.

Meanwhile Monck was back in Norwich hard at work on *The Mancroft Pageant,* his first really large civic show. He had brought Charles Powers from the Abbey to be his stage manager. The Pageant ran June 26 through 29, 1912, and it was another triumph for Monck. By July Monck had returned to work for the Irish Players and staged Yeats's *The Countess Cathleen* with the main company at the Court Theatre in London during the week of July 9. After a brief sojourn in Norwich Monck returned to Dublin to direct the Irish Players' Second Company for a short tour of the provinces.

The second company opened its autumn tour with productions of *The Country Dressmaker* and *The Second Shepherd's Play* at the Abbey Theatre, October 3 through 6, 1912, and Monck toured the provincial cities of Carlow, Maryborough, Tullamore, Kilkenny, Naas, Mullinger, Athlone, and Galway with them during the rest of October. In November the second company was entrusted to A. P. Wilson while Monck joined the main company at the Abbey to prepare for their second tour of the United States of America. On November 22, he produced Yeats's third version of *The Hour Glass,* in which he also played the leading role. This was a poetic version of the script which had been rewritten at rather short notice when it was learned that Gordon Craig would not allow his screens to be used by the Irish Players on their American tour.

Monck's designs for these productions were better liked by the Irish critics than the Craig screens had been and his success in Dublin brought the indignation of Frank Fay, who wrote to a friend on October 27, 1912, "It is astonishing that Dublin can allow an outsider like Monck to be placed in the position that either Will [his brother] or I should have."[64]

The first company had not been very enthusiastic about the prospect of another tour in America but agreed, grudgingly, to a three-month engagement. They left on the steamship *Majestic* on December 19 and after landing in New York took a train to Chicago where they opened at the New Arts Theatre on December 30 for a run of four weeks. Monck's influence on the main company was obvious from the first performance. In an article for the Dublin *Evening Herald* on January 23, 1913, Joseph Holloway told the Dublin public how one Chicago critic responded to opening night. The critic for the *Chicago Daily Tribune,* Percy Hammond, had set out to see the first show with "an inclination to insert discord," and if possible Sara Allgood and Arthur Sinclair were to be his victims, Holloway reported. He quoted Hammond: "Recollections of certain broad, forced moments in their former appearance here rankled into my memory thereof, and it was planned to put Miss Allgood and Mr. Sinclair in their places—as ordinary players striving for 'points' and caring little how they got them." But in this performance of

Maurice Harte, Hammond found that "they hit the mean between too little and too much emphasis, an effective combination of art and artlessness." Holloway commented about this review, "It used to be said of the Irish Players that, no matter how poignant the scene entrusted to them, they showed no sign of being moved, but proceeded with it in their quaint, soft, musical though matter of fact, undertone." This was indeed what Yeats had taught them to do and he was surely right in bringing realism into the performance of the kind of plays he produced. But acting is an art and as such cannot simply be a mechanical reproduction of life. Monck saw to it that art was not lost in the reaction against the excesses of the commercial stage. In this regard Monck did with Yeats's ideas what he had done with Poel's. He recognized the value of the ideas and then interpreted them in a form that was acceptable to the public. There was at least one occasion on this tour, however, when Monck's staging won some undeserved praise for the subtlety of its realism. During a domestic scene in one of the Irish peasant plays, a reviewer commented that, as in real life, the characters tended to drift naturally toward the fireplace. But this was not part of Monck's original intent; "the prompter was there," he later explained.[65]

During their Chicago stay the Irish Players made a brief appearance at the University of Notre Dame, then went on to Pittsburgh, Montreal, Philadelphia, New York, and Boston. They performed a repertory of 22 plays including *The Playboy of the Western World.* Monck seems to have been a great favorite with the critics. Peter Kavanagh wrote in his book *The Story of the Abbey Theatre* that in New York, "the critics gave great praise to everyone associated with the company; Nugent Monck, they singled out as the greatest actor of the group." Kavanagh went on to say, "This was absurd, for Monck had a hard English accent, but American people, particularly the critics, find the English accent irresistible."[66] Judging from Monck's success in Dublin the previous spring it was not so absurd as all that. The production in which Monck was most successful on this tour was Yeats's poetic play *The Countess Cathleen* and it seems more likely that the critics were responding to Monck's speaking of verse, in which he excelled, than to his English accent.

Lady Gregory and Yeats were apparently not so appreciative. In a letter to Lady Gregory discussing the possible inclusion of his own *The Hour Glass* in this tour Yeats said, "Monck could play it finely if he could only keep from tricks, but now that he has remembered these he will always be tricky in this part I suppose."[67] Indeed it was after the pretour performance of this play in Dublin, in which Monck played the Wise Man, that Yeats made the comment which Monck often repeated in later years, "When I see you produce, I want you to play all the parts, but when I see you act, I wonder how an intelligent man can be so bad."[68] In light of the critical response to Monck's acting in both Dublin and America, Joseph Holloway's observation that "Yeats and

Lady Gregory knew nothing whatsoever about acting" seems appropriate.[69] Monck was not a great actor but he was certainly not a bad one.

The tour was apparently not an easy one for Monck and he wrote often to Yeats about his dissatisfaction. On March 7, Yeats wrote to Monck:

> The Abbey company is as difficult to manage as a South American Republic—Fay, Payne, Norre, Connell and Robinson (who was a failure in America) have all failed to get discipline. I know how hard it is to work in an atmosphere of hostility; but I hope you will be able to keep on till the end of the tour. I want you to do whatever Lady Gregory wants and you can. I do not think she could stand the strain of management and this company would never, with you away, obey one of themselves. I think you are probably wasted on present work. I have a few friendly New York notices of *Countess Cathleen* which show that I owe you a fine performance.

Monck did stay on until the end of the tour but he did not return to Dublin with the rest of the company on May 1, 1913. Many years later he would say that his job with the Abbey had been to mediate between the company and the management, who were always at loggerheads, and he added, "I must have done my job very well because both sides hated me by the end."[70] In fact, however, Yeats remained a good friend of Monck's for many years, and as late as 1932 the actress Sara Allgood would write to Monck, "Remember me in your plans for next year. Do think of me in some special part."[71] Monck was probably being more accurate when he said for the BBC, "On returning I was given the opportunity of throwing my lot in with the Abbey Theatre. But although I learned much from that institution—how to run a small theatre cheaply—I felt the limits of the Celtic twilight and my heart was really in the Shakespearian experiments that Mr. William Poel was making."[72]

Certainly, 1912 had been a year to stimulate such an interest. Max Reinhardt's production of *The Miracle,* which Monck saw in the spring of that year, "gave practical shape on a large scale to the principles of Elizabethan staging," Poel said in his *Monthly Letters.* [73] In August, large scale reconstructions of both the Globe and the Fortune Playhouse had been built for the Shakespeare's England Festival at Earl's Court, London. Scenes from Shakespeare's plays were acted in these reconstructions, making this the first attempt at actual working models of these theatres. Finally, in December, just prior to Monck's departure for America, Poel opened an outstanding production of *Troilus and Cressida* at King's Hall, Covent Garden. This was the sort of activity that fired Monck's imagination.

2

Building a Theatre:
1913–1921

While with the Irish Players in Chicago, Monck had met Maurice Browne, founder of the Chicago Little Theatre. During the previous visit of the Irish Players, Browne had asked Lady Gregory's advice about forming a theatre and she told him, "By all means start your own theatre; but make it in your own image. Don't engage professional players; they have been spoiled for your purpose. Engage and train, as we of the Abbey have done, amateurs: shopgirls, school-teachers, counter-jumpers; cut-throat-thieves rather than professionals."[1] Monck of course had set out to do exactly that with the Norwich Players in 1910. But Browne went so far as to secure for his group their own theatre which had opened November 12, 1912, just a few weeks before Monck's arrival in Chicago.

This was an inspiration to Monck, who had long regretted the amount of money which had to be expended on the rental of performance space and who was often frustrated by the last minute rush of moving in. But the inspiration may not have been all one way. Monck indicated in the outline for his autobiography that he intended to write about Browne's production of Schnitzler's *Anatol*. It seems a remarkable coincidence that when Browne wrote his own autobiography in 1955 his only recollection of the production was,

> When we played *Anatol* a Chicago paper commented enviously on the five magnificent sets of velvet curtains with which the five scenes from the play—all that we performed—were hung; the gift, presumably, of a wealthy sponsor. We had used one set of curtains throughout, made of flannelette, with differently coloured lights thrown on it for each scene.[2]

Monck had used exactly this method to change scenes in his production of the *Bethlehem Tableaux* at Norwich in January 1911. Did Browne ask the advice of the Irish Players' manager on how to stretch his meager resources over his first multiple-scene show? Unfortunately, this cannot now be determined with certainty, but it would seem quite likely, given Browne's admiration for the Abbey Theatre. The rarity of such a technique and Monck's availability for consultation at precisely this time do suggest that perhaps more than coincidence was involved. The Chicago Little Theatre was one of the pioneers of modern stage lighting in America; if Monck was instrumental in directing this group toward the ideas of Appia and Craig, it was another of the subtle but significant influences his work had on our contemporary stage.

By the end of the tour, Monck was anxious to follow the example Browne had set, and was determined to secure a permanent home for his amateurs, the Norwich Players.

The Old Music House

While Monck was away with the Irish Players his own Norwich Players had not been inactive. Bridges-Adams, who had assisted Monck with several of his early productions in Norfolk, had taken over as their producer. He took Monck's production of *Job* with the same cast, costumes, set and lights to London where it was produced at King's Hall, Covent Garden, on November 18, 1912. Apparently for the publicity value, William Poel was advertised as the producer, but in fact he took only dress rehearsals and the production remained in all essentials exactly as Monck had originally staged it in March of 1911.[3] The success of the show did a great deal to enhance the reputations of both Poel and the young Bridges-Adams. Princess Christina requested that a special performance of this powerful religious drama be given the following spring.

Bridges-Adams returned with the cast to Norwich where they performed the play at Blackfriars' Hall on February 13 through 14 to keep in practice for the special engagement, which was scheduled for May 8, 1913. It was most likely Monck's hurry to get back in time to oversee this production that caused him to part from the Irish Players before they reached Dublin after their United States tour. The May 8 engagement was another success and the Norwich Players were invited to perform the play in the Shakespeare Memorial Theatre at Stratford-upon-Avon during the following August.

Monck appeared in Poel's final revival of *Everyman* in July 1913. Edith Evans was in the cast in the role of Knowledge. Monck's role is not listed but Ernest Thesiger played Fellowship, the role Monck had had in previous revivals. After this revival, Monck purchased the entire set, properties and costumes from Poel.[4] This material became the mainstay of Monck's work for many years, and as late as 1955 he was still able to revive the play with Poel's original set and ten of these original costumes.[5]

The Stratford-upon-Avon production of *Job* took place on August 15. This production was the young Bridges-Adams's first appearance at the Shakespeare Memorial Theatre, whose fortunes he would direct from 1919 to 1934.

After the summer successes in London and Stratford-upon-Avon, Monck decided to expand his activities in Norwich by producing *Everyman* and his own adaptation of the medieval French romantic epic *Aucassin and Nicolette* at the Norwich Theatre Royal. The *Everyman* production was a faithful revival of Poel's work, so it was to *Aucassin and Nicolette* that Monck really applied his talents. Bridges-Adams, who was still Monck's assistant, painted a beautiful forest setting of blue tree trunks against a gilded sky. Done in aniline dyes on hessian material, it was a backcloth that would often be reused. The design was obviously based on Monck's own backdrop for the 1911 Dublin production of *The Countess Cathleen*; it was strikingly effective and would later find its way to the Old Vic. Great care was taken with the lighting and the production was in all respects Monck's most finished in Norwich up to that date.

It was not a financial success. The Norwich Players' following proved too small to cover the expenses of a theatre as large as the Theatre Royal. But if Monck was at all dismayed by this he left no record of the fact. He was certainly undeterred from his goal of securing a permanent home for his Players. In fact, he had already found a space and on December 20, 1913, he took out a lease for a large room in a building on King Street known as the Old Music House.

Norwich was not an unlikely city for the fostering of new experiments in theatre. It is not a city through which anyone passes on the way to somewhere else, and this isolation generates an independent spirit. In Elizabethan times Norwich vied with Bristol as the most important British city after London. When Shakespeare's fellow actor Will Kemp danced his famous "Nine Daies Wonder" Morris dance, Norwich was his destination. The city has a rich theatre history. "In fact," Poel wrote, "this town's records as regards the early theatre are more full of interesting details than those of any other city out of London."[6] In terms of the availability of a large, educated audience which would not demand recycled London "hits," Monck could hardly have found a better location. Still, his task was not an easy one.

The Old Music House (now known as Wensum Lodge) where Monck set up his new theatre is one of the few surviving Norman dwelling houses in England. The room Monck rented was the upper level of what had once been a great medieval banqueting hall but which had been subdivided sometime in the early nineteenth century. The truss-raftered chestnut roof set off the stage which was roughly 15½ feet wide and 16½ feet deep. On this stage Monck had two 6-inch-square pillars mounted about 6 feet from the front edge and 9½ feet apart. A hessian curtain was hung between these pillars to allow for Monck's method of alternating scenes from front stage to full stage and back again so that sets could be shifted without a break in the action. Lighting was provided by a makeshift row of footlights, and a single arc lamp operated from a rostrum at the rear of the house. The footlights, however, were dispensed with as soon as a second arc lamp was secured.[7]

Outside the theatre was hung the newly designed emblem of the Norwich Players, which has been described as a woodpecker, a cockatoo and a flaming lamp. It is, however, a drawing of the chanticleer of St. Peter, the bird of dawning, symbol of enlightenment, perched on a pedestal studying its part from the book of life for the benefit of mankind.[8] It was drawn by Peggy Kinder and was based on a plate found in John Ruskin's *The Stones of Venice.*[9] This emblem remains the symbol of the Norwich Players' purpose to this day.

Less than three weeks after signing the lease Monck opened his little theatre with *A Twelfth Night Revel.* This was a triple bill of medieval morality plays. In February the Norwich Players performed *Twelfth Night.* It was their first attempt at Shakespeare and their first break from medieval drama. The medieval plays had provided excellent training for the group; the dignity and directness of these plays encouraged a style of acting that was simple, restrained and slightly stylized, and their language demanded a clear intelligent articulation. But a regular season schedule in a permanent theatre could hardly be sustained with such works, and the training would have been of little value if it were applied only to a genre of drama which had such a limited appeal.

After *Twelfth Night,* Monck produced another of his own works, a Molière, a modern play, and two more plays by Shakespeare before closing out the season in June. In August 1914 Monck visited the Memorial Theatre at Stratford-upon-Avon for a last holiday before embarking on the already prepared second season. While he was there, war was declared.[10] Monck hurriedly returned to Norwich to find his band of players either already enlisted or preparing to do so. The Old Music House was closed and Monck went to London to join the war effort.

Monck was 36 years old, one year over the limit for enlisting during the early months of the war. He lied about his age, was accepted into the medical corps and sent to Aldershot for training. In February 1915 he was shipped to Egypt and for the next fourteen months his full energies were given to his work as an operating room orderly for the Royal Army Medical Corps, an especially demanding task during the disastrous Gallipoli campaign (April through December 1915).[11]

But Nugent Monck could not bear the idea of Shakespeare's Tercentenary going by without some appropriate celebration, even if a major war was being waged. By April 1916 he was producing plays for the Fifteenth General Hospital's Music and Drama Society and from that time until his discharge in the spring of 1919 he managed to produce 18 plays by authors from Shakespeare to Sheridan to Shaw.

Monck's productions of Shakespeare with all-male casts during these war years came to the attention of a little-known Shakespearean actor, Robert Atkins, who was serving with the London Regiment in Palestine. The effectiveness of Monck's application of Poel's principles inspired Atkins, who had been an actor for Ben Greet at the Old Vic, to write to that theatre's manager, Miss Lilian Baylis, and propose to produce a season of plays in her theatre using William Poel's methods. Atkins had little, if any, prior contact with Poel or his methods but in Monck he found someone absolutely dedicated to the kind of theatrical art Poel had envisaged without the eccentricities which marred much of Poel's own work.

After the war, Atkins became the producer for the Old Vic, and about the same time another of Monck's admirers, Bridges-Adams, took over at the Memorial Theatre, Stratford-upon-Avon. Poel's theories gained considerable recognition through the work of these three men in those postwar years. All were personal friends of Poel's during this period and Poel's ideas were their inspiration. But when it came to the practical application of Poel's theories to the problems of acting, lighting, staging and designing, Atkins and Adams turned to Nugent Monck.

Return from the First World War

Monck arrived back in Norwich in early June 1919, four and a half years after leaving it. He had £47 to his name and an aged father to support. Producing drama was his profession but conditions had changed considerably during his absence and it was not easy to pick up where he had left off. His little theatre at the Old Music House had been undisturbed but of his dedicated band of Norwich Players only Martin Kinder had returned. Victor Earles, the most promising actor of the group, had died in France. The others survived but the war had taken them to new lives away from Norwich.

Monck immediately set about the task of reforming the Players. On August 27 and 28 he produced *A Midsummer Night's Dream* at Blickling Hall. This was not a Norwich Players production but "a Nugent Monck production," no doubt to raise money to finance the reopening of his theatre. It must have been a financial success because on September 13, 1919, Monck was able to renew his lease on the upper room of the Old Music House.

Figure 2. Monck's Stage at the Old Music House
(From Mariette Soman and F. W. Wheldon, The Norwich Players
[Norwich: Mariette Soman, 1920], p. 4.)

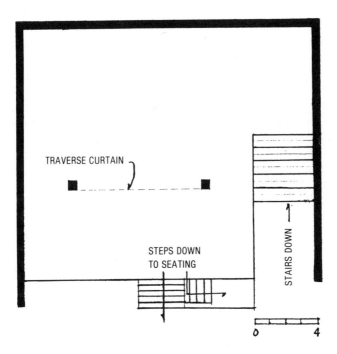

Figure 3. Plan of Stage at the Old Music House
(Plan by William Brainard from author's drawing)

The new group of Norwich Players began their first season at the Old Music House on September 24, 1919, with a production of Shakespeare's *Much Ado about Nothing*. For the first time women were allowed to become members of the group and Monck, too, was now elected. The production received little public attention. The critic for the *Eastern Daily Press,* reviewing the play the next day, briefly welcomed the group back, mentioned the austerity of Monck's prewar work, then added, "It is a very debatable point whether Shakespeare does not suffer considerably by thus adhering to a 'threadbare wardrobe of a bygone time.'"[12] This was typical of the sort of comment which had always been made about Poel and his followers. But debatable or not, this was to be the new direction of the theatre. Prices had soared during the war. In 1917 Henry Irving was forced to withdraw a successful production of *Hamlet* after only two weeks in spite of very good houses because the cost of producing it was double that of a modern play and his theatre simply could not afford it.[13] Films too had grown in popularity during these years and were altering audience expectations in the theatre. Audiences became less tolerant of ineffectual attempts at realistic stage settings and more impatient with the long waits that massive set changes entailed. The theatre could not compete scenically with film realism and its only hope for survival was to present an alternative art form. A return to the Elizabethan conventions with their combination of medieval symbolism and Renaissance pictorial imagery provided one such alternative, and within 10 years Monck was able to prove overwhelmingly that such an approach could be viable both artistically and financially.

Poel had been the first to use this alternative approach and Monck was fast developing it beyond what Poel himself had been able to do. F. W. Wheldon, a critic for one of the Norwich newspapers, provided an excellent illustration of Monck's art and economy from the opening production of *Much Ado about Nothing*. In the church scene, he said:

> The priest accompanied by his acolytes in red came on and stood with his back to the audience, while the curtains opened discovering the whole of the cast who moved slowly forward to the priest, the two principals a little in advance of the rest on a small white stage-cloth. The effect of this cloth was, when Claudio waves the priest on one side, to isolate Claudio and Hero for the tragic scene as no other method on so tiny a stage could possibly do.[14]

In a later review of a less successful Shakespeare, Wheldon describes how "all the effect of a dance was obtained [on this small stage] with figures crossing and recrossing at the back while the action of the play continued at the front."[15] These are examples of the subtle visual beauty for which Monck was justly famous and which went so far to help the actors in his productions.

Monck's tendency towards Poel's habit of severely cutting his Shakespearean scripts was most marked during this period in his career. Wheldon wrote about Monck's Shakespearean productions of this period, "Although the cuts were severe, and to my mind inimical to good acting in all except the principal parts, the idea of each play came out clearly, convincingly and with extraordinary effect."[16] Such cuts were not really inimical to good acting, as for the most part Monck based his cuts on the ability of the performer to sustain the role. The better the performer, the more the lines were left untouched by the blue pencil.[17] But Monck was obsessed with the idea of not boring his audience, and rather than subject them to a poor delivery of great lines, he would cut such lines drastically. Fortunately, while Poel increased the amount of cutting he did in a script as he got older, Monck did the opposite. As he reacquired a core group of excellent performers, he returned many lines to the performed texts.

The production for January 1919 was intended to be John Gay's *The Beggar's Opera*, the first revival in modern times of the now well-known operetta. Unfortunately, the actor who was to play the leading role broke his arm just after rehearsals began and Monck had hurriedly to substitute *The School for Scandal* into his scheduled season. This accident left the honor of staging the first modern revival of *The Beggar's Opera* to Nigel Playfair of the Lyric Theatre, Hammersmith, but *The School for Scandal* proved to be a happy substitute. It was Monck's greatest financial success up to that time and it gave his Norwich Players a much needed boost in morale.

Monck's production of Gay's *The Beggar's Opera* finally appeared on June 14 through 19, 1920, less than two weeks after it was revived at the Lyric Theatre, Hammersmith. The *Eastern Daily Press* critic wrote, "The more considered opinion of the critics appears to be that at the Lyric the play has been interpreted too much in the spirit of broad farce. Mr. Nugent Monck has not erred in that direction. . . . He has invested them [the characters] with grace and sobriety."[18] The Hammersmith production by Nigel Playfair was one of the most important revivals of its day. Playfair was careful to say that the idea of reviving this play was entirely his own, uninfluenced by the fact that Monck, who was his fellow member of the London Shakespeare League, had had the play in rehearsal before Playfair even began work on a production book.[19] Apparently this was one of those remarkable coincidences which occur in the theatre from time to time.

Over the next several years, however, Monck's work with the Norwich Players would provide considerable inspiration for Playfair and his Lyric Theatre in Hammersmith. In 1923, after seeing Monck's production of Toller's *The Machine Wreckers*, which was done for the Stage Society in London, Playfair wrote to Monck,

I want to be allowed to congratulate you on your production for the Stage Society; as far as scenery and the dresses were concerned, it is by far the most satisfying thing I have seen on the English stage for many years, and it makes me very keen to come down and see some of your work in Norwich, and to talk over, if your ambitions lie at all in that direction, the chance of our doing something together in London.[20]

Monck's ambitions did not, it seems, lie in that direction. But early the next year, *The Way of the World,* a play Monck had given its first postwar revival in March of 1923, appeared in the Lyric season and was a great success.

The following year Playfair did a comic opera by Sheridan called *The Duenna,* a play Monck had given its first modern revival in June 1923. Playfair specifically denied any connection between Monck's revival and his own[21] (although Barry Jackson had no hesitation in copying Monck's production at his Birmingham Repertory Theatre), but the pattern of a production having its first postwar revival under Nugent Monck's direction and then appearing in Playfair's program happened with great regularity. By 1926 the influence became undeniable. Playfair went to Norwich to see Monck's production of *Marriage à la Mode* in February of that year. As it happened, the leading actress for the show had contracted ringworm on her left shoulder, which presented a serious problem in a show costumed with eighteenth-century off-the-shoulder dresses. Drawing on his great knowledge of costume, Monck recalled a type of decorative sash sometimes worn by women in prints and paintings of that period. He soon devised such a sash for his leading lady and the problem was solved. Playfair saw this production and was highly complimentary to the cast but said the play would never do for London. By that summer, however, the play was on at the Lyric Theatre. Not to be outdone by Monck, Playfair had every woman in the Lyric cast costumed with one of those decorative sashes.[22]

The next year, when a successful production of *The Beaux' Stratagem* saved the Lyric from financial disaster, it was done with the music Monck had originally used in his revival of the play.[23] In fact, of the nine productions which established the Lyric Theatre's reputation after *The Beggar's Opera,* all but two had been given their first postwar revival by Monck. *The Way of the World, The Duenna, The Rivals, The Beaux' Strategem, Marriage à la Mode, She Stoops to Conquer* and *The Critic* were all seen in Norwich before they were seen anywhere else in England after the war. Only revivals of *Lionel and Clarissa* and *Love in a Village* were first staged at Playfair's Lyric and these were the least successful of the nine major shows.[24] In 1928 Playfair finally conceded Monck's influence on his work. In an impromptu speech given after Monck's premiere production of Bax and Shaw's musical *Waterloo Leave,* "he acknowledged his own indebtedness to Mr. Monck and the Players."[25]

Certainly, it was Playfair's flair and style that made these shows London successes, something which Monck could not have done. But the connection here illustrates the important contribution to theatre made by the Little Theatre Movement which was beginning to grow during these postwar years. These Little Theatres could afford to take chances on plays which the commercial stage dared not risk. Once a group such as Monck's had proven that a long neglected script or a new play could attract an audience, the more creative of the London managers would take a chance on it. In this way the Little Theatres slowly improved the state of theatre art in England. With great courage and energy they introduced innovations in drama and in production methods, and they trained audiences to appreciate these innovations.

Monck's 1920–21 season opened with a production of *Romeo and Juliet* notable only for Monck's extensive cutting of the script. The actor cast for Romeo proved undependable, so with only a few days' rehearsal Monck took the role himself. But he had to edit the text considerably in order to be able to learn it in time, and at 42 he lacked the passion of a young lover. An excellent though straightforward production of *Candida* followed on October 11–16, but it was Monck's production of the *Hippolytus* of Euripides in November that was the great achievement of the season. This production inspired the following observation from the local critic:

> Mr. Monck is not concerned to reproduce archaisms, except so far as they contribute to artistic and dramatic effect. His Shakespeare productions are not a reconstruction of the Elizabethan theatre, nor his mysteries and moralities a harking back to medieval ways of production. He gives his own ideas of the plays he produces, whether they be ancient or modern, informed, of course, by careful study of such material and methods as are available. All true art is the result of an effort of the imagination, and what we witness at the Music House, then, in the way of a production is an imaginative effort, a work of creative art. . . . [H]abitues of the Music House witness drama produced sensibly, sensitively, and, if anything, in an ultra modern way.[26]

This is the first signed review by F. W. Wheldon, whose censorious criticism of Norwich Players performances would eventually lead to his being asked to resign. But he had a great respect for Monck's ideals and his constant criticism prevented any complacency in Monck's work.

The Music House was now operating at ninety-five percent capacity, an indication that the audience was of sufficient size to support a more ambitious venture. In addition, the city fire marshal was beginning to look unfavorably at the audience safety facilities in the Old Music House, and there was a distinct possibility that its license as a playhouse would not be renewed. Monck searched exhaustively for another building.

In March Monck was shown an old derelict building in an alley not far from the city center. The building had a gallery on three sides and perfect acoustics and he decided that it could be converted into the kind of theatre he envisaged. The building, however, was not for lease; it was for sale, a matter of no small importance as the Norwich Players operated from production to production, paying their way and Monck's salary as they went. Members paid no subscriptions and the group did not accumulate funds. Monck had a small legacy of shares which his father had purchased for him in better years, but he was now forty-three and this was all he had set aside for his retirement. He made a determined effort to acquire some financial backers for the purchase but could find no one who did not impose unacceptable conditions. Finally Monck risked all; he borrowed money, using the shares as security, and purchased the old Georgian building and freehold in St. John's Maddermarket Alley for £1,700 on March 24, 1921. Before it could be opened as a theatre, however, an almost equal amount had to be spent on its conversion.

At the Old Music House Monck had been developing his ideas on producing plays simply, with a rapid tempo and an unbroken continuity in the action. Of the ideas on Shakespeare's stagecraft that Poel had espoused, these were the basics that Monck believed had an application to modern drama as well as to the classics. His experiments along these lines, however, had always been hampered by the unsuitable nature of the stage spaces with which he had to work. Now, with his own building he could finally realize his dream of having a theatre in which to perform a wide variety of plays using reasonably similar methods of staging to those which had existed in Shakespeare's day. In recognition of the man who had inspired this dream, Monck invited his old master William Poel to come to Norwich and give advice on the conversion. By August, the necessary plans had been drawn up and the work of converting this derelict hall into the Maddermarket Theatre began.

The Maddermarket Theatre

Norwich is a city which even today maintains much of its medieval character. Its impressive Norman castle keep, set high upon a manmade mound, still dominates the city center, and its cathedral, with the second tallest spire in England, remains one of the most beautiful in the country. But it is the 40 Perpendicular churches which do most to maintain the city's ancient charm; made of the local Norfolk flint, they are an eloquent testament to the wealth and power generated by Norwich's weaving trade from the fourteenth to the eighteenth century. In the shadow of the spire of one of these churches, the fifteenth-century parish church of St. John's, is an area traditionally known as the Maddermarket. Located only a few hundred yards north of the city's present open market, it is thought that here, long before the church was built, madder root was sold to the weavers for the dyeing of cloth. An alleyway runs through the church tower and along the churchyard wall, the same wall over which Will Kemp, Shakespeare's fellow actor, leapt at the end of his "Nine Daies Wonder" dance in 1599. It was halfway down this alley, set back in a courtyard, that Monck found the building he purchased in March of 1921.[27]

Monck's new property had been built in 1794 as a Roman Catholic chapel. The chapel was a rectangular building roughly 42 feet wide and 52 feet long (the building is off square so that exact measurements are not available). It had a plaster barrel-vaulted ceiling and galleries on all but the north side where the altar stood. The galleries were 12 feet high and on the east and west walls were 10 feet deep, but the south gallery was 13 feet deep. Two stairways provided access to the galleries from the back.

In preparing for the conversion of this former chapel, Monck consulted as many books as he could find on the playhouses of Shakespeare's day, most notably W. J. Lawrence's *The Elizabethan Playhouse and Other Studies.*[28] He also gave careful consideration to the numerous suggestions William Poel had made during his brief visit, though many of these were not economically feasible. Having established the basics of what he wanted in his new theatre, Monck entrusted the actual designing to Noel Paul, a Canadian who had studied architecture until the war brought him to England. Monck later wrote that Paul was "a man of taste with an instinctive sense of proportion,"[29] and certainly the proportions of the Maddermarket Theatre have always been one of its greatest assets. The city engineer, W. F. Town, made the necessary architectural drawings from Paul's designs and the conversion began in mid-August.

The most difficult project in this alteration was the building of the Elizabethan stage. While the former chapel's exterior measurements were 52 feet long by 42 feet wide, the thickness of its walls and the internal staircases leading to the galleries made its interior dimensions at ground level just 46 feet by 40 feet. In this space Monck constructed a stage, 3 feet high, with the relatively enormous dimensions, in proportion to the space, of 20 feet in depth by 32 feet in width. It was built along what at that time were the generally accepted lines for an Elizabethan stage.

Of England's seventeenth-century playhouses, the one known as the Fortune built in Cripplegate in 1601 was the most often reconstructed by scholars early in this century. This is primarily because it is the only one for which there are any detailed measurements, its building contract being still extant. It is also easier to reconstruct because it was square, not round like the other public, or open-air, theatres of its day. Monck alleged that his new building was roughly a half scale model of that Fortune Theatre. It was a convenient reference and good publicity but not quite accurate. In reality the design followed more closely W. J. Lawrence's conjectures about Shakespeare's own indoor theatre, the Blackfriars.

At the back of his stage Monck had built an inner stage (or underbalcony), 13½ feet wide by 4¾ feet deep. It was framed by two 9-inch-square pillars which were 18 feet tall. Supported by these pillars 8 feet above the inner stage was a balcony of similar dimensions. Flanking the inner stage and balcony were two stage doors surmounted by lattice windows, extending at an angle to the side galleries, a configuration proposed in Lawrence's *The Elizabethan Playhouse* (pp. 20–21). The resulting structure of inner stage, balcony, entrance doors and windows constituted what was then thought of as the façade of an Elizabethan playhouse's stage.

It was generally considered by scholars that this façade extended across the entire rear of the stage, but the façade Monck had devised could back only the central 20 feet of his 36-foot-wide platform stage because the galleries overhung 6 feet on each side. Shakespeare's Blackfriars Playhouse, being only 4 feet wider than Monck's Maddermarket, would have had a similar problem. It was probably precisely this difficulty which caused Lawrence to conjecture that the side galleries of the Blackfriars Theatre did not extend over the stage area at all. But Monck could hardly have afforded the expense of removing this part of his galleries and he needed the upper floor space for his dressing rooms. So to provide a façade for his entire stage he merely continued the walls, in which the angled doors and windows stood, under their respective galleries to a point on the edge of the stage about 6 feet from the front. It was the solution of a practical man of the theatre and had the special advantage of allowing him to add extra stage doors on each side just under the galleries, thereby giving the Maddermarket stage an entrance pattern that was quite similar to the Inigo Jones 1632 drawing of the Cockpit-in-Court. The disadvantage of this solution was that it made his platform stage, which thrust out over 16 feet beyond the inner stage, seem considerably smaller than it actually was.

The final structure to be added was a large decorative canopy 18 feet above the stage. It was supported at the back by the two pillars which held up the balcony and formed the inner stage. Nine feet directly downstage of these, two more pillars were added to support the front of the canopy. Such canopies were known to exist in the open-air stages of Shakespeare's day where they served to protect the stage façade from the weather as well as possibly providing a place for special effects.[30] They would have been unnecessary in an indoor playhouse, however, and are generally thought not to have been used there. But for Monck such a canopy served several functions; it gave him a place to hang some top lights, provided a convenient location from which to hang his beautiful tapestried set curtains, created a frame for his stage pictures without causing the structural separation between actor and audience which was the great disadvantage of the proscenium arch, and functioned as an effective sounding board for the voices of his less skilled performers.

In front of this stage, at ground level, 170 chairs were placed in eight rows. In the south gallery 36 chairs were distributed in four rows. The exact number of chairs originally in the side galleries is not recorded, but it was probably about 30 on each side, distributed in two rows. The first row in each gallery extended over the stage up to the lattice windows of the rear façade. The second row could run only as far as the front edge of the stage, however, because the dressing rooms had been constructed at this level. When the Maddermarket opened in 1921, then, it had an audience capacity of just over 270 seated around three sides of the stage. But the second row of chairs in each side gallery proved unsatisfactory and was soon removed. After several incidents of audience members in the side galleries dropping things onto the stage during performance, the chairs over the stage too were eliminated. By 1926 there were only 12 chairs in each side gallery and the Maddermarket's capacity had been reduced to 240.[31] In 1930, when cinema tip-up seats were purchased to replace the old Georgian chairs, the seating capacity was further reduced to 230, where it remained for the rest of Monck's career.

If constructed today such a design would not be considered Elizabethan. Modern scholarship has rejected the ideas of an inner stage and of oblique stage doors, for example. The Tudor beaming decoration of the interior of the Maddermarket, too, would no longer be thought of as valid. And the lack of any significant audience along the sides of the stage would be unacceptable in a modern reconstruction.[32] But in 1921, before any of the most significant books on the topic had been written, it was an admirable attempt. Despite its deficiencies as an archeological reconstruction it was undeniably a remarkably efficient stage machine on which Monck could develop his methods.

To ensure maximum publicity for his new venture Monck invited W. B. Yeats to speak at the opening. In accepting the invitation Yeats wrote,

> I feel I know the stage now, but have no longer the heart to write. Very possibly your Elizabethan theatre will give me the heart. I should really like—present tasks finished—to try my hand at a bustling play in the manner of Shakespeare's historical plays with 'trumpets' and 'alarums and excursions,' and resounding defiance and everybody murdered at the end and no damned psychology.[33]

Yeats was not disappointed by his visit. The Maddermarket Theatre opened on September 26, 1921, with a production of *As You Like It*. Yeats spoke during the interval. No detailed report was made of his address to the audience. From the critical response to it, however, it is clear that he launched a firm attack on the proscenium arch, picture frame stage which he believed suitable only for the drama of realism. Poetic drama, he declared, required an intimacy between actor and audience which would allow for the full expression of all the vocal nuances of verse. This could be achieved most effectively with the Elizabethan platform stage and Monck's theatre held great promise for the revival of verse drama. Yeats was sincerely impressed by the Maddermarket. After returning to Dublin he wrote to Monck on October 20, "The spectacle of your plays gave me some new life and imagination,"[34] and about the same time he told a friend, the writer L. A. G. Strong, that he was convinced that it would be in Monck's Maddermarket Theatre that the art of speaking poetry, with its original rhythms and values retained instead of being forced into prose, would be championed.[35]

Yeats was not alone in his appreciation of the Maddermarket Theatre. The next day *The Times* hailed it as "one of the brightest spots in the dramatic history of this country," which, it said, "must afford a great deal of comfort to those who are genuinely concerned for the future of the English stage." It was, it added, "an enterprise that one would like to see emulated in every town and village in the country."[36]

Poel went to see Monck's finished theatre on September 28. "He hated it,"[37] Monck would later say, but Poel himself wrote about the theatre for the *Manchester Guardian* on October 1, 1921, "No-one has got closer to the essentials that give scope for the successful presentation of Elizabethan drama than have Mr. Nugent Monck and his able assistants." He went on to say,

> Norwich is singularly fortunate in having Mr. Nugent Monck as director of the enterprise. In organization, in resource, and in tact, he has proved his efficiency. And he also has a wide knowledge, a philosophic mind, and an historical conscience, which will guard him from unduly indulging in experiments that lie outside the scope of dramatic art.

But there were, of course, critics. Those who accepted Monck's suggestion that this was a half scale model of the Fortune Playhouse found numerous objections to its design. After all, it was not open to the sky, had chairs in the pit, used curtains, and did not have a stage strewn with rushes. But had he admitted the Blackfriars Theatre model, Monck would have been able to invalidate such complaints. The primary criticism of the design, however, was that the stage did not project sufficiently far into the house. This was Poel's major objection although he pointed out, "Yet he has had the courage to bring his actors further into the arena than anyone else so far has done who has been experimenting on Elizabethan lines."[38] But in defense of his design, Monck could easily have pointed to the Fortune Theatre contract, which calls for a stage to thrust out to the center of an open yard which was 55 feet square. At the Maddermarket the equivalent of this open yard was defined by the inner edge of the galleries, and this was a space only 20 feet wide and 37 feet long. His stage thrust out 20 feet, 18 inches beyond the center of this area. The real problem was that Monck's audience was not set up to surround the stage sufficiently. Only 12 people could actually sit along the sides. But the authority Monck had turned to, W. J. Lawrence, had argued that there was no side audience at all at the Blackfriars except for a few nobles who possibly sat on stage, so Monck's choice was not without scholarly support.

The majority of those who had a negative response to the Maddermarket, however, criticized it on more general grounds. The *Sunday Herald* exemplified this position when it stated sarcastically, "If returning to Shakespeare's day is artistic progress, let's have the stage lit by torches; invite the local gentry to lounge about on the stage, and when merry to trip the actors up with their swords; and, above all, let us have female roles played by men."[39] But such criticism was based on misconceptions both of the conditions in the Elizabethan playhouse and of what Monck was actually attempting to do.

The Maddermarket Theatre was not intended to be the Globe, the Fortune, or even the Blackfriars Theatre restored. It was intended to be a theatre where Monck could produce all of Shakespeare's plays on the kind of stage it was thought Shakespeare would have had in mind when he wrote them. Monck clearly defined what he meant by this kind of stage as "a stage designed for fast moving performances with one scene following closely upon another and the words spoken quickly so as to render the play within, as Shakespeare himself put it, 'the two hours' traffic of the stage.'"[40] Whether Elizabethan stages were actually designed for such a mode of staging or not is a question which is still being debated. What cannot be denied, however, is that in 1921 this represented one of the most important movements in modern theatre history. For years producers had been extending their stages past the proscenium as Monck had done at the Abbey, placing action in the house, as Monck had also done, or even dispensing with theatres altogether, doing their plays in parks, churches, or bare halls. But the Maddermarket was the first theatre in England since the Commonwealth to have been designed and built with no trace of a proscenium. It was a true experimental theatre and within 10 years it built an international reputation. In 1931, the noted dramatist and critic St. John Ervine wrote of it, "Norwich has in its Maddermarket Theatre, directed by Mr. Nugent Monck, one of the most interesting experimental theatres in the world."[41]

What was experimental about the Maddermarket? The writer T. R. Barnes explained it for the Cambridge quarterly *Scrutiny* when he wrote that Monck "always wanted an Elizabethan stage; not for sentimental or archeological reasons, but because he believed, and has since triumphantly proved, that it is the cheapest, most flexible and most artistically satisfactory form of stage for a small theatre."[42] From the standpoint of the Elizabethan revival, even so formidable a Shakespearean as G. Wilson Knight later said, "I am not myself in favour of an Elizabethan theatre; to incorporate certain Elizabethan principles with our own seems healthier,"[43] and he used the Maddermarket as an example of how this could best be done. The combination of modern and archaic features gave the Maddermarket a remarkable versatility. Barnes continued in that same *Scrutiny* article, "The peculiarly 'Elizabethan' features of the stage can easily be masked when unnecessary. I have never seen any stage, with or without permanent setting, which can be so completely altered in appearance and atmosphere." To this could be added the comments of the highly experienced producer Norman Marshall, who wrote:

> In fact, one of the best theatres in England for the performance of an ultra-modern expressionistic play is the Maddermarket Theatre at Norwich, which is Elizabethan in its general design without being a laboured and exact reproduction. Probably it was the flexibility of a semi- Elizabethan stage which appealed to Mr. Nugent Monck and suggested to him the idea of building his theatre on these lines. His productions have proved that his theatre is suited to plays of all types and it was here that I saw the best expressionistic production I have yet seen in England. The Maddermarket, because of its flexibility and its atmosphere of intimacy between actor and audience, deserves to rank as one of the few experimental theatres in England. In fact, there are only two others, the Gate Theatre in London, and the Cambridge Festival Theatre.[44]

Monck often said that any play in which setting was not more important than text could be adequately staged in his theatre. In this regard, as Monck confessed, its design owed a great deal to Jacques Copeau's very influential Théâtre du Vieux-Colombier, which had been erected in Paris in 1913. Copeau was a great leader of the modern movement in French theatre, and the Théâtre du Vieux-Colombier was specifically designed for producing plays without resort to more than the most minimal scenery. As Poel had done with his productions for the Elizabethan Stage Society, Copeau used curtains and hangings hung on rods to effect rapid scene changes.[45] (This was the system Monck was interested in perfecting and a discussion of his methods will be taken up in the next chapter.) In 1919 the Théâtre du Vieux-Colombier was remodeled by Louis Jouvet, who built a permanent architectural façade at the back of the stage which, like the Elizabethan designs followed by Monck, provided a raised acting area with an alcove underneath it. As part of this alteration the footlights were removed, the stage was extended past the proscenium arch and direct lighting was employed, thereby putting Copeau's theatre in line with the most modern ideas of lighting, which Monck had been using since 1909. The success of this theatre had confirmed Monck's belief that the Elizabethan stage design could be as useful for modern plays as for the classics; what remained was to establish just how versatile this design might be.

From its opening in 1921 until Monck retired in 1952 the Maddermarket underwent few changes. In the summer of 1926, after a highly successful season, the Caxton Press was evicted from the northeast wing and this area was converted into a greenroom, men's dressing room, and a scene dock. The old vestry was then made into the women's dressing room and the dressing rooms in the galleries were converted into much needed storage closets. In

1927 a large lamp, which Monck had copied from a sixteenth-century German original he had seen on his travels, was hung in the auditorium as a house light. Finally, in January of 1930 all chairs except those in the side galleries were replaced by tilt-up cinema seats. The three rows of the south gallery were raised on tiers and the lighting platform was removed from under that gallery and put up in the back of it, making the lower auditorium seem considerably more spacious.[46] Since 1952 the theatre has undergone two major alterations (one in 1953 and another in 1966) and several small ones. At ground level the auditorium has been extended south to allow for 86 additional seats, and the four southernmost pillars supporting the galleries have been removed. A rehearsal room, costume room, combination bar and coffee bar and several other amenities have been added to the theatre complex, but these are beyond the scope of this study. Those who visit the theatre today, however, should not expect it to have quite the same intimacy it had in Nugent Monck's time.

Figure 4. Exterior of the Former Roman Catholic Chapel of St. John the Baptist, Maddermarket Alley, ca. 1920
The chapel was purchased by Monck in 1921.
(Drawing by Andrew Stephenson)

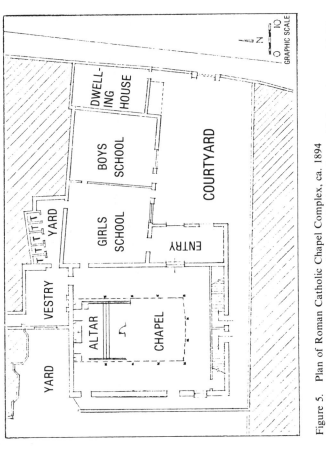

Figure 5.   Plan of Roman Catholic Chapel Complex, ca. 1894
(Plan by William Brainard from author's drawing and information provided by
Andrew Stephenson)

Figure 6. Interior of the Roman Catholic Chapel, ca. 1894
(*Photo*, Eastern Daily Press, *27 September 1971*)

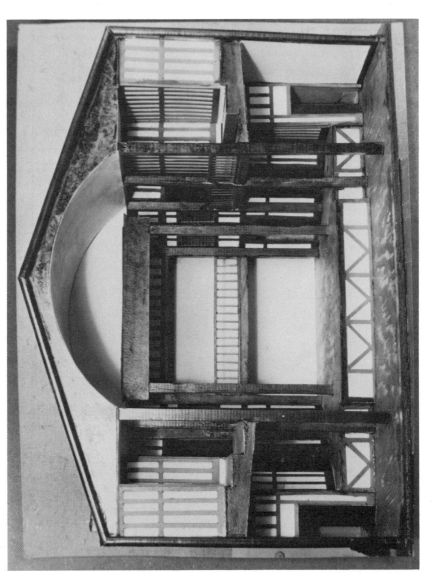

Figure 7. Model of Maddermarket Theatre Stage
(*Photograph courtesy of Jack Hall*)

Figure 8.   Plan of Maddermarket Theatre Stage
(Plan by William Brainard from author's drawing)

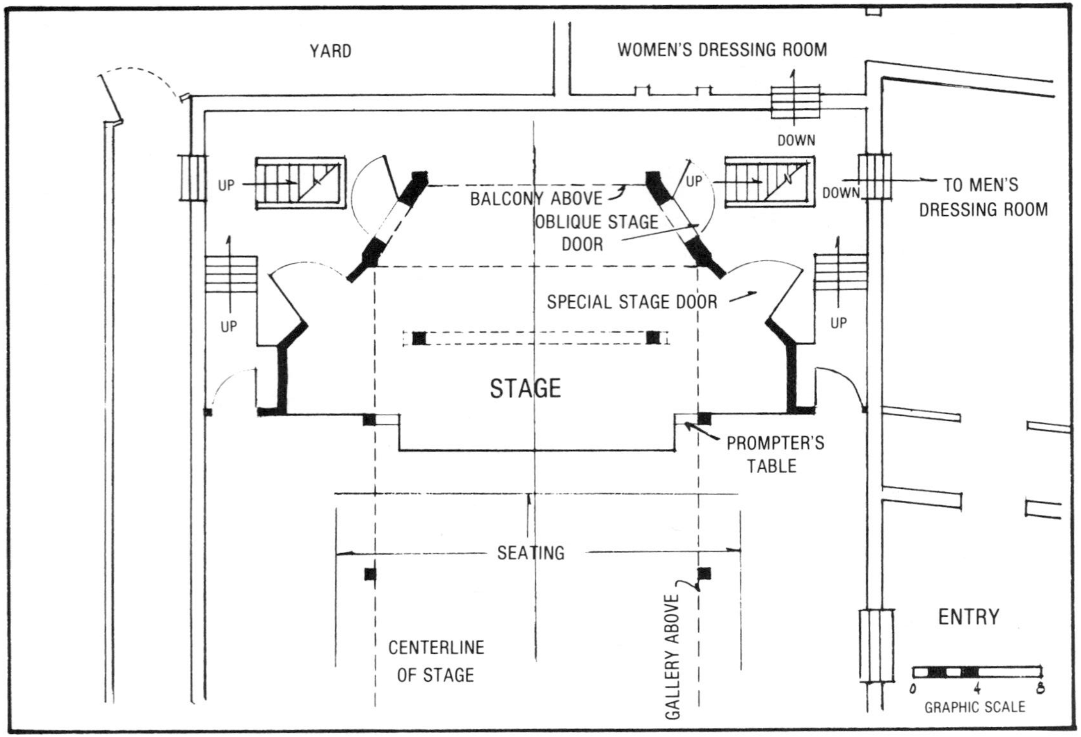

Figure 9.   Interior of Maddermarket Theatre, View of Stage
Note the use of curtains.
(Photo, Tabs, December 1961, p. 22)

Figure 10.   Interior of Maddermarket Theatre, View of Auditorium
Note the lighting platform.
(Photo, Manchester Guardian, *1 October 1921)*

Figure 11. Exterior of Maddermarket Theatre, 1921
(*Courtesy of the Maddermarket Theatre Trust, Ltd.*)

3

Developing the System

After his retirement Monck said of the production of *As You Like It* with which he opened his theatre, "It was not a particularly good performance, for we were all exhausted and had not yet learned the subtleties of our theatre, but the audience was enthusiastic."[1] The audience was enthusiastic indeed. The next day Wheldon wrote, "It is one of the best productions Mr. Monck and the Norwich Players have yet given us. Splendidly rehearsed... beautifully dressed, and cunningly lighted,"[2] and the weekly *Norfolk Chronicle,* after reporting that Monck apologized to the audience for this hurried production, commented, "It was an apology which was gracefully made but quite unnecessary... everyone was thoroughly pleased."[3]

With his first season successfully underway Monck was able to begin testing the capabilities of his Elizabethan stage. During that first season he produced a Greek drama, a group of medieval mysteries, four plays by Shakespeare, one comedy and one tragedy from the Jacobean period, a Molière farce, an eighteenth-century comedy and a modern verse drama by the Cambridge poet John Presland. (See Appendix A.) His stage proved admirably adaptable to all of these, although the reviews indicated that the same could not always be said of his Norwich Players. Still, as Monck and his Players learned the subtleties of their theatre their reputation grew. But before going on to discuss the development of this prestige and influence it may be helpful to explain something of the organization and methods that made it all possible.

Using the Elizabethan Stage

In 1879 Henry Irving wrote in his preface to *Hamlet,* "Shakespeare, if well acted on a bare stage, would certainly afford great intellectual pleasure; but that pleasure will be all the greater if the eye be charmed, at the same time, by scenic illustration in harmony with the poet's ideas."[4] Monck had no fundamental disagreement with this statement; where his approach differed from Irving's was in the consideration of how much scenic illustration could be used while remaining in harmony with the ideas of the poet. For Irving, great ideas beautifully expressed required grand settings wonderfully executed. For Monck, such spectacular scenery conflicted with rather than complemented poetic imagination. Trying to give literal representation to poetic description served only to destroy the illusion which the poetry had intended to create. It was Monck's belief that "we only want on the stage the elemental things. The Japanese theatre has shown that it's not by covering the entire surface that decoration is achieved, but by knowing the one spot, the only spot, where a bird or flower may be hung to give a sense of decoration to the whole."[5] Beyond this suggestion of scenery, Monck said, the color and visual "charm" in a Shakespeare play should be found in the costumes and the grouping.[6] This was the kind of scenic illustration which was truly in harmony with the poet's ideas because it stimulated imagination, and Monck's new theatre was designed for the application of these principles.

In 1921 the recognized features of the Elizabethan stage were a large platform backed by a permanent architectural façade. In that façade were two doors, a balcony and an inner stage or performance space under the balcony that could be closed off with curtains. Details as to the size, shape and exact location of any one of these units were often debated, as were the various proposals for additional units that may have existed on these stages. But on this most basic design there was general agreement and such a stage was ideally suited to Monck's approach. Its permanent architectural façade was in itself suggestive and required only minimal additions to alter its appearance completely, while its three basic acting areas, on two levels, allowed for remarkably varied possibilities of grouping.

Interestingly, there is no historic evidence for the existence of an inner stage in the playhouses of Shakespeare's day. The idea of such a performance space under the balcony had merely been suggested as a possible feature of the Elizabethan playhouses by Edward Capell in 1774. The great Shakespearean Edmund Malone offered it as an acceptable hypothesis in 1780, but when William Archer and W. H. Godfrey included it in their influential reconstruction of the Fortune Theatre in 1907 it became an established part of all subsequent reconstructions.[7] Not until 1940, when G. F. Reynolds published *The Staging of Elizabethan Plays,* was the notion seriously questioned, and not until the mid-1960s was it generally discredited.

But the notion of an inner stage had great appeal to those producers brought up on the conventions of the picture frame stage. Primarily this was because it served as a substitute proscenium arch. Working on the inner stage was like working within a normal proscenium theatre and all the familiar methods and techniques applied. But working on the platform stage meant finding new methods and new techniques. Reynolds pointed out in his above mentioned book (p. 133), "If we assume a permanent rear stage, our natural tendency is to look for scenes in which to use it, and try so far as possible for modern conventions and realism." This was a common tendency among producers who experimented with Elizabethan staging and it reached its logical extreme in 1942 when John Cranford Adams argued in *The Globe Playhouse* that all scenes in Elizabethan dramas which appear to take place indoors were performed either in the inner stage or on the balcony. (With this theory the unimaginative director need stage only half the scenes from *King Lear* on the unfamiliar territory of the platform stage, and with a play like Jonson's *The Alchemist* the platform could be ignored almost completely.) This tendency was not shared by Monck, however. To insist that interior scenes in seventeenth-century dramas be placed in the equivalent of a nineteenth-century box set went against Monck's belief in simple suggestion for stage setting. In addition, such an arrangement would have worked against the intimacy of his platform stage, a feature he considered to be one of his theatre's greatest assets. As the well-known producer Hugh Hunt has explained, "Anyone who has had to deal with production on an Elizabethan stage based on the assumption of balcony and underbalcony [inner stage], such as exists at the Maddermarket Theatre in Norwich, will agree with Dr. Hotson that it is unsatisfactory to play an intimate scene, such as the tomb scene in *Romeo and Juliet,* on the inner stage under the balcony with the whole depth of the platform between the actors and the audience."[8] Hunt might also have added from his own experience at the Maddermarket[9] that this scene pointed to by Hotson was one of the best illustrations of how Monck avoided such an unsatisfactory arrangement and of how effectively the economy of suggestion Monck advocated could be used.

When Monck first produced *Romeo and Juliet* at the Maddermarket in 1925 the reviewer for *The Nation* wrote, "The final scene in Juliet's tomb, where the construction of the Elizabethan Theatre was used to a remarkable effect, was one of the most beautiful spectacles I have had the pleasure to witness on the stage."[10] The critic for *Vogue* called this same scene "positively inspired."[11] Monck had too strong a sense of theatre to put such a scene at the back of his platform in the inner stage. In any event, whether by accident or by conscious design, his inner stage was far too small to accommodate more than the shortest tableau. It was nearly 14 feet wide but less than 5 feet deep, with barely 8 feet of clearance under the balcony. So, to accommodate this tomb scene, Monck employed a movable staircase which connected the balcony with the platform stage in full view of the audience (a solution which Lawrence adopted two years later).[12] The balcony then became ground level for this scene and a heavy-seeming wrought iron gate marked the entrance down into the subterranean burial vaults, which encompassed the full stage. Juliet was positioned on a slab at mid-stage, her head towards the audience. With this arrangement the final emotional speeches of both the young lovers were delivered less than 10 feet from the front row of the audience, while the formal declaration of woe with which the Prince ends the play was delivered from the top of the stairs just before all filed slowly up the staircase and out of view. This was using the Elizabethan stage to great effect and it had required only the staircase, two "slabs" (Tybalt is also dead on stage) and the mock wrought iron gate.

Monck knew how to exploit the intimacy provided by his platform stage and he also knew the value of using his small inner stage or balcony to give a useful remoteness to specific scenes. In *Hamlet,* for example, the Prince entered on the platform in Act III, Scene iii to discover Claudius kneeling at prayer within the inner stage. This left Prince Hamlet the full advantage of the platform stage from which to convey his thoughts of murder to the audience, and all the while the kneeling figure of the King remained clearly within their line of vision. In the bedchamber scene which followed, Hamlet once again used the platform stage as he drove home his message to his mother. The inner stage meanwhile functioned as the fatal hiding place for Polonius. In the final scene of this play Monck employed his movable staircase to connect platform and balcony as he did in the final scene of *Romeo and Juliet.* The King and Queen sat enthroned on the upper level as Hamlet and Laertes dueled below. This allowed the King to move down the stairs as the scene progressed, so that by the time the Queen drank the cup of poison he was too far away to stop her.

Monck realized however that even the most creative use of the three acting areas (platform, inner stage and balcony) on his Elizabethan stage was unlikely to be sufficient to stimulate the imaginations of his audience through 37 plays by Shakespeare, to say nothing of the hundreds of other plays he proposed doing. His audience members had grown up with the elaborate ornamentation of Victorian art and his amateur actors could not be expected to give consistently the quality of performance that can make scenic adjuncts superfluous. The great difficulty with the simplicity of his design methods, Monck admitted, was in avoiding monotony.

> The public . . . will be extremely bored if they see the same people in the same clothes before the same curtains, so that there is no difference between *Twelfth Night, Hamlet,* or *A Midsummer Night's Dream.* The production may look very 'Jacobethan' (as it has unkindly been called) and yet will be no more like the Globe Theatre than a black and white bungalow is like an Elizabethan cottage.

Monck realized that to do the variety of plays he intended to do, "the atmosphere of each play would have to be carefully suggested and contrasted with the previous and subsequent productions."[13] He achieved this contrast with a careful use of lighting, meticulous care in costuming and a unique system of curtains used for scenic decoration.

The idea of an inner stage has its origins in the fact that there are some scenes in Elizabethan plays which need to be "discovered" for the audience. The statue at the end of *The Winter's Tale*, for example, cannot be brought on in full view of the audience; it must be revealed for them from behind a curtain. An analysis of these scenes shows that the space required is not very large,[14] but the need for even the smallest curtained space necessitates a decision on how this might have been managed in the theatres of Shakespeare's day. The concept of an inner stage offered the most attractive solution, but it was not the only theory put forward.

By the late nineteenth century the need to reduce the time spent waiting for scene changes had given rise to a policy of occasionally playing a short scene on the narrow strip of stage in front of the main curtain while a set was being changed behind it.[15] The scenes in classic plays like those of Shakespeare were at times even rearranged to facilitate this procedure. In 1880 a seventeenth-century drawing of the interior of the Elizabethan Swan Theatre was discovered at a library in Utrecht. This so-called de Witt drawing shows two large stage posts supporting a canopy that covers about half the stage. It seemed a quite reasonable theory to suppose that a curtain was hung between these posts,[16] for such an arrangement allowed short scenes to be played before a closed curtain while sets were changed behind them, exactly as was being done on modern proscenium arch stages. But just as a theoretical inner stage tempted some to find more and more uses for it, so this notion of a "traverse curtain" inspired what became known as the alternation theory. The alternation theory suggests that Elizabethan plays were designed to be played in an alternating pattern of one scene played in front of these closed traverse curtains followed by another scene played with the curtains open. Those scenes staged in front of the curtains required no set or large properties, while those staged with the curtains open did require such things. This theory can be made to work to a remarkable extent in most Elizabethan plays and it is basically what Monck had used at the Old Music House, but it is not without its drawbacks. When rigidly applied it becomes predictable and monotonous and at times requires the same rearrangement of scenes which the proscenium arch theatres had found necessary. On the commercial stage it led to the ridiculous situation pointed out by Norman Marshall for *The Bookman*. All too often, he said, vital scenes were forced onto the narrow strip of stage in front of the curtain while the set was changed rather noisily behind it. A trivial scene which followed then ended up in a dominant position with a full scenic complement. This unbalanced the play.[17] In a reconstructed Elizabethan theatre this problem was coupled with the realization that if the curtains were indeed hung between the stage posts a large portion of the audience would see behind them, because in the Elizabethan playhouses the audience sat around three sides of the platform.

To solve both problems, of balance and of sightlines, Monck adopted the policy of hanging his traverse curtains halfway back between the posts and the rear façade even though he had little in the way of side audience with which to be concerned. This position left ample room even when the curtains were closed for the staging of any important scene. When the curtains were open the scene being played could encompass the entire stage, but large properties such as a banqueting table or a royal throne would remain behind the curtain line for easy removal when the curtains closed. Monck realized that his system would still become unavoidably repetitious if strictly applied over a long period even if the use of his balcony and small inner stage were taken into account. Monck had learned from Poel's experiments and from his own work at the Old Music House that the traverse curtain created a flat, monotonous line. To vary this he added two more sets of curtains. One set moved in a shallow arc across the back of the stage while another set formed an angular juncture at the center of the façade. When all three of these sets of curtains were fully opened the balcony and inner stage were exposed, each having its own set of curtains, the two sets often being matched. "And such curtains!" wrote Christine Orr for *The Scots Observer*: "They are hessian, hand-dyed, but they give a medieval richness. One showed a jade and russet wood, another scenes on a tapestry, some were neutral and dun."[18] Every scene could be given a distinctive shape and color by altering the pattern of the open or closed curtains and each production could be given its own distinctive setting by changing the color of these curtains. The critic for *The Garrick Magazine* gave an illustration of how efficiently and effectively this system worked when he described Monck's 1926 production of *Twelfth Night*:

> The street scenes (e.g., Sebastian and Antonio) were played in front of the [traverse] curtain on the apron stage ... curtains were then drawn back, and we had Lady Olivia's garden; the space below the balcony was a wall, with Malvolio's dungeon in the middle, while the balcony itself was transformed into a formal hedge behind which the conspirators listen to Malvolio's reading the letter ... curtains were closed, other long curtains were drawn quickly round in a semi-circle completely to hide Olivia's garden, and there was the Duke's Palace. Three settings. What about the scene inside Olivia's house where Toby and Aguecheek carouse and Malvolio interrupts? [II,i.] It was played in the garden. Malvolio, with nightcap and candle complete, interrupts and harangues from the lattice window above.[19]

The Maddermarket stage, then, provided numerous acting areas. These were the forestage (in front of the traverse), the middle stage (between the traverse and rear façade), the inner stage and the balcony. Then of course there was the full stage which could be backed by the curved curtains, the angled curtains, or the façade with various arrangements of open or closed balcony and inner stage curtains. Two stage doors led onto each side of the stage, with further entrances into the inner stage and balcony for a total of eight entrances so the flow of the actors would not be impeded.

The real secret to the speed and extraordinary continuity in Monck's shows was in the manipulation of those five sets of curtains. All curtains were opened or closed by the actors in character in full view of the audience. With the closing lines of a scene a performer could open a set of curtains as he exited, exposing the next scene, or draw a set of curtains, closing off the scene as it ended. When this seemed inappropriate, those entering for the next scene could expose their setting or close off the previous setting as they arrived on stage. It was a frankly theatrical convention. "All theatrical entertainment is a convention," Monck once said, "and it is the artist's job to make us accept that convention."[20] Monck certainly did his job very well, for even the most ardent critics of his productions seemed unperturbed by this technique.

Reviewing Monck's production of *All's Well That Ends Well* in 1924, a London critic wrote:

> The manipulation of the traverse in change of scene by the actors themselves in full view of the audience, it is claimed, becomes part of the exposition, merges emotionally in the action. There were illustrations in this production of its doing so—one in particular, where Helena as she slung back the enclosing curtains, punctuated the speech thereby with fine effect. It can easily be conceived how the novice especially will recover natural gestures of expression with this muscular action.[21]

This was the theory and in practice it seems to have worked effectively without distracting the audience. Certainly no other method could allow for one scene to follow the next with any greater speed. The modern tendency in Shakespearean productions is to have the actors or costumed attendants bring on the few properties needed for various scenes. This can be made interesting in its own right, but it cannot "merge emotionally in the action," nor can it be as quick as Monck's method was. Isolation of scenes with lighting can be as rapid but can only be effective on a large stage, set well away from the audience. Only the use of a revolving stage comes reasonably close to achieving the same results, but it is still slower and is considerably less economical.

Monck demanded that the last line of a scene in his productions be treated as if it were the cue for the first line of the next and he expected the one to follow the other as if they were in the same scene. The idea of a traverse curtain on the Elizabethan stage had no historical validity and Monck knew it. But as he used it, it allowed him to change scenes in which large properties such as beds or tables had been used or simply to indicate a change of location without losing a single moment's time. Norman Marshall pointed out that with this method Monck's Players were able to perform nearly the full text of

Romeo and Juliet in two hours and 15 minutes including a 10-minute intermission. This was one hour less than it took to produce a drastically cut version at Stratford-upon-Avon in 1948. Marshall used the beginning of Act II of the play to illustrate how Monck's system was used. Benvolio and Mercutio came on in front of the closed traverse curtains searching for Romeo after the dance, Marshall said. Romeo entered through the middle of the curtains just in time to watch them leave. As Romeo spoke, "He jests at scars that never felt a wound," he flung open the stage right curtain. He then crossed and opened the stage left curtain and, as he did so, revealed Juliet on her balcony.[22] It was an unashamedly theatrical approach which was remarkably effective and efficient.

But the system was not without difficulties. The curtains were large, 17 feet high and nearly as wide. They were hung by metal rings which slid on metal rods. The experienced Norwich Players learned to open or close a curtain in one swift, even stroke that minimized the noise distraction. The less experienced, however, would drag the curtains into place or use several swishing movements to get them there. In the noise lines would be lost. Just before the highly acclaimed *Hamlet* of March 1924, Monck managed to cut down on the noise by having each ring wrapped with twine. But this caused greater friction, making it nearly impossible to close the curtains in one smooth motion. The noise problem was not really solved until the end of the 1926–27 season when Monck was able to purchase brass rods and sliders for his curtains. But it was still up to the actors to learn to manipulate the curtains effectively.

Dressing the Elizabethan Stage

The curtains were gorgeously dyed. Reviews mentioned such colors as light fawn, deep purple and rose red; patterns selected for comment include blue and buff, yellow and green, and orange and brown. In front of these sumptuous hangings the actors performed in costumes which were equally luxurious.

"Dresses were chosen not only to suit the player who was to wear them, but to suit the lighting, the set, and the producer's conception of the part,"[23] a critic said of one of Monck's productions. When it came to Shakespeare's plays, Monck, like Poel before him, conceived of all the characters from Troilus to Hamlet as essentially Elizabethan people and he dressed them accordingly. "It is wrong to dress *Hamlet* in early Danish costume. If you shut your eyes and listen to the verse you realize it is the language of the 16th and 17th centuries. And the philosophy behind the play is clearly not from an early Danish civilization, it is strictly Elizabethan," Monck once said in a lecture.[24]

It can be argued, of course, that it is the exceptional audience member who can distinguish between philosophy which is strictly Elizabethan and that which might be essentially early Danish, but the fact remains that in Shakespeare's day his plays were costumed in the dress of his own period. If it is true, as Poel had argued, that the best way to come to the clearest understanding of Shakespeare's plays is to see them staged in a manner which is as similar as possible to the stagecraft of Shakespeare's own day, Elizabethan costuming cannot be neglected for it was an essential element of that stagecraft.

In the early days of Poel's experiments he came under heavy criticism for using such costuming. William Archer thought it antiquarian nonsense and challenged anyone to try producing *Julius Caesar* in this fashion without making it totally ridiculous.[25] Monck took up the challenge in January of 1926 and he found that the Elizabethan dress made the play "full of the rough, buccaneering spirit of the Elizabethans—not the majestic solemnity of classical tragedy with which stage tradition has invested it."[26] Far from making the play ridiculous, this use of the kind of costume Shakespeare had intended helped to make Shakespeare's anachronistic references to things like doublets in the play less distracting and more meaningful.

Poel had come to believe that costuming was not a very significant concern in the Elizabethan theatres;[27] but Monck recognized that costuming was of primary importance in Shakespearean stagecraft. From the beginning of his career Monck worked hard to learn all he could about period, color and cut, and he worked consistently to build up an extensive wardrobe for his Players. He spent nearly £100 every year on costumes at the Maddermarket. This was nearly twice his average expenditure for scenery and in many years was more than he paid out in salaries.[28] In his book *Shakespeare's Stage* (p. 91), Alois Nagler wrote, "It has been reckoned that the value of the costumes stocked in an Elizabethan theatre considerably exceeded that of the building." Monck's Maddermarket was clearly in this Elizabethan tradition; when Monck transferred the title of his theatre over to a trust in 1952 it contained over 4,000 costumes insured for £10,000, nearly twice the value of the building itself.

Monck's longtime costume mistress, Madeleine Havers, once commented about this wardrobe, "But it's not nearly so large as our electrician makes it seem. I put my bits and pieces together in some sort of colour scheme, some sort of style, and the slides do the rest."[29] Under Monck's careful guidance the Maddermarket electrician, William (Billy) Hewett, made the lighting an integral part of the Maddermarket scenic design. Once, when confronted with the Elizabethan stage and costumes of Monck's 1924 *Hamlet* production, a local critic queried, "Are the Norwich Players aiming at a presentation of the Shakespeare play itself, or at a production of an

Elizabethan presentation of it?"[30] Monck might have responded that the best way to do the former was with the latter, but there was never any debate that the stage lighting he used with such effect owed nothing to the Elizabethans.

After a production of *The Trojan Women* in 1925 a local reviewer wrote,

> And I would remind my readers that here in Norwich we may see a development which will profoundly influence the future art of the theatre.... here is one essential part of the producer's art which is in process of being perfected, and that is effective lighting. Dressing, grouping, and scenery form, in fact, the canvas on which he works his harmonies of coloured light.[31]

Previously this same critic had commented, "At each successive production we seem to be watching a master painter actually working in line, silhouette, and colour on a canvas before our eyes."[32] Monck had indeed been one of the earliest practitioners of the now universally practiced method known as "direct lighting." By 1921 probably no producer in England had more experience with this method than did Nugent Monck. The above quotations were typical of the response Monck's lighting effects inspired. To this day Monck's stage lighting is the first production element recalled by those who saw his shows, and it was the one element most consistently singled out for praise by the reviewers during his lifetime. It has also been the most elusive element for anyone to describe.

In lighting, as in setting, Monck was against realism, especially the kind of pseudorealism which tended to put an even level of illumination over the entire stage. Because Monck was an eminently practical producer, part of his objection to realism in both lighting and setting was based on the economic fact that realistic scenery was very expensive and realistic lighting required a great deal of electrical power and equipment.[33] But more importantly for Monck, realism did not satisfy his artistic sensibilities. Lighting was for Monck "the great new gift to the theatre," and he believed in using it for emotional effect.[34] To achieve this effect required a careful use of shadow and color, not simply uniform visibility.

"Figures should move from shadow to light and back to shadow in keeping with the mood and flow of the play,"[35] he would say, and this is what he tried to do at the Maddermarket. These shadows were not simply a matter of dark spaces on a white lit stage, but carefully plotted variegations of color. Describing Monck's production of *Doctor Faustus* done in the Chapter House of Canterbury Cathedral in 1929, the *Morning Post* critic wrote, "The stage reflected mingled lights of yellow and gold, blue and green, or red and blue, according to the significance of the text at any moment." The critic then went on to add the very important point that "the changes were not made restlessly, but in harmonious company with the varying intensities and moods of the enactment."[36]

Not all people react to the same color in the same way, and Monck was well aware of this.[37] Part of his artistic talent was the ability to find the one color that communicated the desired mood to the largest portion of the audience. Monck had a real feeling for color in light and an unusual understanding of how it affected his curtains and costumes. As early as 1911 he had experimented with completely altering the color of his scenic curtains simply with the use of lighting. It was an effect he used beautifully at least one other time, when he did *Julius Caesar* in 1926. But normally his use of lights consisted of washing the carefully selected and detailed costumes and curtains of his stage pictures with a deep, vibrant color that made them look richer than they ever could have under a bright, near white illumination.

For some though, Monck carried his desire for soft lights too far and failed to light the stage sufficiently. On the rare occasion when his stage lighting was criticized, it was for being too dark. This was especially a problem when Monck went from the tiny confines of his Maddermarket Theatre to work in one of the large theatres of London or at the Shakespeare Memorial Theatre.

"How he manages to obtain his effects of light and half light and his very lovely shapes of colour remains only known to himself. One wishes he would share his secret with some of the London producers," wrote the critic for the *Eastern Evening News* after one of Monck's productions.[38] Unfortunately the secret remains undiscovered. Certainly only the slightest hint is given by the remarkably primitive equipment with which he had to work. When the theatre first opened the *Daily Express* reported on July 27, 1921, "The lighting was projected from a limelight chamber at the rear of the pit and from a batten in the flies." The light that was projected from the rear of the pit was from one of the old carbon arcs which had been used at the Music House. The throw from these lamps was not adjustable so it could provide only general illumination. What was worse, it operated on 240 volt direct current, the standard current in those days, which tended to fluctuate markedly during a production, causing noticeable changes in the brightness of the light. All other light on the stage came not from one batten but from six. These battens were simply a row of ordinary lightbulbs hung from side to side above the stage. There were two battens above the platform (tucked out of sight under the canopy), two above the balcony, and two above the inner stage. Each lamp in a batten was dipped in shellac which was colored either blue, amber or rose pink. These colors were alternated along the batten and each color on each batten was controlled by a separate switch. During the run of the show all these lamps had to be taken down, scraped clean, and reshellacked to maintain the intensity of the color.[39] Most of the switches which controlled the lights were operated from a "lighting booth" which was located near the lattice window above the stage left entrance. Other switches, all of which were simple on-off devices with no dimming capabilities, were located near the stage right door and had to be operated by the actors as they entered or exited.

The lighting complemented the system of curtains in maintaining the rapid pace of Monck's production method. The swish of a curtain, a flick of a switch, and the next scene was in progress without a moment's delay. But this original lighting was not sufficient for Monck's needs, though he did manage to get some remarkable effects from it. As soon as he could afford it, two 1,000 watt projector spotlights were purchased and added to the pillars at each rear corner of the house. The front of each of these instruments was fitted with a box which contained three plates of colored glass. By the use of an ingenious system of strings manipulated from the rear lighting platform these colored plates could be raised or lowered from in front of the projected beam of light. Thus the color of the lights could be changed from blue to amber to rose pink or any combination thereof at any time.

There was a penalty for this economical system of lighting, however. Like the carbon arc lamp, it tended to be rather noisy. The sliding in and out of the glass plates could not be muffled. Furthermore, the string used was simply ordinary picture hanging string. It was not uncommon for one of the strings to be burnt through by the heat of the instruments, thereby dropping the glass plate into the box with a thud and also making any further color change during the show very awkward.[40] But for the most part this basic system worked to great effect throughout Monck's 31 years at the Maddermarket.

In November of 1925 some improvements were made in the system.[41] Four rheostat single-way dimmers were purchased and with some careful ingenuity in replugging after each scene nearly all the lights used in a show could be faded in or out rather than simply being switched on or off. During the following August, in 1926, with the help of a grant from the Carnegie Fund, Monck was able to have the entire system rewired. The switches which had been controlled by the actors were moved to the stage left lighting booth; a set of lights was added to the back of each stage pillar, functioning as side light for the rear stage and as front light for the inner stage, and a number of extra plug-ins for special effects lights were provided. Finally in January 1930 the lighting platform for the carbon arc was moved up to the rear of the south gallery and two additional 1,000 watt spotlights were installed along that gallery's front edge.

The Actors

As far back as 1895 Bernard Shaw had written, "I have never, I hope, underrated the importance of the amateur; but I am now beginning to cling to him as the saviour of theatrical art."[42] By 1918 William Poel was prepared to add, "There can be little doubt that in the present condition of the professional stage, amateurs are sometimes the better actors of Shakespeare."[43] Admittedly Poel, at least, was speaking out of a certain amount of self-interest as amateurs were usually the only actors with whom he could afford to work. But still these were not absurd assertions; the style of production advocated by these two men required a new acting technique and as Poel pointed out, "To suit my purpose I found that the modernly-trained actor had generally very much to unlearn."[44] Monck had been one of the first to attempt to train young talent for the changing demands that were to be made on the actor's art. His success with this at the Abbey Theatre was considerable but the conditions of his work with the Norwich Players were somewhat different and deserve closer scrutiny.

There were two basic problems with the average professional actor as far as the new movement in which Monck was involved was concerned. The motto of this new movement was "the play's the thing," but for the old school of professional actors the production was the thing and the actors' performance was usually more important than the material being performed. In "The Art of Rehearsal," Bernard Shaw put the case this way:

> The beginning and end of the business from the author's point of view is the art of making the audience believe that the real things are happening to real people. But the actor, male or female, may want the audience to believe that it is witnessing a magnificent display of acting by a great artist; and when the attempt to do this fails the effect is disastrous, because then there is neither play nor great acting: the play is not credible nor the acting fascinating. To your star actor a part is a mere *"cheval de bataille"*: the play does not exist except as a mounting block. That is why comparatively humble actors, who do not dare think they can succeed apart from the play, often give much better representations than star casts.[45]

Monck dedicated a great deal of his energy to maintaining this sense of humility toward the script in his actors. That he succeeded is indicated by the local critic's tribute, "Let us note this of the Norwich Players, . . . they seldom have the presumption to attempt to improve on Shakespeare."[46]

The second problem with professional actors was that the training they received was in a technique designed specifically for the vast auditoriums of the commercial theatres. In the intimate confines of the new theatres such a technique seemed self-conscious and stagy, with an unnecessary amount of overemphasis and underlining. Monck's job as a producer then had to be to develop in his company a technique suitable to a stage which brought his actors into considerably closer contact with their audience than a proscenium arch theatre would require.

Monck had chosen to do this work with amateurs rather than to develop his own young professional troupe, "not because he deprecated professionalism but because the kind of theatre he wished to do could not support a paid company."[47] This was in fact true. Working along similar lines but with young professionals, Barry Jackson lost over £100,000 with his Birmingham Repertory Company. J. B. Fagan at the Oxford Playhouse and Peter Godfrey at the Gate Theatre in London both went bankrupt trying to train young professionals in the new methods. Even the innovative Leeds Civic Playhouse, which Monck had helped to start, found itself in serious financial difficulties soon after its amateur company became professional.[48] Both the inappropriate training received by most professional actors (at least for his purposes) and economic reality encouraged Monck to keep his acting company amateur. But the Norwich Players were no ordinary group of amateur performers.

Writing in a series of articles entitled "Theatre to Remember," Burgoyne Miller said in *The Bookman,* "To say that the company is composed of amateurs might mislead some into thinking of the horrors of charity theatricals," but, he went on,

> the Norwich Players, responding to the genius of the producer, would put many professional companies to shame by the standard of their acting and most of them by the degree of their dramatic intelligence. . . . A band of enthusiasts, they form a single entity, a living instrument which the producer may use at will for his interpretation of the dramatic masterpieces of all ages and countries.[49]

This is an indication not only of what the Norwich Players had achieved by 1931, but also of the two most significant factors which led to that achievement.

The first of these factors was their constant association with a gifted producer. In a letter of recommendation written for Monck in 1940 Norman Marshall wrote,

> In England the Maddermarket Theatre is unique in being, so far as I know, the only permanent amateur company under the direction of a professional producer, and as a result of Mr. Monck's work there, the Maddermarket is generally acknowledged to be the most distinguished amateur organization in this country.[50]

The second factor was the quality of the scripts Monck chose for his amateurs to perform. In an anonymous article about the Maddermarket which appeared in *Time and Tide* the author commented, "We have already too many theatres filled with actors whose technical equipment is superior to the material they have to work upon. Let us be thankful for one theatre where the material is always of the best quality."[51] With the opportunity to be involved with as many as 10 productions of scripts of outstanding quality per year under the direction of a producer of Monck's abilities, a core group of Norwich Players developed who were of an unusually high caliber. But developing such a group was not an easy process.

During the early years of the Maddermarket's operation the critic for the local *Eastern Daily Press* was F. W. Wheldon. He did not allow Monck or the Players to become complacent or self-satisfied in their new home. After their third Maddermarket production, *She Stoops to Conquer,* done in November 1921, Wheldon wrote, "The more one sees of Mr. Nugent Monck's productions, the more one admires his flair for dress, lighting, and scenic effects. But it would be well for him to take as much pains with his human material as he does with his properties."[52] Wheldon took the Norwich Players very seriously and was anxious for their success. "I write always as a Norwich Player and I am anxious always to see the Norwich Players live up to their high reputation,"[53] he wrote. But eighteen months later he still found it necessary to comment, "I fear it is inescapable that Mr. Monck can do wonders with paint and canvas, with light and colour and all dull inanimate and abstract things, but he cannot control or direct or fire the actors."[54]

Each such criticism made by Wheldon, it should be noted, received a flood of protest in the letters column from audience members who disagreed strongly with his point of view. The protest after the latter review was so strong that Wheldon resigned his post as critic. But to a certain extent his criticism was valid. Over the years the one uniform criticism of the Norwich Players was that they consistently underplayed emotion. The Victorian actors, it seems, had been very demonstrative in the expression of emotion and audiences had come to expect this in acting. But it was Monck's belief that in order to avoid rivalry with the cinema, "there will be less noisy action on the stage, less movement, and characterisation will be given by the modulation of the voice, the word said (and more possibly by the words left unsaid)."[55] This belief caused him to direct his actors towards an acting style that was even more reserved than the intimacy of his theatre required.

Wheldon was perhaps too tied to the old methods of acting to be a good critic of Monck's work; but even his replacement, Arthur Batchelor, a man completely open to the new methods, had some sharp criticism of the acting in the January 1924 production of *Antony and Cleopatra.* The major characters were admirably handled, he reported, but many of the minor roles were very poorly done. They must learn to avoid the barnstorming of the Victorian professionals on the one hand and the staccato, schoolboard arithmetic lesson on the other. "The fact is that the setting, grouping, and lighting at the Maddermarket are such an unfailing delight to the eye that the ear craves an equal satisfaction."[56] During these early years, however, Monck had been building his company and by the end of 1924 he had a consistent core group of performers firmly established at the Maddermarket. From that point on the standards of acting rose steadily.

By 1925 a London critic was able to say of the Norwich Players:

> The company act like a team, and like professionals; and indeed, with the tradition and the solid experience that they have behind them, they are a great deal better versed in the technique of their art than many professionals under whom I have suffered. The Norwich Players know how to move and how to stand still; they have more than a hazy notion how to speak; above all, they know how to listen. They know, in fact, everything that a first-rate coach can teach them.[57]

By the time they appeared in London in a production of *The Lady from the Sea* the *Daily News* could refer to them as "probably the most important body of amateur actors in England," and the *Daily Telegraph* reviewer added, "It must be remembered that these particular amateurs have acquired a breadth of experience which many professionals might envy."[58]

None of this is to suggest that the Norwich Players were superior to the better professional companies in the country. "It is not to be thought that the acting throughout, high as it is, reaches the level of the best productions in London," cautioned the critic for the *Christian Science Monitor.* "But," he went on, "what the Players lack in 'finish,' that vague word, they make up by a more acute sensibility and sincerity."[59] A critic for the *Festival Theatre Review,* the magazine of the very avant-garde Cambridge Festival Theatre, put it another way. Seeing the Norwich Players he said, "is like eating fresh vegetables after tinned: tinned may be selected and unexceptionable, but fresh vegetables, if they are fresh, are very fresh: it's a relief not to be able to foresee the next five gestures and every intonation."[60] The Norwich Players were clearly in the forefront of the most modern movements in acting and, while they could not compete with professionals on the large commercial stage, at their peak only the best professionals could have outshone them within the intimate confines of their own Maddermarket Theatre.

The Discipline

The Guild of the Norwich Players was set up from the beginning to appeal only to those who were interested in acting as an art form which required discipline and not to those who were merely interested in playing before their friends. As the well-known Norwich author R. H. Mottram once said of Monck, "His methods consist partly of picking out the best plays and entrusting them to actors who would make considerable sacrifices to play in them."[61] And the sacrifices Monck required were indeed considerable.

One of the most significant sacrifices Monck required of his Players was anonymity. The policy of actors appearing in roles without being given public recognition for their work was not unique to the Norwich Players. It was an early policy with the Irish Players in Dublin, the Marlowe Society in Cambridge and the Stoneland Players, among others. But no other group has maintained this policy throughout its history, as the Norwich Players have done to this day.

The arguments for actors appearing anonymously are many and varied. Originally this policy was part of the revolt against the excesses of the star system. Audiences in the new theatres were to come to see plays, not individual performers, and to ensure that they did so they were provided with only the title of the play and the names of the characters without reference to those who impersonated these characters. Monck originally adopted this policy when working with the English Drama Society in London. There it was a matter of moral principles, for he was working with religious drama and, like Poel with the *Everyman* production, he did not believe it appropriate for actors' names to be connected with the religious figures they portrayed.

As the Norwich Players drifted away from the exclusive presentation of religious drama, however, other reasons for maintaining this anonymity developed. Anonymity did a great deal to encourage ensemble acting, for example. Praise under such a policy could be won only by the group, not by individuals. This insured that the name of the Norwich Players was always more important than the name of any single performer and it prevented individual players from thinking themselves indispensable.

But there was another, equally practical reason for Monck's long insistence on adherence to anonymity. If it helped to keep successful performers from valuing themselves too highly, it was also a great insulator for those who were not so successful.[62] A review which states that "the character Orlando tended to lose his diction in the emotional scenes" is informative and constructive. But when a reviewer comments, "Mr. John Smith as Orlando . . . " an element of personality is brought into the criticism that can be devastating to young egos. Monck knew it would take a long time to develop his company and to train an audience to appreciate the new style. He also knew that to do the variety of plays he intended to do with the relatively small group of actors at his disposal a certain amount of miscasting would be inevitable. This was all the more reason for him to protect his amateurs from criticism that could be personal and destructive. A further benefit of this policy has been described by Andrew Stephenson. It was part of Monck's training, he said, that "one week you may be playing the lead, and the next, the third footman." Anonymity was a great help with this because "if your name doesn't appear in the programme then your pride isn't hurt."[63]

In later years when Monck's own reputation was firmly established he used this part of his training technique to its fullest advantage. Rather than being primarily concerned with achieving 10 financial or directorial successes each year, he used casting to control and improve his actors. Actors were sometimes assigned roles not primarily on the basis of what they could do best, but on the basis of what would be best for them and the Players. The audience, of course, got less impressive performances on occasion, but they benefited in the long run because the actors expanded their talents and the organization was not fragmented by self-seeking egotists. For over 75 years now each succeeding generation of Norwich Players has been convinced of the wisdom of maintaining Monck's policy of anonymity. Its equalizing effect and the fact that it discourages self-important actors from joining the Players have certainly been largely responsible for the group's longevity.

It was many years before the local newspaper reviewers could finally be persuaded to respect Monck's policy of anonymity, and the policy was never without its critics. One of the most representative criticisms appeared in the *Manchester Guardian,* July 10, 1929:

> Even the actors remain anonymous. The rule is made to create the impression of a united company, a kind of compact and distinct world, and also to avoid clapping, flowers, speeches, and the other vanities of a perverse universe. At the same time it also suggests a slight affectation. The Maddermarket is supported by a regular audience not numbering more than a thousand, all of whom know the actors either well or by sight. Thus the attempt at anonymity is a trifle comic, since if I know Miss Jones you don't disguise her by saying— and repeating—that she exists only as Portia.

This is certainly a valid argument, yet from a strictly practical standpoint one might argue that, for that part of the audience (and of the newspaper readership) who were not regulars Monck's justifications of this policy were still applicable. For those 1,000 who were regulars (the figure was actually closer to 500) there was hardly any need to waste the money required for publicizing the names or to waste the time required for announcing the numerous last minute cast changes which are inevitable in amateur organizations. In addition, anonymity ensured that no one avoided a play merely because a favorite performer was not announced as having a leading part.

Along with this anonymity the actors agreed never to take curtain calls. Again, this emphasized the importance of the play over the players. "Surely it's a pity to see Macbeth or Hamlet come to life again just to bow," Monck said; "the better the performance the greater the pity."[64] The audience were to leave the theatre with their meditation on the ideas presented by the play undisturbed. Commenting on this in *The Other Theatre* (p. 97), Marshall wrote:

> As a member of the audience, I personally dislike this. It always seems to me arrogant and ungracious for the actors not to respond to the applause of the audience by bowing their thanks. It is absurd to say that calls destroy the illusion. The whole essence of the theatre is that it is a game of make-believe. Not even a small child in the audience believes that the actor who dies in the play is really dead. When the final curtain falls the game of make-believe is over and it is right and proper that the actors and the audience should thank one another.

It would certainly have been exceedingly difficult for Monck to justify this rule against curtain calls on the grounds that curtain calls destroyed theatrical illusion. His frank convention of having the actors open and close the curtains in character and in full view of the audience already had the equivalent effect without any harm being done to the enjoyment of the play. Nor was his convention of having a prompter sitting in full view of the audience with the promptbook resting on the edge of the stage conducive to any illusion of reality. But the prompter's conspicuous presence was an added incentive for the learning of lines and the lack of curtain calls also encouraged discipline by keeping the actors secondary to the script.

Monck himself, however, did not work anonymously. He often said that he regretted that his name was so much in the public eye, but legally someone's name had to appear on the program so that in the event of trouble the police would know whom to call. But it was not until the 1940s when his theatre had been turned over to a trust that the programs referred to Monck as the lessee of the Maddermarket. Before that time the programs always carried the phrase "The Norwich Players under the direction of Nugent Monck" below the theatre title. Even when the Norwich Players appeared outside of Monck's theatre he was always properly billed as producer. In the early years on the rare occasion when someone else would produce at the Maddermarket that person received no credit in the production's program. But the program for the show immediately prior to a guest producer's appearance usually carried a notice that Monck would be away and clearly listed the name of the person replacing him.

After 1931 there was no longer any pretence that the producer would maintain the same anonymity as the Players and guest producers' names always appeared on the program. Why this should be so is not exactly clear. The Maddermarket guest producers were usually professionals and Monck may somehow have considered that they deserved billing even when none of the amateurs received any. Perhaps too it was simply an honest admission of the reality pointed out by the *Daily Telegraph* reviewer W. A. D. in his review of *Pericles* on November 10, 1929. He wrote, "The real quality of the performance consists not in the acting at all, but in the groupings, the movement, and the touch of style which showed in the manipulation of the curtains and so on. To put it briefly, the Maddermarket is a producer's theatre. One goes to it to see Mr. Monck's work." This was undeniably true. It was Monck's exceptional ability that made the Norwich Players outstanding and they were "invited" to do the plays he selected in the theatre he owned. R. H. wrote for *The Garrick Magazine.*

> Mr. Monck, for lack of a better word, is an autocrat.... Yet the word "autocrat" is quite a misnomer, for surely no autocrat ever worked himself so unsparingly, with so sure a touch and yet so modest an attitude. "All the mistakes are mine," he whimsically remarked; the credit, apparently, he leaves to the Players.[65]

And indeed Monck never failed to give the highest praise to the Norwich Players or to express his deep appreciation of their loyalty and unselfish dedication whenever he spoke of his work at the Maddermarket. It is probably for this reason that no Norwich Player ever criticized him, at least in print, for not working anonymously as they did; and to question the right of other producers to be named on the program would have been to question the reason for Monck's name being there.

The Training

Constant performance in high quality plays gave the Norwich Players an enviable range of experience; anonymity and the lack of curtain calls encouraged teamwork. But it was Monck's ability to maintain a strict discipline that accounts for most of the success of the Norwich Players. Maintaining discipline in any voluntary organization is always an enormous task, but this is especially true in a community theatre where there is usually a chronic shortage of actors. Numerous Players have commented that they were first introduced to Monck by a friend only to find themselves measured for costumes and wigs, presented with scripts for small walk-on roles and caught up in the world of the Maddermarket before the meeting was over.[66] With his considerable charm Monck was always able to cast any play he had chosen to do, so he never let the fear of losing an actor keep him from demanding the same obedience from everyone. "Monck frankly confesses to 'bullying any actor who is guilty of disloyalty to his fellow actors through gross carelessness or unpunctuality,'" wrote the editor for the Adult Education Committee's report, *The Drama in Adult Education* (p. 182). "Actors are infused with a spirit of loyalty to the group and trained in self-discipline."

Robert Speaight wrote in his biography, *William Poel* (p. 3), "Poel had the intransigence of a saint, and his refusal to work under normal theatrical conditions meant that he could rarely acquire the best actors and never had the time to initiate them fully into his methods." Monck too was unable to work with the best actors, but he made certain that he had time to teach his methods to the actors he had. It took roughly three years to do this with amateurs, he always said. It was Monck's belief that anyone who had sufficient desire to learn could be taught to act and it was part of his method to test that desire soundly. Later Monck would recall for the *News Chronicle* on November 16, 1953, "I demanded of my actors two things, that they bring with them absolute obedience and their own grease paint. In return I refused to let any of them speak a line until I had trained them for three years."

This was of course one of the typical exaggerations for effect for which Monck was so well noted, but it expresses the spirit with which he worked. New members were not allowed simply to come in and perform the roles which appealed to them. Every potential Norwich Player had to prove a willingness to contribute to all aspects of production before earning the privilege of acting in major roles. Even after this privilege was earned it was not guaranteed. An actor playing Hamlet one month was expected to play a servant the next or even to be an usher if necessary. Furthermore, having played Hamlet once was no assurance of being assigned the same role again when the play was revived. Actors were invited to act in Monck's theatre in the plays he selected. The only certainty was that refusal to participate in the hard work of running the theatre would ensure that no future invitation to act at the Maddermarket would be extended. By the same token, however, loyalty to Monck and to the Norwich Players was wholeheartedly rewarded.

Three years of small roles and production support work were usually sufficient to sort out the dedicated from the self-seeking and during those three years the dedicated performer would have gained a fairly complete knowledge of Monck's methods and of the working of the theatre. In the years after World War I when Monck was just beginning to rebuild the Norwich Players he was very dictatorial in rehearsals. F. W. Wheldon wrote in 1920:

> The producer comes to the first rehearsal with a complete idea in his mind, and his sometimes witty, always vivacious and revealing comment on the characters at once places the actors *en rapport* with the idea of the play.... The producer imposes his own idea of the play, and of each individual part, on the actors at the very beginning. Nugent Monck gives you the impression that his conviction of each character is the only one which will fit in perfectly with his complete conception of the play.[67]

But once he had trained a core group of performers he was able to take a more liberal approach. Barbara Wilkes, who designed all of Monck's productions for the last 20 years of his career, stated in *"The Scene wherein We Play In"* (p. 13), "From my experience of Monck's producing, I would say he tends to let the play shape itself at first, drawing his inspiration as he goes along, keeping his ideas fluid for at least the first week or so." Madeleine Havers, a woman who had been both actress and costume mistress for Monck long enough to experience the change in his approach firsthand, elaborated on the same page:

> When he started, very much earlier, he did try to do every flick of an eyelash with intonation, until he found he was producing various versions of WNM [Walter Nugent Monck]. Then he started to wait, and watch to see what you had to contribute, and he became past master at spotting what you were trying to get at, and showing you how to get it.

Years of experience made Monck's control of his productions imperceptible, sometimes even to his actors. "An experienced producer knows how to get the best results from his actors without forcing his views on them, by inspiring and guiding what seems to be their own creation—what is their own creation (born of his lucidity and enthusiasm) into channels that will best present the spirit of the play."[68] Regardless of any seeming lack of direction from Monck, the end product, what finally appeared on stage, somehow always bore his unique stamp. Subtly (and sometimes not so subtly) he always got what he wanted from his performers.

Monck never made notes during rehearsals. He had a remarkable visual memory and made corrections on the spot. He never gave line readings unless it was in a highly exaggerated manner so that the actor, rather timidly trying to reproduce Monck's reading, would hit about the right emphasis. Normally he just repeated gibberish as he used his considerable mimic talent to demonstrate precisely what he desired.

> He wouldn't talk to you about the psychology of a part. We never heard of "motivation" or method acting in those days. Instead, he would jump on the stage and without bothering about the "words" of your part would say "er, something—something—something—something" but you could see by his manner, expression and walk the character as he wanted you to play it.[69]

What Monck taught his actors by his mimic actions was a semistylization of movement.[70] "Stylised acting kept the essentials of movement, but held the movement as long as the emotion lasted,"[71] he said. His method of semistylization was closer to naturalistic acting, he contended, but he insisted that his players stand still or move in a precise manner on stage. To go along with this and to allow for the abilities of the actors he had, Monck was careful not to fill his shows with clever bits of business. Nothing was worse than clever business badly handled, he realized, and he made the amount of business in a scene commensurate with the actors' abilities to handle it.[72] Indeed a large part of Monck's great talent as a producer was in his ability to help his actors and to adjust to their needs. Stephenson has said of Monck's producing:

> He could visualize what his groups would look like, how they drew together and how they faded away. He had an acute ear for the rhythm and scansion of lines. . . . He created moods and atmosphere which inspired his sometimes inexperienced cast to excel themselves. . . . If he found a player could not do what he wanted he would modify his demands, and if he found a player's conception of the part differed from his, and he thought the player would give a better performance if he followed his own interpretation, then Monck would adapt his production to the player's vision.[73]

Monck's careful stage management too was of the greatest assistance to his performers. "There is always a space for you to go to and a reason for getting there," an actor who worked for Monck at Stratford-upon-Avon is reported to have said, "and when you have to go off, you are always near your exit."[74]

Certainly the real triumph of Monck's work with the Norwich Players however was not in his teaching of movement but in his ultimate success in training them to speak verse. "The old school of acting Shakespeare involved singing the lines with a booming voice and a bravura declamation that invariably sacrificed sense to vocal talent," wrote Norman Marshall.[75] The modern idea, he continued, "was to be natural at all costs and involved the most ingenious methods of making the finest verse sound exactly like prose." Like Poel, Monck had always believed in an approach halfway between these extremes. "It is essential that people shall hear quite clearly and that rhythm shall be given to the prose and verse," he said.[76] Monck was helped in achieving clarity by the almost perfect acoustics of his Maddermarket Theatre and he was helped in achieving the proper rhythms by the fact that his amateurs were generally free from the improper training of both the old and new schools of verse speaking.

> It may seem extraordinary that most of the young people who come to me at the Maddermarket have some feeling for verse speaking, or fairly soon acquire a sense of rhythm, while among professionals I have found this sense often completely lacking— sometimes this is due to a wanton desire to give fresh interpretation, fresh impulse to a hackneyed part, feeling that the words would seem more natural if they sounded like prose.[77]

By 1927 when Monck's training process was at last showing results, the critic for *The Nation* could say, "In any case the Maddermarket Theatre is almost the only place of entertainment where squeamish persons can hear blank verse recited in a manner which does not make one feel rather sick. This instruction in elocution has been one of Mr. Monck's greatest achievements."[78] Monck was a firm believer that all dialogue on stage, whether verse or prose, should be spoken swiftly and with clarity and that pauses should be used sparingly and only for definite effect, but he saw no need to go to Poel's extremes of orchestrating all the voices.

If lighting was the one production element for which Monck was consistently praised, the rapid, clear delivery of lines was the one aspect for which his Players were most generally congratulated. Even when they performed outdoors, as when they played *Everyman* before the west door of Canterbury Cathedral in 1929, their staunchest critics still praised them for their vocal delivery.

Unfortunately, as with Monck's lighting effects, no one has really been able to explain how this training was done. Monck seems to have possessed an uncanny ability to know exactly what comment to make and when to make it in order to get a performer to respond in the desired way. There was no systematic approach but rather a constant exposure to corrections over several years, until, without really knowing how, actors and actresses found they were speaking as Monck wanted them to speak.

In general Monck's approach to actor training was very simple: "I ask of my actors sincerity. I require them to study the play with a view to finding out what the author meant and try to instill in them the capacity to reproduce the emotion which they first felt when reading the part. I never allow anyone to express an emotion which he has not felt."[79] He never defined his method of achieving this except to say that there are

> certain rules and exercises of simple nature which will prevent the novice making a fool of himself, such as learning to stand still intelligently, and not fidget; to speak clearly and swiftly, not shouting but knowing that you are heard by the whole audience: the use of inflexions and slight pauses, but particularly in English, the tones of the voice.[80]

Apparently he adapted his approach to fit each individual performer. The results were that the Norwich Players achieved an excellence in performance which was far above average. What they ultimately learned was an acting style designed specifically for the theatre in which they worked and the production method which was uniquely Monck's own.

4

Building a Reputation:
1921-1928

"In these days when theatre forms and staging are so much discussed it is useful to remind ourselves that in the now far away 1920s even Britain had its experiments. Perhaps the most famous of all these was the Elizabethan Theatre of Nugent Monck, the Maddermarket."[1] The name of the Maddermarket and the work Monck did there have been so far forgotten that it is difficult to believe such a statement could have been made only 25 years ago. Yet the local Norwich author Eric Fowler surely was right when he wrote concerning Monck, "His influence, from his little theatre in the provinces, was international. Indeed, in the 1920s and 30s Norwich became better known abroad for the Maddermarket Theatre than for anything else it did or possessed."[2]

Monck's reputation and that of his theatre were international. It was an extraordinary achievement made all the more extraordinary by the fact that Monck was working in an isolated provincial city using only amateur performers. Those who wished to see his work had to undertake the long journey to Norwich because Monck rarely produced drama elsewhere. Yet over the years numerous important people of the theatre made the pilgrimage to Norwich and came away inspired by what they saw. But as with so many important ventures, while others recognized its importance those closest to it were slow to realize its significance.

Early Recognition

The first London critic to venture to Norwich to see Monck's work was the formidable Shakespearean Herbert Farjeon, who went to see *The Taming of the Shrew* in February 1922 when the Norwich Players were still far from coming to terms with their new theatre. His comments are recorded in his book *The Shakespeare Scene*. "The Maddermarket Theatre in Norwich is a revelation," he declared. "Nothing could seem less antiquarian. You do not look on at the feast through a crack in the wall. You are actually present at it. You come upon it as you might come upon a fight in the street." The approach had won him over completely. Of the specific performance he added,

> We do not say that the performance at the Maddermarket achieves perfection. The play was cut, because Norwich likes to be in bed by ten o'clock. The lighting of the front of the platform was unsatisfactory. The players quite often stressed wrong words. But here was perfection almost within grasp. Shakespeare was out of his coffin even if he was still rubbing his eyes at the unaccustomed sight of the brave old world.

He ended by saying, "It is safe to predict that, before long, many Londoners will make the pilgrimage to Norwich, and they will not return from it empty minded."[3] He was right on both counts. By the next season *The Times, The Nation, The Stage* and the *Observer* all regularly carried reviews of Maddermarket shows. The *Daily Telegraph* and *Morning Post* soon followed suit and numerous other papers, including the American-based *Christian Science Monitor,* periodically ran articles on Monck's productions.

The attention the Maddermarket received was due primarily to its uniqueness and to the outstanding quality of Monck's staging. But partly, too, it was due to an ever-increasing dissatisfaction with the commercial stage and the consequent search for fresh ideas and new approaches. Norman Marshall, writing of this period, stated, "Nearly everything that was worthwhile in the English theatre in the period between the two wars was due to the influence of these rebel organizations." Their story, he said, is

> a record of how the English theatre was saved from stagnation and sterility by the small group of producers, players, and playgoers who, supported by many of the dramatic critics, refused to accept the drab monotony imposed upon the theatre by the managers and by the Censor, seemingly united in a determination to keep the theatre in a state of arrested development.[4]

Monck himself, however, took a somewhat broader view of the situation. In a 1928 lecture Monck said that the professional stage was at a low ebb because of the rivalry from cinema, which was able to provide cheaper entertainment with greater comfort to the audience.[5] Cinema, he went on, was training audiences to use their eyes, not particularly their brains or their ears. As a consequence plays written primarily to be heard, especially the classics, were being dropped from professional repertories because people would not make the effort to listen. Since the lower one goes intellectually the more popular an entertainment becomes, he contended, the professional theatre usually replaced these "plays to be heard" with material of a rather low artistic standard. The future hope for the theatre, Monck believed, was the wireless, which might again train people to listen; but until that time it was the responsibility of the amateur societies to win back the intelligent audience and revive interest in the art of drama. The professional theatre could not afford such a crusade, Monck said; only amateurs were free from the financial responsibilities that make such an educational undertaking impossible for professionals.

Monck, then, saw his financially viable amateur organization as a crusade. He admired those professionals who tried and failed, usually at substantial cost to themselves, to raise the standards of the professional theatre, but they created only a brief stir which soon died away. Monck realized that in the long run those groups which could survive long enough to establish a tradition would have a more lasting impact on artistic standards.

One of those professionals who struggled bravely against stagnation in the theatre was Barry Jackson, who ran the Birmingham Repertory Theatre from 1913 to 1935 and lost a personal fortune of £100,000 in the process. Jackson began his distinguished career in theatre in 1907 when he founded a group of amateurs called the Pilgrim Players. The Pilgrim Players were formed for the specific purpose of performing *The Interlude of Youth*[6] which Monck had adapted and revived in 1906. In November 1922 Jackson went to Norwich to see another of Monck's original revivals, *The Duenna* by Sheridan and Linley. This comic opera had been so long forgotten that Monck had to search for the original score in the British Museum,[7] yet in its own day it was easily as popular as *The Beggar's Opera*. Jackson was enthralled by Monck's work and by the Maddermarket. After his visit he wrote to Monck, "In my hurry to get away on Friday night, I am afraid that I did not convey to you and the company the tremendous joy your theatre and performance gave me."

From this visit on Monck and Jackson became the closest of friends and Jackson returned to the Maddermarket on numerous occasions to see Monck's work there. On December 3, 1928 he came to lecture on "The History of the Birmingham Repertory Theatre." The next day the *Eastern Daily Press* reviewer noted, "The life history of the Birmingham venture seems not unlike that of the Norwich Players 'writ large' with this difference, that there were signs of a certain despondency and rather a gloomy outlook on the future from Sir Barry, an outlook which we trust and believe the Players do not share." The Players did not share that outlook, though at times they seemed to get little more support from their Norwich public than Jackson was getting from his in Birmingham.[8] In a 1949 lecture at the Maddermarket Jackson reprimanded the citizens of Norwich for this, saying that they did not realize how famous the Maddermarket was and that it had made Norwich one of the theatrical attractions of the country.[9] In 1946 Jackson became the director of the Shakespeare Memorial Theatre and as one of his first official acts he invited his longtime friend, Nugent Monck, to produce the opening production of that season. That same year he participated in a BBC radio broadcast in honor of Monck and the Maddermarket and in 1953 he paid tribute to Monck again in a BBC broadcast commemorating Monck's retirement. Unfortunately no recordings or transcripts of Jackson's comments in these broadcasts have survived,[10] but when Monck died in 1958 Jackson wrote to the local newspaper:

> Nugent Monck's work at the Maddermarket Theatre spread much further than the confines of Norwich, and the drama generally owes him an enormous debt of gratitude. He was completely catholic in his tastes, and his treatment of all branches of dramatic literature showed the man's tremendous integrity especially in the classical field. He was completely fearless in his approach, and never failed to treat his authors with absolute honesty. His work with the famous William Poel affected his own approach to William Shakespeare whose plays he produced as they should be—swiftly, surely and with no nonsense. I personally mourn the loss of a very sincere friend.[11]

After *The Duenna* in November 1922 the Norwich Players struggled through the rest of their season performing *Henry IV, Part I; The School for Scandal; Othello; The Way of the World* and *Doctor Faustus.* It was a difficult time financially. During several nights of *Henry IV, Part I* there were more actors on stage than people in the audience. To help support himself through these trying times Monck accepted his first job in London since he had left there twelve years before. He produced Ernst Toller's *The Machine Wreckers* for the prestigious Stage Society at the Kingsway Theatre May 6, 7, 13 and 14, 1923. The following *Manchester Guardian* review of May 8 was typical of the positive response Monck's work received in the press:

> When Reinhardt produced *The Machine Wreckers* in Berlin last year, he had all the resources of a great spectacular playhouse wherewith to translate the feverish poetry of the Bavarian Communist Ernst Toller into its appropriate setting of mob-misery, mob-conflict, and mob-defeat. This week-end the play has been given by the Stage Society on one of the smallest London stages, that of the Kingsway Theatre, and the success with which the frenzy was embodied in small compass is a fine tribute to the capacities of the producer, Mr. Nugent Monck, of the Maddermarket Theatre, Norwich. He has not only discovered an efficient technique for the manipulation of quick movements of scene but he has also shown, particularly in the factory episode, a very shrewd knowledge of how much to hint in terms of light and shadow and how much to leave to the imagination. We realize now how the Elizabethan formula of a fore-stage with a room behind can contribute to modern poetic drama by giving it ease and speed of movement, and we realize too that it is perfectly possible with taste and judgement and good generalship to give spectacular tragedy full justice in a narrow lodging.

The most interesting point in this review in terms of Monck's development of an economical production method is its reference to his discovery of "an efficient technique for the manipulation of quick movements of scene." The *Pall Mall Gazette* gave some hint as to how this was achieved when it said, "Mr. Monck managed to give us eleven episodes without any fuss upon a grey-walled stage by the simple device of old-fashioned 'flats' duly 'joined.'"[12] Undoubtedly this is a reference to Monck's first use of the special two-sided flats he introduced to the Maddermarket eighteen months later for his first production of *All's Well That Ends Well.*

These flats were painted on both sides, with a different scene on each. When secured with hinges to the permanent gallery posts they could be opened or closed to change scene. In combination with Monck's system of curtains this gave added versatility to his stage, with the additional advantages that more painted scenery could be employed and that the manipulation of these flats was quieter than the manipulation of the curtains.

Not everyone, of course, was as taken with Monck's production of *The Machine Wreckers* as was the critic for the *Manchester Guardian.* The critics for the *Herald,* the *Express* and *The London Mercury* all found Monck's production far "too gentlemanly" for the rugged emotion called for by the script.[13] This was perhaps Monck's only serious weak spot as a producer. After his retirement he freely admitted, "I have always tried to give a gentlemanly entertainment at the Maddermarket. You see a good play without fuss, you come without fuss and you leave without fuss."[14] There are many plays, however, that are anything but gentlemanly; they demand fuss. Monck never quite came to terms with such plays. His productions appealed to the genteel, but those looking for a more emotionally demonstrative experience in theatre at times found Monck's productions rather too tame.

Monck began his 1923–24 season with a determined effort to build an audience sufficient to sustain his new theatre. His 1920–21 season had been his most successful and had prompted him to make the risky move to larger premises. That success was probably attributable in part to the series of weekly lectures, readings and concerts he had given the previous autumn and had continued semiweekly during the spring of 1920. In 1919, when the Norwich Players performed Wednesday to Saturday, these lectures appeared every Wednesday when a performance was not running. During the following season, when their schedule was expanded to playing Monday to Saturday, such lectures were moved to Monday. Monck probably never realized that this had helped his season not only by the added income it produced but also by the fact that it made the Old Music House the habitual place to which a certain group of people went on Monday night. After moving into the Maddermarket, at any rate, Monck dropped the extra work of the lectures while he concentrated on setting up the operation of his new venture. Occasionally lectures or recitals were given but there was not the consistency of scheduling which would have made going to the Maddermarket on Monday night a habitual activity.

To develop the Maddermarket's reputation as a center for cultural activities Monck announced an extraordinary series of lecture-performances to be given one Thursday each month throughout their third season. He was to lecture on Sanskrit drama, followed by a simple staging of the Indian classic *Śakuntalā*; on Japanese Noh drama, followed by two short plays, *Hantan* and *Nishikigi*; on medieval drama, followed by the tenth-century *Paphnutius*; on the *commedia dell'arte,* followed by Monck's own adaptation of an old scenario which he called *The Magic Casement*; on pastorals, followed by one Elizabethan example of the genre; and finally he was to lecture on eighteenth-century European drama, after which two scenes from the Italian *Philip II* were to be performed. In addition, a recital of Greek drama was to be given by Penelope Wheeler in November and a full production of *Everyman* during Easter week. It was a remarkably ambitious undertaking but the entire series was given and Monck, being the perfectionist he was when it came to staging, turned these lecture-performances into fully costumed productions. They were good training for the Players, very well received by the audience and of considerable educational value to the community. But they were also an enormous drain on the energies of the Norwich Players who had in the meantime eight regular season shows to perform, including five by Shakespeare: *Cymbeline; Henry IV, Part II; Antony and Cleopatra; Hamlet* and *The Merry Wives of Windsor*. The experiment was never repeated.

Shaw had once advised Monck:

> I must warn you against the notion that the general public could be got at by adequate advertisement by any method whatever. First rate art cannot be pushed beyond a certain percentage of the population. It is not that the rest are ignorant or indifferent: they very actively dislike it and resent it; and forcing it on them—even if you could—would be as cruel as making little children go to church.[15]

The Maddermarket's history bore out the truth of Shaw's belief. But faced with the need to make his venture pay it remained for Monck to try constantly to discover just how high that mysterious "certain percentage" might be. Two more seasons went by before Monck finally found a program that was successful in building his audience.

Of the five Shakespearean plays done that season, *Hamlet,* which ran March 31 to April 5, 1924, was the outstanding success. Convinced by Poel's argument that Shakespeare originally conceived of Prince Hamlet not as a man in his thirties but rather as a young university student, Monck gave the role to a young Cambridge University scholar. The *Norwich Mercury* was laudatory: "We have never seen Hamlet more powerfully performed by amateurs.... It is no misuse of praise to say that the production ran the best of professional efforts very closely."[16] London critics were equally impressed. Francis Birrell wrote for *The Nation,* "They gave a performance of Shakespearian tragedy that I have never seen approached on the London stage."[17] A year later the critic for *Vogue* remarked, "The *Hamlet* given there last year was the best that I have seen, for Mr. Monck is a producer of extraordinary talent."[18] Monck and the Norwich Players had settled in to their new home at last.

The *Hamlet* success in March and April was followed by an even greater financial success in May. The Norwich Players performed Bernard Shaw's *Getting Married* with the author himself in attendance. During the previous summer Monck had written to Shaw asking the author's advice about certain changes in staging that were needed in order to perform the play on the Maddermarket stage. Shaw's response, dated August 4, 1923, contained some very interesting remarks about his published stage directions. He wrote:

> In dealing with my stage directions you must always allow for the difficulties raised by my determination never to mention the stage in my printed books. I had to make this rule to get away from the old "Stabs her RC: sees ghost up C (biz); and exit RUE," which made plays unreadable and unsaleable before I started reforming them for the press. But to make this possible and at the same time make my printed versions practicable prompt copies, I have to define positions on the stage by specifications which are quite inessential. For instance, I call a certain chair a Chippendale chair so that when I write "The colonel sits down in the Chippendale chair" the producer may know which chair I mean, and the reader will not be upset by such an absurdity as "sits chair B." But it does not matter two straws whether the chair is Chippendale or Sheraton. The producer must use his common sense to decide what is essential and what not.

In regard to this particular production Shaw illustrated his meaning by referring to the large "Glastonbury clock" which is mentioned in the text. This would be a characteristic piece of furniture, he said, but nobody takes the time from it (as presumably it does not work) so it is unnecessary. The producer needed only to make clear to his cast where the clock should be, Shaw pointed out, so that references made to the clock in the stage directions would make sense.

Sometime between this August letter and the following April Shaw decided to travel to Norwich to see for himself just what Monck would do with the play. Years later Monck would tell a reporter for the *Observer* that he was never sure if Shaw liked the production.[19] By all the contemporary accounts, while the production may have been a well-deserved financial success for the Norwich Players, it was not their best artistic effort even though they were playing for the famous author himself. But whether Shaw admired this particular production or not, he certainly admired Monck's efforts and seems to have maintained a special interest in the Maddermarket for the remainder of his life.

When in 1928 the local critic Arthur Batchelor stated in his review of Monck's production of *Heartbreak House*, "G. B. S. claims that these prefaces of his are a serious effort to convey the full content of the play,"[20] Shaw took the time to respond. In a letter published in the *Eastern Daily Press* on May 1, 1928, he wrote:

For the sake of the Maddermarket Theatre which Mr. Nugent Monck has made one of the most remarkable artistic theatres in England, I must not allow it to be supposed that the citizens of Norwich cannot enjoy themselves there when one of my plays is being performed unless they read a treatise of 30,000 words or so first at a cost in money of several shillings for a copy of the book. I can assure them that most of the plays were written and performed long before the prefaces were thought of. When there is any connexion at all between them it is the play that creates interest in the preface, and not the preface that creates interest in the play.... I rather implore playgoers not to come to the play with their heads full of the preface, thereby confusing their attention by trying to discover relationships between the two that do not exist. The play is a work complete in itself; and so is the preface.

In 1933 Shaw paid another visit to the Maddermarket, this time to see Monck's production of Shakespeare's *Henry VI, Parts I, II* and *III*. He attended both because he had never seen the plays performed and because he wished to pay tribute to Monck's achievement of having finally staged all of the plays attributed to Shakespeare. The production took two evenings and Shaw attended the opening nights, June 19 and 20. It is characteristic of Monck that although he knew well in advance that Shaw intended to be present at these performances, no announcement was made about it and no mention was made in the program of what Monck had personally achieved with this production.

In 1940, when Shaw heard that Monck might be forced by the war to take a job in South Africa, a job offer Monck declined, he wrote to Monck on May 22:

Dear Nugent Monck,

It is with something like dismay that I learn that the war has struck your wonderful theatre dead, and that you are forced to begin life afresh in a part of the world younger than Norwich, which is still in the days of Alfred the Great.

There is nothing in British theatrical history more extraordinary than your creation of the Maddermarket Theatre out of nothing, with no money and no municipal support, and its maintenance for so many years in an apparently hopeless *milieu,* planning, managing, producing, financing without finances, and doing everything outside the acting (without professional actors) except sweeping the stage and sitting in the pay box—if indeed you have always been spared these extremities.

You have produced all Shakespeare's plays and I think all of mine, with everything else of cultural importance in modern drama. And you have met all your business obligations like the Bank of England. How did you do it—out of nothing but your own wits [?]

I have lost no opportunity of urging your right to official recognition, and shall continue to do so, war or no war.

faithfully [*sic*], G. Bernard Shaw

It was a sincere expression of admiration from a man who was known to be sparing in his praise. Shaw continued to work for Monck's official recognition after the war. On November 22, 1945, he wrote to Monck, "Shall I ask the Labour Party to give you the next theatre Knighthood? Your consent must be assured. They should make you an Abbot, or give you the O.M."

"Whatever people say," Monck later said of Shaw, "he was kind and courteous to me. I was always struck by his courtesy, not in an exaggerated way but in the small graces of life. I was naturally a little shy of him because he was a great figure, but I never found he made any attempt to embarrass me."[21]

Experiments and Development

The artistic success of *Hamlet* followed by the financial success of *Getting Married* could not have come at a more opportune time for Monck and his theatre. Even with those successes the 1923–24 season proved to be the Maddermarket's worst financial showing until the 1939–40 season, which was carried on during the opening months of World War II. The venture might well have collapsed completely without the boost these productions provided; for while Monck's reputation outside Norwich was growing steadily, within Norwich he was still treated with indifference. Yeats, Poel, Farjeon, Atkins, Playfair, Jackson and now Shaw had all come to see the Maddermarket and gone away impressed by Monck's work there. Still, only a few of the local residents realized its importance or appreciated its value.

The Players opened their 1924–25 season with *All's Well That Ends Well*. The poor financial showing of the previous season did not prompt Monck into a more conservative approach. A great many producers would have justified to themselves putting on a few "safe" London successes at this point. Monck, however, entered into this fourth season with a drive for experimentation. *All's Well That Ends Well*, hardly one of Shakespeare's more popular dramas, was staged using the new system of reversible flats. The next day the *Morning Post*, in a highly favorable review, stated in a congratulatory manner, "The play, ... as produced tonight, gave a sense of being remarkably *slow-running*" (italics mine). Upon returning to London, it was an embarrassed critic who had to explain to his readers that there had been a serious error in the transmission of his review, which should have said that the play was "remarkably *smooth-running*."[22] Incidentally, Monck took the role of Lavatch, the clown, in this play and his performance won praise both from the *Morning Post* and *The Times*.

All's Well That Ends Well was followed by Sheridan's comedy *The Critic*. This is a risky period piece. It has some very funny scenes but is also full of topical allusions to Georgian London which mean little to audiences of today. Monck further courted disaster with this show by continuing his scenic experimentation. In March of 1923 he staged *The Way of the World* using a false proscenium. Door flats, decorated like the proscenium arch doors of the Georgian theatres, were placed at shallow angles between the side galleries and the stage post which supported the canopy. This proved unsatisfactory, however, because the resulting proscenium arch was only 14 feet wide. For *The Critic* a new approach was tried. The stage area beneath the galleries was closed off by a façade containing a door and a box seat on each side, one of which served as a musicians' stall. This created a beautiful period setting while not cutting down stage space unduly. It was an artistic triumph, but audiences remained small.[23]

In November Monck went further still with his experiments by producing a premiere play by none other than his severest critic, F. W. Wheldon. The gamble paid off, however, as Wheldon's *The Red King* attracted the first really good opening-night house the Maddermarket had had since its opening.[24] The season continued with the first modern revival of Wycherley's *The Gentleman Dancing-Master* and then finally settled down with the more popular selections of *Romeo and Juliet, The Tempest, Macbeth* and Drinkwater's *Mary Stuart*. But even these were not done in any conventional manner. *Romeo and Juliet* contained the much-admired tomb scene which the critics for *Vogue* and *The Nation* praised so highly. Making the entire platform into the subterranean vault of the Capulet family was taking full advantage of the Elizabethan stage and the entire production, the critics said, was a great relief from the romantic extravaganza which the management of Drury Lane had recently made of the play.[25] *The Tempest* also received wide acclaim, especially for the effectiveness of its opening storm scene. In this scene the ship's company appeared on the balcony while Ariel and a group of sea nymphs danced wildly on the stage under a richly lit green net cloth which billowed up and down with their motion. This created a striking, yet simple, effect of a turbulent sea. *Macbeth* too was staged in a challenging manner, being costumed completely in Elizabethan dress rather than in the usual medieval Scottish garb.

This experimental season of Monck's ended in June with a special benefit production to raise money in order to clear the theatre's debts. Once again Monck chose to maintain the standards he had set for his theatre rather than play for safety by staging a light comedy. For this benefit he chose to do Browning's *Pippa Passes* and Sheridan's *St. Patrick's Day, or the Scheming Lieutenant* which he produced under the short title *The Scheming Lieutenant*. The first play had only one previous production in England and that was by Monck in 1909. Most reviewers enjoyed the productions a great deal, but the Norwich public was not to be won with such unknown dramas and sufficient money was not raised to free the Maddermarket from debt. The season brought in £200 more than the previous one, however, and Monck was sufficiently encouraged by this to invest an additional £400 into having his building repainted throughout.[26]

Overall, the artistic standards of Monck's producing remained significantly higher during this fourth season than the acting standards of the Norwich Players. But the number of Norwich Players who could match Monck's high standards with their acting was increasing steadily and the acting was therefore becoming more consistent throughout each cast and from one production to the next. Meanwhile, Monck's work and theirs continued to win recognition. In a book entitled *The New Spirit in the European Theatre, 1914–1925,* Huntley Carter had referred to them as "probably the foremost amateur theatrical organization in this country."[27] Meanwhile, in July 1925 Monck and his Players were awarded a Bronze Medal by the French government for the designs and models they displayed in the International Exhibition of Industrial and Decorative Arts held in Paris that summer.[28] Their exhibit included a scale model of the Maddermarket; designs for *Cymbeline, Hamlet, The School for Scandal* and *The Tempest* done by their regular designer Owen Paul Smyth; and two photographs of their extremely successful *A Midsummer Night's Dream.* Upon its return from France the exhibition was sent to Oxford University where it was featured in the University Extension Lectures Committee's conference on "Drama, Ancient, Mediaeval and Modern."[29] From there it went to London where, along with two of Monck's tapestried curtains, it was honored with a place in the Whitechapel Art Gallery.[30]

To help finance his theatre Monck began to take on more outside work during his fifth season, 1925–26. Before the season opened he produced a revival of his own work, *The Masque of Anne Boleyn,* at its original site, Blickling Hall. On September 14 he returned there with a special evening of scenes from Shakespeare, after which he opened his new season at the Maddermarket with *Measure for Measure,* running September 21–26. In October Monck left for York where he produced *The Duchess of Malfi* for the Everyman Theatre Company in York's medieval Guild Hall. This production was for the most part a revival of his 1922 production of the play at Norwich and the local Yorkshire critics were much impressed by its effectiveness. "The lighting, costumes and general 'decor' of the piece were arresting and effective," wrote the critic for the *Yorkshire Evening Press* on November 25. The Maddermarket backcloths, he said, were "inspiring" in reds, greens and blues, and "reminded one that after all sable is not the only hue." Monck was in York to replace the Theatre's usual producer, Charles F. Smith, so that Smith could get his new project, the Leeds Civic Playhouse, underway.

The Leeds Civic Playhouse opened on October 23, 1925 and no-ticket performances with a collection at the end were its hallmark. Monck had apparently worked closely with Smith and his partner, James G. Gregson, on the establishment of the Leeds theatre.[31] How he met Smith is not known, but Gregson had been playing the lead in a play called *T'Marsdens or Young Imeson* in London when Monck's *The Machine Wreckers* production was such a success in 1923. Unfortunately there are no records of just what advice Monck gave these two men concerning the Leeds Civic Playhouse or of how significantly his work influenced them. In 1928, however, they invited Monck to revive his Maddermarket production of *The Tempest* at Leeds. Monck's anticipated appearance as producer for the Leeds Civic Playhouse was announced early that year (1928) in their program for a production of *Canon in Residence* by F. A. Rice. In this announcement Smith wrote, "Some time ago I asked a very distinguished producer a characteristically indiscreet question: 'Who in your opinion are the three greatest producers of this generation?' "Gordon Craig, Granville Barker, and Nugent Monck,' was the prompt reply."[32] While it is unfortunate that the "distinguished producer" cannot be identified, Smith's admiration of Monck was obvious. This same admiration would later be shared by another Leeds Civic Playhouse producer, Norman Marshall, who later wrote in *The Other Theatre,* "Monck at his best deserves to be ranked among the first half-dozen producers in England."[33]

While Monck was in York the Norwich Players were left in the care of his longtime friend, the actress Isabel Roland. She directed and played the leading role in the Maddermarket production of *The Trojan Women,* which ran along with Monck's *The Magic Casement* November 30 to December 5. If Monck had anything at all to do with this production it could not have been to do more than set the lights at dress rehearsal, since *The Duchess of Malfi* had opened in York on November 24 and by December 7 Monck was opening another production in Oxford.

The appearance of the Maddermarket designs in Oxford in August 1925 apparently inspired a young man named R. L. Stuart to solicit Monck's help with the founding of an Oxford University Opera Club. Monck agreed to produce their opening production and on January 7 through 9, 1925 they gave the first production in England of Monteverdi's 1607 composition, *Orfeo.*[34] It was a good, though not outstanding, production. Monck had the musical training and artistic skills to be a great producer of opera, but his ideas about simplicity and continuity in production were in conflict with what audiences expected in opera staging.

In January 1926 Monck was back in his own theatre doing *Julius Caesar,* which was followed by the production of *Marriage à la Mode* that Nigel Playfair took to his Lyric Theatre, Hammersmith, complete with Monck's special costume innovations. The remainder of the season was uneventful except that it was scheduled to close with *King Lear,* but casting problems forced *Twelfth Night* to be substituted in its place. It was a fortunate substitution, as *Twelfth Night* was the greatest financial success of the year.

In the February 1, 1925 issue of *Vogue* the drama critic wrote, "Mr. Monck is a producer of extraordinary talent.... If there are any readers of *Vogue* living in or near Norwich who do not realize that they have a theatre which we in London greatly envy, let me beg them at once to investigate. There are even some of us so perverse and high-brow as to prefer it to Drury Lane." The *Vogue* readership around Norwich did not flock to investigate the

Maddermarket in any significant numbers, but in July 1926 Monck got his chance to show a large portion of the community what he and the Players were capable of doing. He wrote and staged for the city corporation *The Norwich Pageant* using his own Norwich Players in the speaking roles, supported by 1,000 local citizens.

Gaining Publicity

The Norwich Pageant was presented in July 1926. In ten beautifully choreographed scenes Monck covered the history of Norwich from the departure of the Romans to the suppression of the 1745 rebellion. The Norwich Players scored a particular triumph with their performance of *Abraham and Isaac,* which was part of Scene iv, and the entire program was carefully timed to end after dusk so that the closing grand finale could be played under colored floodlights. (The presentation of an actual medieval play and the use of colored floodlights were the special hallmarks of Monck's pageants and pageantlike productions.) The local reviewers were enthralled but they were not the only ones who were impressed. E. S. A., writing for *The Spectator* on July 31, declared:

> For years I have seen them; the coming of the Romans, trouble with the Druids, the inevitable arrival of Elizabeth on a white palfrey,... but I have never come away with any lasting feeling except that of astonishment at the incomprehensible desire of the English (so self-conscious in other respects) to dress up. In Norwich, for the first time, I have seen a pageant produced and performed as it should be ... where most pageant masters are just good showmen, Mr. Monck brought to his work the genius of a master-mind of the theatre.

The critic for the *Daily Telegraph* was equally laudatory. Writing of the grand finale in his July 22 review he said, "In all that had gone before it was possible to feel the influence of a man of vision—one, moreover, who had the power to project his vision in tangible and coherent form. But here his perception was at its finest. The grouping of the figures, of colours, and of movements was like the deft and delicate orchestration of a Mozart Symphony."

For once, too, the production was not merely an artistic success for Monck; he was paid £100 for his labors plus 10 percent of the profits. This was equal to fully half the yearly income his work at the Maddermarket had been generating. But more importantly, in the three days of performance nearly 15,000 local people saw the work of Monck and the Players. Applications to join the Norwich Players poured in and Norfolk people seemed finally ready to investigate the Maddermarket.[35]

In August Monck announced his 1926–27 season, which was to begin with the previously postponed production of *King Lear*. At the end of that month Monck received a letter from Colyton in Devon: "I am hoping to make an expedition to Norwich to see the first or second performance of your *King Lear*, for I am doing a preface to the play and sight of it on stage will be helpful, I know."[36] The letter was from Harley Granville-Barker and the series of prefaces on which he was working were to become the single most important influence on Shakespearean staging in this century. The visit apparently served its purpose, for on October 4 Barker wrote thanking Monck for making the trip pleasant and profitable, saying "I gathered a lot about the end of *Lear* as W[illiam] S[hakespeare] meant it to be." But Barker goes on to add an interesting criticism:

> I think—if I may say so—you could have been as courageous over Act III—though I know when one thinks in cold blood of "Blow, winds, and crack your cheeks . . ." with nothing to help it—! I daresay Burbage exlaimed "Ludd my dear Shakespeare, what will they make of this?" To which W. S. "Never you mind. Plunge in and try. It'll go." And I expect it did.

What Barker objected to was Monck's use of lightning effects in this particular scene, as he explained in a letter dated October 7, 1926. "I could of course have 'pieced out your *Lear's* imperfections with my thought,'" he wrote, "but really I don't think there'd have been any more—not as much—need to as there was with limelight. Anyhow—I cursed you when you turned it on." Barker then advised Monck,

> Given that stage, I think you must stand or fall by the technique that belongs to it—and I believe you'll stand—rhetoric—no backs to the audience—entrances and exits—discoveries seldom. Movement to counterbalance the standing still for the sake of the speeches coming off the chest. And I suspect you know that the 17th cent. man wasn't a very noble actor, was an "amateur" in many ways. But he looked *fine* and *he could speak verse.*

This final comment was, it seems, a compliment for the "amateur" Norwich Players, for he went on to say of their ability to handle verse, "You've evidently got your people to love and—apparently!—understand it. You can trust in this I'm sure." But his injunction against playing with backs to the audience hit at Monck's pet theory of staging. It was Monck's belief that when a speaker's back was to the audience, the audience's attention was focused on the faces of the listeners on stage. He found that this produced a very desirable emotional response from the audience and he liked to use it at climactic moments in his productions.[37] One wonders what reason Barker could have given for objecting to this. On a stage which is surrounded on at least three sides by the audience, as the Elizabethan stage certainly was, the actors must invariably have had their backs turned to some parts of the audience from time to time. And what could he have meant by saying the seventeenth-century actor "was an 'amateur' in many ways"?

Regardless, when Barker's *Preface to King Lear* appeared in the summer of 1927, his appreciation of Monck's work showed through to such an extent that *The Times* book reviewer commented, "Mr. Granville-Barker begins by pointing out that none of the dead and very few of the living critics can ever have seen *King Lear* acted. They have only seen adaptations from the play of the same title, for the Maddermarket Theatre at Norwich appears to be the only place at which Shakespeare's *King Lear* has been acted, since the seventeenth century, as Shakespeare meant it to be acted."[38]

This production of *King Lear* broke all attendance records for the Maddermarket, thanks in part, no doubt, to the interest generated by the Norwich Pageant. But there was at least one critic who was not favorably impressed. After establishing his objectivity by declaring "Shakespeare cannot be properly given on the Anglo-Saxon stage," "Globe-Trotter," the roving reporter for the *Toronto Globe,* wrote of the Maddermarket *Lear,*

> The actors were amateurs, lines were not well delivered, the directing was not particularly intelligent, and full advantage was not taken of the platform stage's rich resources. Scenes were telescoped and mangled in the same old way, and poetry was sacrificed to scenic effects, because the producer seemed afraid to trust this beautiful instrument, the Elizabethan stage.[39]

That Monck did not give his Shakespearean productions over entirely to what was then thought to be the austerity of Elizabethan staging there can be no doubt. This had been the main thrust of Barker's criticism. But while "Globe-Trotter" accused the players of poor delivery Barker had praised them for their verse handling. Barker also did not find Monck's cutting of the play nearly so unsatisfactory. On November 11, 1926 he wrote to Monck, "Could you tell me the exact playing time of your *Lear* and the number of lines you cut. I am convinced—in fact your production was full evidence—that played as it should be, it is not so long." Monck apparently responded that he cut 750 of the play's 3,340 lines and that the play ran just two and one-half hours. Barker did not find this excessive; the Folio, he pointed out, will give authority for cutting at least 200 lines.[40] Certainly this is not the mangling and telescoping of scenes which "Globe-Trotter" suggests. But throughout Monck's career there was always a wide divergence of opinion as to the extent to which he cut Shakespeare's plays for performance.

There seem to have been several reasons for this divergence of opinion. The first was a fundamental discrepancy between theory and practice which Monck inherited from William Poel. The primary principle of Shakespearean staging which Poel taught to his followers was the presentation of "the full text in its proper order without interpolation or rearrangement." But Poel admitted that in actual practice, "I have consistently throughout my productions made alterations and reconstructions when the plays are considered to be unactable or are not being acted, and when it seemed to me that the success of the performance needed some alteration in the play."[41] Unfortunately, as Poel's career progressed he became obsessed with seeing allusions to the Essex rebellion in all Elizabethan drama and he also became more self-indulgent of his other idiosyncrasies, such as putting women in men's roles. To make his productions "successful" under these conditions he often edited his texts so severely that poetry, meter and story line were lost.

Monck never cut his plays this ruthlessly but, like Poel, he realized that his audience was not quite ready for the ideal of Shakespeare's plays being performed unabridged. *"King Lear* and *Hamlet* are too long for a general audience," Monck once reported, "but the balance of these plays is completely lost when they are shortened, so the producer must make up his mind what is to be sacrificed and console himself with the thought that if people enjoy the performance they may read the whole play at home, but that if they are bored they will certainly prevent others from coming to see them."[42] It was undoubtedly this consideration that caused Monck to write in his program for *Antony and Cleopatra* in 1924, "The Producer regrets that in order to shorten the play he has been obliged to omit the Pompey scenes."

But while Monck realized that it would take some time for audiences to learn to appreciate Shakespeare played in full, he also realized the importance of constantly advocating a policy of producing the plays with the full text even if he did not always practice such a policy himself. This probably explains why just four months after his *Antony and Cleopatra* program noted that all the Pompey scenes were cut Monck told a local reporter that the Norwich Players had given 18 of Shakespeare's plays and "in each case they had tried to give the full text except for the cuts to make them suitable to a Cathedral city."[43]

The inevitable result of this gap between theory and practice was that Monck often actually did cut more lines from Shakespeare than he admitted. On January 6, 1925 the *Observer* wrote of Monck's production of *Romeo and Juliet*:

> The cutting deserves a word or two of comment. Some of the play is obviously much the better for being cut. The sprightliness of the Romeo-Benvolio-Mercutio set means nothing whatever to a present-day audience, except for an occasional indecency and the pure silliness of such a remark as the "Here comes Romeo, like a dried herring, without his roe…" But no one has any legitimate complaint for the puns and the indecency disappearing. Mr. Monck took them out, and, I am glad to say, left in instead the curious little domestic colloquies between the servants that give so vivid a touch to Capulet's feasts. But cutting [lines from] the balcony scene, Juliet's 'Gallop apace' speech, and Romeo's last speeches in the tomb is a very different matter. Here, in the Mecca of true Shakespearians, I was surprised to find these things rather ruthlessly slashed.

Yet, only three months later on March 18, *The Times* reported on Monck's authority that, "Mr. Monck gives during his season of six or seven months each year nine or ten plays, all presented faithfully, with a minimum of 'cutting.'"

There is no doubt that Monck cut Shakespeare's plays rather significantly for their first performances at the Maddermarket. But as the competence of his Players increased and as he became more confident of his audiences' ability to listen he played more and more of the complete texts. This restoration of the integrity of the text was not always noticed, however, because of Monck's unique methods of staging. Everything about Monck's stagecraft was designed for a smooth-flowing, rapid-paced performance. The effect was intended to be exactly what the *Eastern Evening News* critic experienced at Monck's 1947 production of *Othello*. The critic wrote, "There is nothing to divert our attention from it, nor to give us relaxation; the plot drives us relentlessly on from crisis to crisis."[44] This swiftness often made Monck's productions seem to be cut more significantly than they actually were. They could even appear rearranged at times, as one scene followed the next with unfamiliar rapidity. Under Monck's method "Globe-Trotter" might very well have mistaken full text scenes for telescoped versions. As a final confusing factor in all this, when war broke out in 1939 considerations of curfew regulations and problems with casting forced Monck to cut his texts severely again. Unfortunately these war and postwar productions have been fresher in the minds of those who have written about Monck since his death than the productions of his prewar days, but those postwar productions do not represent Monck's best work.[45]

Monck's failure to adhere to the policy of performing Shakespeare's plays uncut did not significantly damage his reputation as a producer of Shakespeare's plays. His reputation continued to grow both in that area and as a producer of plays by living authors. In the busy year of 1926 he had been featured in Gordon Craig's widely read journal, *The Mask*. It was a characteristically eccentric article by Craig himself entitled "The Chances for and against Good Theatres in the Provincial Centres in England, with Special Reference to the Maddermarket Theatre of Norwich." Craig began the article by saying, "I had often heard of Nugent Monck as being an extremely able man in theatrical things. I had heard this from dramatists who are always to be relied on to recognize those who have helped them."[46] Most likely Craig heard this from W. B. Yeats and Lady Gregory, both of whom he knew well. Shaw too may have attested to Monck's capabilities.

Soon after the appearance of Craig's article, however, several more authors joined the pilgrimage to see their work done at the Maddermarket. Ashley Dukes, Laurence Housman, Clifford Bax and Martin Shaw all came to see Monck produce their plays and all left greatly impressed by what they saw. In 1936 when the Norwich Players were celebrating their twenty-fifth year under Monck's direction Dukes would pay tribute to Monck saying, "There is one distinction that English writers for the stage must especially prize. That is a production of one of their own plays by Nugent Monck at the Maddermarket Theatre."[47]

In December 1926 Monck returned to Oxford and the Oxford University Opera Club to stage their second major production, *Alceste,* by the eighteenth-century composer Gluck. But Monck's major outside effort for the year came in July when he produced his own work, *Robert, King of Sicily,* for the Leeds Civic Playhouse in the ruins of the twelfth-century Kirkstall Abbey with a cast of over 600.

The production was billed as a "Community Drama." It was intended to be a hybrid entertainment combining the best features of the two most widespread movements in British theatre at that time, pageants and the Little Theatres. Pageants were popular, democratic spectacles but usually had little else to recommend them. The Little Theatres brought high artistic ideals to thousands but they remained fundamentally elitist. Community Drama was intended to combine the scope of a pageant with the artistic standards and form of a play. Those experienced amateurs who were part of the Little Theatre movement would take the speaking roles while ample opportunities were provided for other enthusiasts in the crowd scenes. In this production 72 speaking roles were taken by members of the Leeds Civic Playhouse Company.

It was a grand plan which did not quite succeed. Critics were confused and tried to force it into the old molds of pageant or play. It was not quite spectacular enough to be outstanding as the former and not quite literary enough to be outstanding as the latter. It was an artistic success, though Monck's producing won more praise than his playwriting, but not a success sufficient to inspire others to attempt such a challenge. Monck was the only producer in England who had been highly successful both at staging in the most intimate of theatres and at producing the grandest of pageants. It is unlikely that anyone could have been more successful with this venture or even have done as well as he did. "Community Drama" did not catch on in England. But smaller scale pageantlike productions are still given in the old Cistercian Abbey at Kirkstall Park in Leeds, attesting to the impact of Monck's original production there in 1927.

Monck's monthly schedule of productions at the Maddermarket continued in spite of this extra activity. On September 26, 1927 the seventh Maddermarket season opened with *The Taming of the Shrew,* which Monck produced as usual with Shakespeare's Christopher Sly introduction and the epilogue from the earlier play *The Taming of a Shrew*. The financial success of that season was a musical comedy by Clifford Bax and Martin Shaw called *Mr. Pepys*, which was done in January 1928.

Monck's reputation continued to grow and in March he was asked to bring his Players to London to perform *The Lady from the Sea* for the London Arts Theatre Club as part of their Ibsen Festival. For the first time the Norwich Players outshone their producer. Critics for *The Times*, the *Morning Post*, the *Daily Mail* and the *Daily Telegraph* were unanimous in their praise of the acting when the reviews came out on March 25 (though overelocution of lines was mentioned as a slight fault), but Monck's production elements, they agreed, lacked cohesion. Monck chose to costume this 1888 play in the dress of that period. The first act was staged with beautifully detailed period furniture but combined with the costumes this gave the play a sense of being rather artificial. The second act, which takes place at a "view point" on a cliff overlooking the fjord, was then given a strangely Cubist background that clashed totally with what had gone before. Monck had difficulty whenever he was forced to work behind a proscenium arch and this production was no exception, but such errors in design were strangely uncharacteristic of his work. What is more, the critics also complained of unduly long intervals between the acts, a criticism never before made of one of Monck's shows. Clearly this was atypical of Monck's usual production efforts.

Figure 12. *As You Like It*, 1921
Inaugural production at the Maddermarket. Monck is in jester costume *(far left)*.
(Photo, Daily Mirror, *1 October 1921)*

Figure 13. *A Midsummer Night's Dream,* 1923
(*Courtesy of the Maddermarket Theatre Trust, Ltd.*)

Figure 14.   *Othello*, 1923
(*Courtesy of the Maddermarket Theatre Trust, Ltd.*)

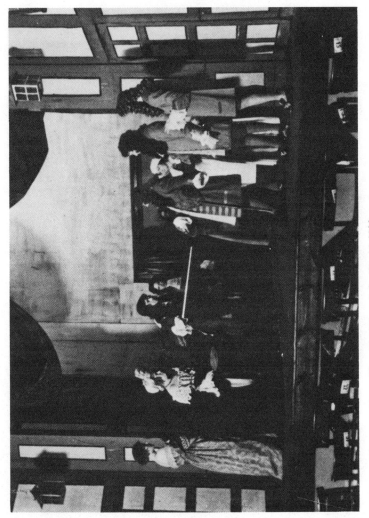

Figure 15. *The Way of the World,* 1923
(*Courtesy of the Maddermarket Theatre Trust, Ltd.*)

Figure 16.   *Marriage à la Mode*, 1926
(*Courtesy of the Maddermarket Theatre Trust, Ltd.*)

5

Achievements and Influence: 1929-1933

By the end of the 1927-28 season Monck and the Norwich Players had established an international reputation. Monck had staged nearly seventy plays in almost eighty productions since the Maddermarket's opening. While maintaining a grueling production schedule of ten plays per year (with actors who had to earn their livings with other employment), he had produced seven additional plays in neighborhood communities, three productions in London, two operas in Oxford, and one major production each in St. Albans, York and Leeds. He gave testimony for a major Board of Education Committee report, lectured at Oxford, and served as an advisor on the founding of the Leeds Civic Playhouse. Numerous producers and playwrights came to the Maddermarket and left greatly impressed. Less prestigious visitors came from as far as India to see the tiny theatre that was making Norwich famous.[1] Maddermarket designs had won an award in Paris and were exhibited in Oxford and London. The Norwich Players had received one offer to tour America and another to tour Germany (both of which had to be declined).[2] They had received considerable praise from the London press and were the first amateur society to be invited to perform at the London Theatre Arts Club. But in spite of this substantial achievement the Maddermarket audience showed no sign of increasing. The sudden upsurge in attendance prompted by the success of the Norwich Pageant in 1926 had quickly dissipated and by the end of the 1927-28 season production profits were again showing a definite decline. Fame had not brought fortune to Monck or to the Maddermarket.

Maddermarket Mondays

Monck had long struggled with the problem of developing an audience. For years, reviewers had commented on the small houses on opening nights. The conservative Norwich public apparently waited for the reviews to come out before buying their tickets. This meant that the financial success of a play depended on the personal opinion of only one or two people. Monck was confident in his work and believed if more opinions were circulated by the word of mouth of a large first-night audience, his venture would stand a better chance. He also realized that a full house on opening night would inspire his actors to better performances. For their part, the critics reprimanded the audiences for not being more adventurous and attending the performances before the reviews appeared. Monck tried numerous approaches to solving this problem, most of which were attempts to educate his audience.

In his very successful 1919–20 season he drew a large first-night audience by maintaining a series of lectures which took place every week when the company was idle, on the same night on which the plays normally opened. After that season Monck continued to offer lectures, readings, dance and music recitals, and other forms of entertainment that would keep the name of his theatre synonymous in the public mind with art, culture and intelligence. But these programs were not given on a consistent basis, or when they were, as with the 1923–24 lecture-performance series, they were not given on the same night on which his plays regularly opened. In 1925 he experimented with a specially invited audience for the opening of *Hedda Gabler*. In April 1926 he hit on a more successful approach when he made the first night of *The Cherry Orchard* a benefit night for the local hospital. This provided the desired full house on opening night, and as a result the play was unusually well attended throughout the week in spite of having received only very average reviews. But giving away all profits for the first night in order to attract larger audiences for the remainder of the week was not a financially viable way to run a theatre. So with the next production, *Twelfth Night,* Monck changed the opening night to Friday, thereby hoping to attract a larger first-night crowd and to maximize profits with two additional performances per run. The increase in profits, however, did not prove sufficient to warrant the extra strain this put on his amateur casts and the experiment was not attempted again until the 1940s.

In the summer of 1928, Monck announced a new attempt, based on the idea of the Theatre Guild's subscription program. For a very modest price a patron would receive tickets to the first five opening nights in the season. In addition, the patron would be entitled to attend eight special performances of various kinds without charge and all were to occur on Monday nights. The series did not have a very auspicious beginning.

For the inaugural production of this series, *Henry V,* Monck had invited an old friend, the actor Henry Ainley, to come and play the minor role of the Chorus. Ainley had been an actor of considerable stature in London until alcoholism had forced him to withdraw from the stage in 1924. By 1928, however, he had improved his condition and was prepared to reenter the theatre.

Ainley was to appear anonymously at the Maddermarket, but on the Sunday before opening night, the Norwich Player cast in the title role became seriously ill. Ainley agreed to read the role, and Monck chose to advertise the fact the next day when he notified the press that the leading role would be read. Ainley performed brilliantly and hardly needed the book by the week's end. After this production Ainley went to London where he became a great success in St. John Ervine's *The First Mrs. Fraser* early the next year.

The near cancellation of *Henry V* was followed by the actual cancellation of Sir Nigel Playfair's lecture, which was to be next on the schedule. Fortunately, the actress Penelope Wheeler was available and was quickly substituted, performing a reading of *Medea*. The remainder of the series went without incident, but at its completion the new local critic Charles Rigby wrote, "It must be remembered that the Mondays were this year an experiment. As an experiment they were successful. As anything else, they are, perhaps, open to criticism."[3]

Monck continued the series through February, March and April 1929 on the same terms, apparently with considerably more success (though no financial records are available for this season or the next). For the 1929–30 season, at any rate, he was able to change the program so that subscriptions ran for an entire season, September to June, but included only six "occasional" free Monday recitals. In this form the Maddermarket Monday program was a remarkable success and remained a vital part of the theatre's operation until the 1946–47 season. In that season it was replaced by a broader program in which half of the seats for every performance were sold to subscribers (under the original plan all Monday night seats were sold but no others), and the free recital program was terminated.

Having finally developed a method for improving his audience base in the Norwich area, Monck was freer than ever to concentrate on his producing. In October he went to Yorkshire where he produced *The Tempest* for the Leeds Civic Playhouse at the Albert Hall. The production received considerable attention, and the general consensus of the reviewers was that Monck's staging was far superior to the acting. But even the staging had problems the first night because the lighting had not been sufficiently rehearsed. These were not Monck's own well-trained actors or technicians and Monck had already returned to Norwich where he was opening two plays in his own theatre. (Lessing's *Minna von Barnhelm* and Shaw's *Man of Destiny* were done at the Maddermarket October 22 through 27.) The Leeds *Yorkshire Weekly Post* of October 26 said of Monck's work, "What cuts in the play there inevitably are, are the work of a producer who is also a scholar and whose greatest contribution to the theatre to-day has been his study and reinterpretation of Shakespeare." The more widely circulated *Amateur Stage* commented about this production, on December 28, "It was produced in the Elizabethan manner, by the producer who understands the playwright Shakespeare better, perhaps, than any producer in England to-day." So, despite deficiencies in acting and first night lighting, Monck's stature as a producer of Shakespeare's plays continued to grow.

Back in Norwich, Monck ran a remarkably adventurous program which included a world premiere musical comedy, a version of Schubert's ballet *Rosamunde,* Chekhov's *Uncle Vanya,* a week of *The Merchant of Venice* in repertory with St. John Ervine's *The Lady of Belmont,* Bruno Frank's *The Twelve Thousand,* Dryden's *All for Love,* and Pirandello's *Six Characters in Search of an Author,* as well as the first production of Ashley Dukes's *The Fountain Head.* It was the most adventurous program he had ever undertaken, and, amazingly, all the shows received very favorable reviews. The most daring play of the season, at least for Norwich, was *Six Characters in Search of an Author.* It was reviewed by *The Festival Theatre Review,* the magazine of the Cambridge Festival Theatre. "I recommend everyone interested in theatre to beg, borrow or steal a car and go over to Norwich," the reviewer began. He then went on to say of the production:

> Mr. Nugent Monck played all the time for simplicity: the stage was not littered with realistic stage clutter: the play's "players" were an ordinary everyday company, without make-up (though here the size of the theatre made things easier); the players were allowed to be just people earning a living on the stage instead of a lot of actors acting being actors: the setting was nothing at all: the lighting unobtrusively effective. Last and best, the play never dawdled.[4]

In the summer of 1929, Monck and the Norwich Players took on two major productions which won them overwhelming acclaim. The first was a production of *Henry VIII,* staged in the garden of the Bishop's Palace next to Norwich Cathedral. The production, which ran from July 8 to 13, was a great success both artistically and financially. It had been intended as the final attempt to clear all the Maddermarket debts, and it did. All the reviews, including those in the *London Referee,* the *Shanghai Times,* the *Christian Science Monitor,* and the *Argus* of Melbourne, Australia, commented favorably on the artistry of the production and publicized Monck's work worldwide.[5] But Monck and the Norwich Players received their most general acclaim with their next appearance, when they performed *Everyman* and *Doctor Faustus* at the first Canterbury Festival.

The Canterbury Festival was a week of music and drama held in the precincts of the great mother cathedral of the Church of England. By 1935 the festival would have sufficient prestige to inspire T. S. Eliot to write *Murder in the Cathedral* specifically for it, but in 1929 it was just beginning.

Monck's reputation as an outstanding producer and successful experimenter with religious drama prompted the Cathedral's Dean, Dr. G. K. Bell, to approach him about supervising the drama portion of the proposed festival. This invitation was something of a personal triumph for Monck. The work in religious drama he had so doggedly pursued for 20 years was finally beginning to receive some official acceptance.

For the Festival, which ran from August 19 through 24, Monck chose to produce *Everyman* and *Doctor Faustus* in repertory with the Norwich Players taking the major roles. *Everyman* was performed outdoors on a platform stage set up just in front of the west porch of the Cathedral, while *Doctor Faustus* was done inside the Chapter House on a stage arranged just below the massive stained glass windows of the east wall.

The production of *Everyman* was given mixed reviews by the critics, who were impressed by the Players but not by the play. The critic for the *Daily Chronicle* probably summed up the general consensus when he wrote,

> It was a brilliant achievement by the Norwich company. After that one is bound to raise questions...As an attempt to revive the old-time association between the drama and religion it was too violent a backward jump in time and method...One felt that one was getting an undesired glimpse of another world, and one it was impossible to regard without feelings of thankfulness that it had ceased to exist.[6]

Clearly the naive religious moral of this medieval play did not have the appeal for the postwar British that it had had for the late Victorians.

The production of *Doctor Faustus,* however, was widely acclaimed. This play had a special appeal for the Festival as its author, Christopher Marlowe, was born in Canterbury and educated within the precincts of the Cathedral. Monck staged it and lit it beautifully on a stage similar to that of the Maddermarket but without a balcony. The critics were very complimentary and especially singled out the Norwich Player who took the title role for a magnificent performance. The perfect elocution of all the players was also much admired as it had been in *Everyman*; for this production, however, it was an even greater achievement because the Chapter House acoustics are very poor.[7]

This first Canterbury Festival received extensive newspaper coverage and the Norwich Players' part in it finally established them as the most widely known and respected Little Theatre group in the British Isles. Over 200 newspapers ran articles on the Festival. These articles appeared not only in England, but as far afield as Brussels, Bombay and Boston. From Montreal to Ceylon the Norwich Players' contribution under Monck's direction was enthusiastically praised.[8] Over 6,000 people had seen their work and left with impressions of a level of performance that was uniformly exceptional. The Norwich Players had set a standard by which other groups would gauge their own work.

The Reputation

In Norwich the newspapers frankly admitted, "Norwich is known chiefly in the United States, for example, not for its old streets, its cathedral, or even for its manufacturing, but as the place where they run the Maddermarket Theatre."[9] To attest to that fact, in the United States papers as small as the Springfield, Massachusetts *Sunday Union* were carrying articles on the Maddermarket. In an article which appeared in that paper on August 4, 1929, Alice Wildey said, after recounting her 118-mile drive from London to Norwich, "I went from a sense of duty. I went because I knew this to be one of the most famous Little Theatres in England and Nugent Monck, one of the best-known producers of England." Even in India the *Madras Mail* was reporting, "Such theatres as the Leeds Civic [now professional], the Oxford Playhouse, and the Cambridge Festival Theatre, are already well known. But increasing attention has been drawn to them this year by the excellent performance of the Norwich Players."[10] This was a considerable achievement for an amateur company. It is also an interesting reflection on the wisdom of Monck's choice to work with amateurs that by 1933 all of the other theatres mentioned by the *Madras Mail* had closed.

The relationship between the Maddermarket and the Cambridge Festival Theatre is an especially interesting one. In his book, *Theatre Prospects,* Tyrone Guthrie asserted that the first step in breaking away from extreme naturalism should be made with the classics, "plays of unexceptionable quality." With a new play, he argued, "the novelty of technique is apt to overwhelm the significance of what is being expressed"; such was the fate of Expressionism.[11] There were two alternative approaches to handling the classics, he continued; one was to reproduce conscientiously the originals which were not naturalistic, and the other was to apply a contemporary viewpoint with as little reference to the past as possible. In eastern England during the late twenties and early thirties both these methods were being thoroughly explored, the former by Monck at the Maddermarket and the latter by Terence Gray at the Cambridge Festival Theatre.

When the Festival Theatre's lighting designer, Harold Ridge, published his first book in 1930, he referred to the Maddermarket as "the first amateur repertory company of real standing."[12] But the theatre's director, Terence Gray, was not so impressed by an approach to theatre which was at the opposite pole from his own. He commented in Ridge's book:

> Cannot Max Reinhardt, Jessner or Hilar make more of Shakespeare, producing him with all the forces of modern continental stagecraft at their command, than can some archaeologist reviving the conditions of the Elizabethan stage? True, I would rather see *Hamlet* done by Nugent Monck at the Maddermarket than by any trade theatre producer in a West End playhouse, but I would rather see it done by Jessner in a Gothic cathedral than by Monck in his reconstruction of an Elizabethan theatre.[13]

It is ironic that Gray then went on to advocate a theatre with no separation between actors and audience and a technique which was not tied to realism, ideas with which Monck had already been experimenting for a quarter of a century.

In October 1931, Gray had an opportunity to illustrate further the differences between his kind of theatre and Monck's when Peter Godfrey's production of *From Morn to Midnight* was staged at Gray's Cambridge Festival Theatre during the same week that Monck was producing the play in Norwich. In a letter to Charles Rigby, the critic for the *Eastern Daily Press,* Gray said:

> Peter Godfrey's treatment of *From Morn to Midnight* was in every respect exactly the opposite of that of Mr. Monck. Godfrey's production . . . is entirely formalized, strident, full of rhythms, and intensely exciting. . . presentational and personal, the audience being addressed throughout. Mr. Monck placed the Salvation Army audience and all on the stage so that the theatre audience could observe it objectively; it was restrained and passive. In this theatre [Cambridge] the Theatre audience is the Salvation Army meeting and the noise and excitement is [*sic*] tremendous.[14]

It is certainly a debatable point as to whether the audience would appreciate being part of the Salvation Army meeting as depicted in this play. As is done with the crowd in Shakespeare's *Julius Caesar,* which Mark Antony manipulates so blatantly, the author of the play seems to be making a critical statement about this group. To make the audience part of it (for the sake of theatricality) may well cause them to miss the author's intention.

By 1933, Gray seems to have come to a better understanding of Monck's work and its importance. On January 17 of that year, Charles Rigby wrote for the *Eastern Daily Press,* "In a talk I had lately with Mr. Terence Gray . . . that clever producer could not find words to express his admiration of the subtlety of Mr. Monck's production." Gray's admiration was widely shared; when he announced the closure of the Cambridge Festival Theatre the following month, the *Daily Telegraph* reported on February 24, 1933, "Its closing down is all the more unfortunate as it has now perfected a style of production quite unique in this country, based on the Habinia Players of Japan. This, and the presentation of rare plays, . . . has won for the Festival a position to rank with the Maddermarket Theatre of Norwich." Monck's Maddermarket was the standard against which even such a well-known venture as the Cambridge Festival Theatre could legitimately be measured in the early 1930s.

The success of the Canterbury Festival and its subsequent publicity for Monck and his Players were followed by a long string of successful and influential productions. After the season opened at the Maddermarket in September, the world press continued to report on the activities there. The November production of Shakespeare's seldom performed play *Pericles* was the most interesting production of that season. "A Greek story, in a Persian setting, with Elizabethan music, Mr. Nugent Monck has done many wonderful things at the Maddermarket but none quite so wonderful as this," declared a local critic.[15] *The Times* agreed and even the reviewer for the *Times of Bombay,* after severely criticizing the Old Vic production of *Richard II* which featured the new young actor, John Gielgud, said, "There was more profit and pleasure to be had by students of Shakespeare at the revival of *Pericles* this week by the Norwich Players."[16] George Benthal, who was producing at the Shakespeare Memorial Theatre, also made the pilgrimage to Norwich to see Monck's famous theatre. He went away much impressed, and the critic who travelled with him wrote for *The Shakespeare Pictorial,* "Four hundred miles was not too far to journey to pay tribute to such creative effort. The material difficulties must be great and the undaunted courage which keeps the flame burning deserves the salute of every student of Shakespeare."[17]

Monck had cut the first act of this play, eliminating what he considered to be the pointless story of incest with which the plot begins. The production opened with a storm and a series of storms forced the action on. Inspired by the British Museum's recently acquired sixteenth-century Persian manuscript, the *Khamsa of Nizami,* Monck chose to costume this production in Persian dress. It was in every way an ideal vehicle for Monck's talents, for the fantastic romantic tale allowed for considerable masquelike elements to be incorporated into the production. A sword dance, a scene of Pericles serenading Thaisa on her balcony, and many songs were added. The visual impact of this "gorgeous Eastern fairy tale" was unforgettable, the local critic exclaimed.[18]

In January 1930 Monck was back in London and back at producing opera. Robert Stuart, who had founded the Oxford Opera Club in 1925 and had invited Monck to produce *Orfeo* for them in December of that year and *Alceste* in December of 1926, was now in London and had organized the London Festival of Opera. Seven operas were produced in three weeks, all by different producers. Monck's production was Mozart's *La Finta Giardiniera,* which ran January 8, 10, and 12 (Norman Marshall produced Handel's *Julius Caesar* during the other three nights of the week). The opera was translated by Stuart and conducted by Leslie Howard, who also wrote the music for Act I, which is missing from Mozart's score. Sets and costumes were executed by Monck's own actor-designers, Andrew Stephenson and Doris Lane, whose "ravishing Watteau-esque costumes and settings"[19] won unanimous praise from all the critics. In fact, the entire production was acclaimed as the greatest success of the Festival, with Marshall's *Julius Caesar* production running a close second.

With Monck's long training in music and his great talent for the visual aspects of staging, producing opera would seem the natural showcase for his talents. But his sense of theatre rebelled at the staginess of opera and he constantly worked against allowing the singers to come downstage to perform. The one consistent criticism of all three of his operatic productions was that the singers were much too often upstage, with the result that the voices did not come across as easily as they should. In spite of this failing, *La Finta Giardiniera* was another great success for Monck and his staff.

It was about the time of this festival that Monck received the script to a morality play written by a young schoolmaster at the Preparatory School, Limpsfield, Surrey. Monck was much impressed by the author's talent and wrote encouragingly to the young man, inviting him to come see the Maddermarket during preparations for the production of *Othello,* which was given the third week of January.[20] The young man, Christopher Harris, came to Norwich, spent several days with Monck, and the following year gave up his teaching post to pursue an illustrious career in theatre under the name of Christopher Fry.

The year 1930 was the most hectic of Monck's career. *Othello* was followed by two performances of *The Chester Mysteries* at the Bishop's Palace, Norwich, February 21 and 22. These were followed immediately on February 24 by a week's run of an interesting double bill, Shaw's *The Devil's Disciple* and General John Burgoyne's 1788 masque *The Maid of the Oaks* (General Burgoyne is featured as a character in Shaw's play). On March 31 through April 5 *Richard II* was produced, and in May a new play by John Davison, *The Shadows of Strife,* was staged. Monck then became involved in a wild flurry of activities over the summer when he produced two pageants, lectured for the British Drama League's summer drama school, produced a very influential production of *Love's Labour's Lost,* and went on a theatre tour of Germany and Austria.

The revival of civic pageantry in England had begun in 1905 when the popular dramatist, Louis N. Parker, was commissioned to write a play to commemorate the twelfth centenary of the founding of Sherborne Abbey near Ealdhelm, Dorset. On a bright summer's day, some 250 performers acted Parker's "folk-play" against a background of trees and old walls. Before the opening, however, it had been recognized that "folk-play" was not a genre with which to sell tickets, so "pageant" became the descriptive term for the publicity fliers. In the audience for one of the performances of this first pageant was the young Nugent Monck.[21] Pageants enjoyed an enormous popularity from that time up to the Great War, but suffered a significant decline in the early to mid-1920s. By 1930, however, pageantry was experiencing a real renaissance; at least seven were produced in the summer of that year alone.[22] In this revival Monck was recognized as preeminent, producing two of the seven pageants done in 1930 and significantly influencing a third at Windsor Castle, where Monck's trademark of staging a medieval mystery play as part of the action was used to good effect.

Speed, variety, color and a careful attention to detail were the elements of production to which critic after critic pointed as putting Monck's pageants far above those of other producers in the country. The staging of simple medieval religious dramas within these grand displays made an effective contrast which was characteristic of Monck's work. His careful arranging of finales so that they would often occur after dusk when beautiful artificial lighting could be employed was another distinguishing feature of his pageantry. Monck was also consistently courageous in his selection of scenes, which he chose not for their historic importance but for their dramatic content and ability to give a sense of history. This was in marked contrast to the endless dull scenes of the granting of city charters that were seemingly obligatory selections in the pageants staged by others.

Monck staged nine major pageants in his career and numerous pageantlike productions. Besides the previously discussed *Mancroft Pageant* (1912), *Norwich Pageant* (1926), *Leeds Pageant* (1927), and the two pageants of 1930 at Northampton and Ipswich mentioned here, he directed pageants at Ramsgate (1934), Nottingham (1935), Chester (1937), and Manchester (1938), the last of which used some 8,000 performers. Of these *The Ipswich Pageant* of 1930 was the most interesting in terms of Monck's work in Shakespearean staging. Monck wrote the book for this pageant, which was also known as *The Wolsey Pageant*. Cardinal Wolsey was born at Ipswich and the pageant was in commemoration of the four hundredth anniversary of his death. Monck built his pageant around the Shakespeare and Fletcher play *Henry VIII*, in which Cardinal Wolsey is a major figure. He had produced the play on a grand scale in Norwich the previous summer, but had remained faithful to the rather slight script. At Ipswich Monck gave himself free rein and produced an artistic spectacle that was "magnificent in conception, triumphantly beautiful in execution, and profoundly inspiring in effect," according to a local critic.[23] London critics had flocked to the play because of the presence of the Prince of Wales at Thursday's matinee and they agreed with this assessment. *The Times* reported on June 24, "Mr. Monck is a remarkably clever inventor of pageantry, and the best things in the Ipswich pageant are his and not Shakespeare's."

Monck, then, was capable of producing the kind of overwhelmingly theatrical productions which Terence Gray admired in the work of Reinhardt, Jessner, and Hilar, and he both enjoyed doing it and profited financially from it. (In 1938, for example, his salary for one pageant was double his net income from an entire Maddermarket season.) But this was not the true art of theatre for Monck. Pageantry, like film, had its place, but within the theatre Monck believed the play must not be overshadowed by the production. When dealing with inferior works as he sometimes did it was not always possible to prevent such overshadowing, but he avoided the temptation to make the Maddermarket a mere showcase for his ability to create striking effects.

The Ipswich Pageant closed on June 28, 1930, and Monck continued his feverish pace by opening a production of *Love's Labour's Lost* in Norwich on July 14. The production was planned for the gardens of the Strangers' Hall Museum which occupy the lots to the west of the theatre. It attracted only average critical attention but it epitomized more than any other the extent of Monck's influence on the staging of Shakespeare. On stage for this show in the role of Sir Nathaniel was Andrew Leigh, recently retired director of the Old Vic. The set and costumes on that stage were designed by Owen P. Smyth and Peter Taylor Smith, artists trained by Monck, who were now members of the Old Vic staff. And in the audience was a young producer just up from the Cambridge Festival Theatre, Tyrone Guthrie, whose career would be significantly influenced by this production.

Monck had a powerful influence on the Old Vic Theatre's producers between the wars. Robert Atkins, who directed the Old Vic from 1920 to 1925, had been inspired to apply for that post by Monck's productions in Egypt. His successor, Andrew Leigh, has left no record of his association with Monck but was obviously sufficiently impressed by Monck's work to be willing to travel to Norwich to perform in a Maddermarket show without pay. Leigh's successor, Harcourt Williams, who took over the post in 1929, owed his early success there to Monck and the experiments done at the Maddermarket, though Williams himself may not have been fully aware of that fact.

Harcourt Williams was undoubtedly first exposed to the work of the Maddermarket in 1922 when his wife, the actress Jean Sterling Mackinlay, performed there. But it was in 1929, when Williams arrived at the Old Vic, that he had most occasion to be grateful for the pioneer work Monck had done in Norwich. By the time of Williams's arrival at the Old Vic, Owen Paul Smyth, a talented artist who had learned set design under Monck's careful guidance, was already making a name for himself in that theatre. At the end of Smyth's first season, 1928–29, the art critic Horace Shipp wrote,

> One other recruit to the London theatre, whose work must be watched, is Mr. Owen P. Smyth, who graduated from the Maddermarket Theatre at Norwich and is doing delightful work for the Old Vic. In the Surreyside home of Shakespeare there is little chance of erring on the side of expensiveness, and Mr. Smyth knows just what are the elements sufficient to convey a scene. His seashore set for the first and last acts of *The Vikings* was a veritable triumph of big results from small means.[24]

Smyth had obviously assimilated Monck's ideas and methods very well, and his long apprenticeship at the Maddermarket, 1921 through 1928, was excellent training.

Williams's career as a producer, on the other hand, had a very inauspicious start at the Old Vic. The first three productions he staged there failed so miserably that he tendered his resignation to the theatre's manager,

Lilian Baylis. It was at this juncture that Nugent Monck's expertise came to his rescue. Smyth persuaded Williams to do *A Midsummer Night's Dream.* For this production Smyth basically recreated the Maddermarket set designs of 1923.[25] Meanwhile, Peter Taylor Smith, who normally only acted at the Old Vic, helped recreate the costumes which Monck had based originally on Inigo Jones's designs for Thomas Campion's *The Lord's Masque.* The production was a triumph and on the strength of this success Williams decided to continue as the Old Vic's producer. Williams did not acknowledge this debt to Monck in his own account of these events;[26] apparently he did not realize the true source of the ideas which made this show so successful. Even his rejection of Mendelssohn's music in favor of Elizabethan tunes, an innovation to which he pointed with apparent pride, was something Monck had done consistently since 1910. And the careful reader might recognize in his description of Smyth's "glorious wood with a silver sky" the set Monck had originally designed himself at the Abbey Theatre for the 1911 production of *The Countess Cathleen.* With one change, a golden sky, Monck used this set on several occasions, including the 1923 production of *A Midsummer Night's Dream.*

Monck's subtle influence continued to find its way into Williams's work from this production onward. In 1931 Williams opened his production of *Henry IV, Part I* with Falstaff in bed, an unusual opening Monck had devised in 1922. Williams's production of *The Taming of the Shrew* also followed Monck in the practice, unusual at that time, of retaining the Christopher Sly prologue and filling it out with the epilogue from the earlier anonymous work, *The Taming of a Shrew.* Later that season Monck's skill and experience were again of significant assistance to Williams in his production of *Antony and Cleopatra.* Williams said of this production, "I decided to abandon realism and, hanging on the coat-tails of Harley Granville-Barker and William Poel, and with the help of Paul Smyth, we achieved a rapid sequence of events almost kaleidoscopic in effect. For costumes we went to the pictures of Paul [*sic*] Veronese and Tiepolo."[27] Williams, who was a personal friend of Granville-Barker, undoubtedly got his inspiration from that source. But Smyth, who was responsible for the visual effectiveness of those ideas, made the trip down to Norwich to work out the practical details of this venture with his old master Nugent Monck.[28] The resultant kaleidoscopic effect came by way of Monck's 1924 production of the play while the costuming owed much to Monck's *Julius Caesar* of 1926 and his *Coriolanus* of 1928, in which there had already been experiments with the Veronese and Tiepolo models. It was little wonder that the Old Vic's legendary manager, Lilian Baylis, wrote to Monck on November 24, 1931, "I'd love to try to pick your brains, I know a little of what those who work for you think of you and often wish we could work together."[29]

Muriel St. Clare Byrne has said that Harcourt Williams's great contribution to staging was that he managed to fuse the ideas of Poel, Barker, and Craig with the best traditions of Irving, Tree, and Alexander.[30] For over 25 years, by this time, Monck had been experimenting, trying to determine exactly where the pendulum should balance between the extremes represented by these two groups of producers. It is taking nothing away from the reputation of Harcourt Williams then to point out that his success in this fusion owed a great deal to Monck's long years of experience, as translated through the considerable artistic talent of Owen P. Smyth with the assistance of Peter Taylor Smith.

When Williams left the Old Vic in 1933 he recommended as his replacement the young producer Tyrone Guthrie. This recommendation was made on the strength of a production Guthrie had done at the Westminster Theatre that year. The production was of *Love's Labour's Lost* and Guthrie has said of it:

Most of the good ideas in my production were culled from Monck's at Norwich. I have no shame in confessing this. No art is completely original; there are always influences. The artist is rarely conscious of the most important and significant influences. But in matters of style, in the externals, artists, especially young artists, invariably imitate what they admire. From Monck I absorbed various points of style, and a point of view about this particular play.... I look upon this kind of theft as a compliment to the person whose ideas are used:... And now I confess my debt to Nugent Monck, not with a blush but with pride that I had the sense to pick so good a model.[31]

Numerous producers had paid Monck a similar compliment from time to time. W. Bridges-Adams, Robert Atkins, Barry Jackson, Nigel Playfair, Harcourt Williams; the list reads like a *Who's Who* of what Norman Marshall calls "the other theatre." That not all of them have been so frank in confessing their debt as Tyrone Guthrie is probably best explained in Guthrie's own words, "The artist is rarely conscious of the most important and significant influences." But Guthrie spoke for all of these and many lesser-known producers when he wrote to Monck in 1953, "You will be remembered by many, as well as myself, as one of the strong professional 'influences' that directed their attention and taste in the way you thought it should go." And he added on a personal note, "Your *Love's Labour's Lost*...remains the Shakespeare production which I have enjoyed easily the best of any I've seen anywhere and one that one could see in a second was on the right lines."[32]

Guthrie had occasion to see a number of other productions at the Maddermarket, especially during the years of World War II when he was working in close association with the Council for the Encouragement of Music and the Arts, CEMA. After the war he referred to these productions as "some of the most interesting productions of Shakespeare I have ever seen."[33]

Figure 17. *Love's Labour's Lost*, 1930
Outdoor performance, Strangers' Hall garden.
(Courtesy of the Maddermarket Theatre Trust, Ltd.)

But the 1930 production of *Love's Labour's Lost* represented Monck's work at its peak; what Guthrie saw after this date was not often of so high a quality.

Continued Experiments

Monck opened the 1930–31 season with a most successful production of *Hamlet* but the greatest success of the season was the December production of Shaw's *Saint Joan*. This production brought in the best box office results in the Maddermarket's first ten years. This was happily followed by the Maddermarket's second greatest financial success in that period, the January 1931 run of Elroy Flecker's *Hassan*.

In February Monck returned to London where, with a cast of professional actors and a few Norwich Players, he produced the premiere of a play by a new playwright, John McCreery, titled *The Force of Circumstance*. The play was performed at the Grafton Theatre, Tottenham Court Road. Monck's production got very good reviews and the play itself, while not overly impressive, was generally considered to be an admirable first attempt.[34] But if Monck believed he had finally found a playwright to write plays specifically for the Maddermarket, his hopes were soon dashed. During Thursday's performance of the play John McCreery jumped in front of an electric trolley and was killed; he was twenty-four. Monck brought the production to Norwich on February 23 through 28; it was the first and only time a professional company acted as part of the Maddermarket's regular season. A poor financial showing for the venture merely confirmed what Monck already realized: the work he was attempting to do could not support a professional organization. So Monck returned to his regular season and before it was over, he added two more productions to the list of Shakespeare's plays he had staged, *Macbeth* in March and *Timon of Athens* in June. He was now only five plays away from completing the Shakespeare canon of 37 plays.

Outside Norwich, Monck's reputation and that of his theatre continued to grow. Geoffrey Whitworth, founder of the British Drama League, referred to the Maddermarket as one of the two most important amateur theatres in Britain, the other being the Un-named Society of Manchester.[35] In one of a series of articles surveying British theatre for *The Bookman* in 1931, Burgoyne Miller wrote, "On the Continent of course Nugent Monck's name is known as one of the greatest of English producers." He then went on to say, "While fully acknowledging the good work which is done at such places as the Old Vic and the Stratford Theatre, I am still convinced that the Maddermarket is the only theatre in England where Shakespeare is perfectly interpreted."[36] Miller attributed this to the Maddermarket's Elizabethan stage, the intelligence of its audience, and to the fact that the Norwich Players had reasonable time for rehearsals, something which was denied professional actors of Shakespeare.

The 1931–32 season marked the tenth anniversary of the Maddermarket and the twentieth year for the Players. The Maddermarket's inaugural production of *As You Like It* was revived to open a season which showed no shift in policy except that it was perhaps weighted more heavily toward comedy than past seasons had been. *Titus Andronicus* in December and *Richard III* in June brought Monck two productions closer to his goal of completing the Shakespeare canon while another Shaw play, *The Apple Cart*, set a new box office record. Monck stayed away from any outside work for this and the following two seasons, concentrating instead on improving his reputation in Norwich and pursuing some of his personal goals.

In April 1932 Monck staged his own musical adaptation of Gogol's *The Marriage.* This production was followed in May by two productions which represented both Monck's first return to playwriting in over 20 years and yet another attempt by him to find a playwright for his theatre. *The Heavens Shall Laugh* by Nugent Monck was produced in repertory with *Worship No More* by Hilary Gardner, May 16–21, 1932. Gardner had been a young actor in *The Force of Circumstance,* Monck's last attempt to encourage a promising young playwright. This production of Gardner's play received encouraging reviews, but except for a one-act comedy, *2/6 and 3/6,* which Monck produced in 1933, Gardner wrote only one other play for the Maddermarket, *Dark Shadow,* which was not done until 1947.

Monck's play of course received the bulk of the critical attention and the majority of critics seemed in agreement with Charles Rigby when he wrote, "There is, of course, some fine stuff in *The Heavens Shall Laugh* but taking it purely at its face value and as it stands, it would be idle to pretend that the play is much more than a passing diversion."[37]

But if Monck did not improve his stature as a playwright in 1932 he certainly increased his reputation as an adaptor when he brought out his version of Bunyan's epic, *The Pilgrim's Progress.* Produced on the tiny Maddermarket stage with a cast of 66 characters, the play received outstanding reviews and for the first time in Maddermarket history people queued daily outside the box office for tickets. Monck's version became the standard one used for many years in England; it was produced by numerous groups and was the version selected by the BBC for its broadcast of Bunyan's classic on September 4, 1943.

Despite the success of *The Pilgrim's Progress* and a succession of positive reviews by the local critics which had lasted for a season and a half, by 1933 the Maddermarket was facing serious financial difficulties. It was not alone; the Depression was by now worldwide, and theatre after theatre announced its forthcoming closure. The Leeds Civic Playhouse announced in January that it could not continue its operation, the Cambridge Festival Theatre made a similar announcement in February, and the Manchester Repertory Theatre announced its anticipated closure soon after. Nigel Playfair's Lyric Theatre, Hammersmith, had already closed in 1932, and the London Gate Theatre under Peter Godfrey was in financial difficulty and ceased its activity before the end of 1934.

Throughout the country theatre audiences were defecting to the much cheaper talking pictures. In Norwich, Monck's faithful following of some 600 audience members remained dependable but there was no increase in this number while expenses were going up steadily. Monck steadfastly refused to bow to the economic pressure and begin staging recent West End comedies in order to attract a larger audience. Indeed, in March he staged two evenings of medieval plays and in April a week of *Oedipus Rex,* knowing full well that neither would draw an audience. But these were great plays and he wanted to see them performed.

Monck had always tried to encourage the young to appreciate the great drama he worked so hard to put on the stage. Before the First World War and immediately after he had produced scenes from Shakespeare with the local grammar school students every summer. But during the war and throughout the 1920s young people ceased to be encouraged to go to the theatre.[38] Those so actively involved in community theatre thoughout the country had been trained to appreciate this art before the first war and were consequently now predominantly middle-aged. This created a paradoxical situation. A predominantly middle-aged audience suggested to the young that the Maddermarket was a dull "highbrow" establishment which was to be avoided. The only way to change this was to get a younger audience but getting the young into the theatre in order to dispel the very image that was keeping them away was not an easy task.

This "highbrow" image had plagued Monck's efforts in Norwich from the start. When he opened the Music House in 1914 the *Eastern Daily Press* remarked,

> The little playhouse which Mr. Nugent Monck has secured for his company of Norwich Players was opened last night under circumstances that should give cause for pleasure to all who have any taste for what is beautiful in things artistic. It cannot be pretended that the number of such persons is large, but it ought to be sufficient to secure the permanent running of the modest-sized building which Mr. Monck has taken on a three year lease.[39]

The number was sufficient, but Monck later made a telling comment about them when he explained that the Music House was opened "with no capital and nothing but enthusiasm and the help of a small audience, who, if they did not love us very much, hated the people who did not love us more. There is nothing like using us as a stick with which to beat the bourgeois."[40] The press bore some of the responsibility for this; for many years in an attempt to encourage support for Monck's efforts they had tried to shame people into attendance by dwelling on the great cultural importance of the classic drama Monck produced, neglecting to point out that such drama had become classic because of the quality of its entertainment value.

When the Maddermarket opened in 1921 the problem remained. After describing the opening of this "Elizabethan Playhouse," the *Morning Post* critic added,

> Whether the audience bore as much resemblance to their Elizabethan predecessors is a matter of some doubt. But probably in course of time the Norwich Players will grow their own Elizabethan audience, and we shall have our plays performed in the cheerful and lively manner which has been so admirably depicted in *The Knight of the Burning Pestle.*[41]

It was most likely merely wishful thinking however that caused Monck to report a few months later, "Gradually the high-browism of the audience is being broken down. The younger people are taking it up and are enjoying it."[42] Meanwhile the critics continued to beat the bourgeois with Monck's art. "I take the Norwich Players at their own valuation," wrote F. W. Wheldon; "it is a Highbrow institution, and a very good thing that it should be."[43] But if this really was the valuation of the Norwich Players it was not a valuation Monck wished to publicize. When Wheldon was replaced by Arthur Batchelor in 1924, Monck encouraged Batchelor to write such comments as "I cannot conceive a more delightful or less 'highbrow' method of acquiring knowledge."[44]

But by this time it was not so much the critics who were encouraging the highbrow image of the Maddermarket as it was the inherent characteristics of Monck's own objectives and the organization which he had developed to achieve them. "First rate art cannot be pushed beyond a certain percentage of the population,"[45] Shaw had advised Monck, and what Monck was attempting was first rate art. The avowed purpose of the Norwich Players was "to produce plays of literary and artistic merit in the best and most vital manner possible, and to bring such within reach of everyone."[46] Monck's disclaimer that the Players did not give highbrow programs but programs which any intelligent person with average grammar school or public school education could enjoy did not convince the general public.

Monck was well aware of the situation with which he was faced. "You cannot have high-class drama without a highbrow audience," he admitted in 1926. But he had a plan for overcoming this. "You must begin not particularly by amusing the top, but by very slowly interesting people of—should we say a lively intelligence and not too much culture? They are by far the easiest people to play to. Cultured people come already bored and that after all is their form of amusement."[47]

Monck had an almost religious belief in the value of drama and a nearly evangelical approach to educating his audience. "If amateurs did good, sincere work, their audience would come," he believed. "First they may come to scoff, then they may come to complain, but gradually they would come because the theatre was giving them things they could find nowhere else. Drama has an aesthetic value of unique importance and they would be grateful to the amateurs for providing it while the amateurs would be doing a great thing for civilization."[48] This was perhaps true but only for a very limited portion of society. Shaw was being more realistic when, after warning Monck of the limited appeal the work he had set himself would have, he added, "It is not that the rest are ignorant or indifferent: they very actively dislike it and resent it."[49]

" 'You have educated your actors,' said one American lady visitor [to Monck], 'but my God, you've educated your audience.' " This was a quote often pointed to with pride by the Norwich Players.[50] But the education his audience received worked against the audience response for which the Maddermarket was designed. When, back in 1928, Monck explained that Schnitzler's *An Episode* was being added at the last minute to the musical comedy *Mr. Pepys* because that comedy proved too short in a theatre where the audience did not applaud or demand encores, the local critic had responded,

> I was a little surprised at some of Mr. Monck's remarks on the failure of his audience to applaud or call for encores. I had always imagined that it was a praiseworthy Maddermarket tradition not to.... Overmuch applause and insistence on one or more encores has been a curse elsewhere in Norwich. Surely it would be a pity if the habit extended to the Maddermarket.[51]

Monck's own policy of allowing no breaks in the action and no curtain calls at the end did more than anything else to encourage this restrained response. What his policies had taught his audience was summarized by R. F. Lush, who wrote:

> At nine out of ten modern plays Mr. Nugent Monck contrives to offer us a new criticism of life. We suspend judgement—not on the players but on the author's new view of an old problem—until he has reached his conclusion. When it is over, we go away still thinking. We might show our appreciation by applauding then; sometimes we do; more often we forget. But that is ... our undemonstrative tribute to the producer. "The Play's the Thing." Mr. Nugent Monck knows it; his players are never allowed to forget it; and it is to the credit of Norwich that he has found an audience who will continue to go to the Maddermarket because they know it too.[52]

Audience response and the players' reaction are vital elements of the theatrical experience however and Monck never ceased to stress the importance of the audience's role in "making up the entity of the theatre by supplying that mass emotion which alone can make art a reality."[53] It is, then, one of the great ironies of Monck's career that while he had built the best theatre of his day for the interplay of actor and audience, he operated it on a basis that discouraged that interplay from taking place.

Completing the Shakespeare Canon

The 1933 season ended in June with the accomplishment of one of Monck's most cherished goals. On June 19, 1933, Monck staged *Henry VI, Part I*, with the first two acts of *Henry VI, Part II*, and the following night the remaining three acts of *Henry VI, Part II*, were performed with *Henry VI, Part III*. George Bernard Shaw made a special trip to Norwich in honor of this occasion, for with these two performances Monck had personally produced for the public every play generally attributed to William Shakespeare. The following January, Hugh Hunt reported in the international theatre magazine, *Theatre World*, "Mr. Monck has produced the whole of Shakespeare's dramatic works, and in so doing became the first producer in the world, except perhaps Shakespeare himself, to complete this magnificent cycle in one theatre and by one company."[54] By the time Monck retired in 1952 only two other producers had accomplished this same feat; they were Monck's friend and admirer Robert Atkins, and the director of America's Pasadena Playhouse, Gilmore Brown.[55]

It was characteristic of Monck not to make any announcement concerning his achievement either in the press or in the theatre programs. It was, after all, not a goal he had set in order to win public acclaim but rather a personal commitment to apply his theories on Shakespeare's stagecraft to all the existing plays in order to see for himself how they would succeed. The critical response to this production was typical of comments made about all the Shakespearean productions Monck had done. The critic G. B. R., writing for the *Norwich Mercury,* identified the essence of Monck's art when he wrote,

> There is much of the best of cinematic art in this production. There is simplicity of character and device, directness of plot, counterplot and subplot, rapid changes of scene, and above all, movement, movement all the time. Whether rapidly through clash of arms or moving slowly through the scheming of the war lords, the story moves unceasingly to its climax.[56]

Ultimately every element of Monck's production was designed to drive the plot on to its climax. As with a good book which a reader cannot put down until the final page is turned, Monck wanted his audiences to be swept along by the story that was being told for them on the stage. But this method could not be a merely slapdash affair run on the premise that if one moved one's play along fast enough the audience would not notice mistakes. Every detail had to be meticulously correct so that the audience's attention would not be called to errors and they could concentrate on the fast moving plot. In these *Henry VI* plays, for example, Basil Maine has written, "Perhaps the greatest danger in presenting such a play lies in the endless shedding of blood." This was the kind of detail to which Monck paid careful attention with the result, as Maine pointed out, that "here each death was an experience, separate in its poignancy. We were affected no less by Jack Cade's end than by Warwick's."[57] The variety here was as important as the detail, or more precisely was a result of the detail. This variety was a primary element in the audience's perception of speed, for a boring presentation will seem long no matter how rapidly it moves. On this point, Charles Rigby wrote concerning the *Henry VI* productions,

> It is when you mention the producer that you come to the greatest element of all in this memorable production. The twenty scenes are a sheer masterpiece of resource and artistic feeling. It was, indeed, impossible to conceive the settings, colours, and dresses in greater variety or perfection. There is extraordinary use of the same materials so that they never seem alike.[58]

This is where Monck's work varied most significantly from that of William Poel. Poel had come to believe by 1921 that "on the Elizabethan stage . . . there was no attraction to be got out of scenery, costume, lighting or even action, for these varied but little in appearance whatever was the play acted."[59] This belief however was more the result of Poel's own obsession with vocal orchestration in productions than of any real examination of the evidence. Monck, on the other hand, was convinced that there was a great deal of variety in the visual elements of Shakespeare's stage, and the more of Shakespeare's plays he produced the more convinced he became that no audience, whether Elizabethan or modern, would have continued to attend the theatre if there was as little visual variety as Poel suggested. With costuming and action, Monck had found that there were few limits to what Elizabethan conventions, as he understood them, would allow. Scenery, he knew, had to be very simple in its beauty and able to be altered easily and rapidly. But when it came to lighting, the Elizabethan evidence was not even considered by Monck. His lighting was frankly acknowledged as modern, but it was a modern technique that Monck believed complemented Shakespeare's stagecraft as he understood it and in no way detracted from it, so he felt justified in its use.[60]

Monck was fifty-four in 1933. The theatre he had firmly established in Norwich, the international reputation he had won, and the personal goals he had achieved had all come at a great cost to energy and artistic ability. He was exhausted by the strain and was only too happy to accept a request from the outgoing president of the Oxford University Dramatic Society that Monck take him on as a stage manager for the 1933–34 season.

Hugh Hunt came to the Maddermarket on the advice of Sir Barry Jackson and Poet Laureate John Masefield.[61] He could not have come at a better time for Monck, but he could have arrived in more productive times as far as his own education was concerned; Monck was tired and his health was failing. Hunt served as stage manager under Monck for *Romeo and Juliet, Gloriana, A Doll's House, The School for Scandal,* and *The Winter's Tale.* Of these, *A Doll's House* received the first really negative review a Maddermarket production had got from a Norwich critic in two years.[62] *The School for Scandal,* which had been a great success when done previously, got only polite reviews. Hunt's only real opportunity to see Monck's work at its normal level of excellence came when he helped with Monck's January 1934 production of *The Winter's Tale.* Finally the reviews indicated that Monck's work was back to its old standard. Monck was able to exert himself on this production because he had made the decision to cancel the remainder of his announced season and turn his theatre over to Hunt. Hunt took up the leadership of the Norwich Players with great enthusiasm, producing John Masefield's *End and Beginning,* with the author in attendance, in a double bill with *The Forced Marriage.* Productions of *Much Ado about Nothing, Strife, Macbeth, On the Rocks,* and *Children in Uniform* followed. In addition he formed the Associate Players, or the "second eleven" as they were affectionately called, and staged studio productions of *The Parting* and *Gammer Gurton's Needle* with them.

Hunt's half season at the Maddermarket was a great success, so much so that he was invited to become producer of the Croyden Repertory Theatre, where he replaced Henry Cass, who was at that time taking over the position of director of the Old Vic from Tyrone Guthrie. Interestingly, Hunt too would make the move to the Old Vic in 1948 after doing excellent work at the Abbey Theatre and the Bristol Old Vic. This would mean that of the six producers who directed the Old Vic company between 1920 and 1953 only Henry Cass, who served for two seasons, cannot be shown to have been directly influenced by the artistry of Nugent Monck.

While under the spell of the Maddermarket milieu, Hunt wrote for *Theatre World,* "I firmly believe that when the history of the 20th century amateur movement in this country comes to be written, it will be shown that the Norwich Players have been one of the most important factors in the renaissance of the drama."[63] Years after his experience there, when he was director of the Old Vic, his opinion had changed very little. In 1950 he told a Norwich crowd, "You have here one of the best foundations for a civic theatre in the kingdom, where I and others learned all we know about the theatre."[64] And when Monck retired in 1952 Hunt wrote, "To him I owe a personal debt of gratitude, as do many others, for it was he who first taught me the craft of Shakespearian production, and the value of teamwork and loyalty to the theatre."[65]

6

Recognition and Retirement:
1934–1958

While Hugh Hunt had the Maddermarket Theatre under lease Nugent Monck was off on a tour of Europe. Upon returning to Norwich in the late summer of 1934 he made this significant observation, "At Berlin the Germans seem to be very sorry for themselves and have a strong feeling that they are crushed . . . They cannot see why they lost the war. They are desperately hard up." Outside Berlin, he said, he was struck by the spectacle of what seemed like millions of young Germans drilling with their packs full. "Nominally the whole world is at peace, and one wonders what these Germans are doing it for,"[1] he said. In just over five years all of Western Europe would cease to wonder.

Monck returned to Norwich refreshed and determined to revitalize his company. Economically the world was on its way to recovery and the next five years, up to the outbreak of war, were exceptionally profitable ones for the Maddermarket. But the period of Monck's greatest artistic achievements and influence was over. He did some excellent work during the remainder of his career but was no longer able to do it consistently. Meanwhile, the ideas of simplicity and speed which he had championed for so long were becoming widely accepted. The contrast between what Monck did and general practice was becoming less sharp and Monck's work consequently seemed less extraordinary.

Monck had every reason to be proud of his achievements and of the contribution he had personally made to the development of theatre in England. But he was not one ever to rest on his laurels and he continued to take on new challenges.

The Last Resurgence

Monck opened his 1934–35 season with a lavishly Elizabethan *Antony and Cleopatra* along the lines of the 1932 production that he had worked out with Owen Paul Smyth for the Old Vic. It was not an outstanding success, however;

Figure 18. *The Taming of the Shrew*, 1927
(*Courtesy of the Maddermarket Theatre Trust, Ltd.*)

Figure 19. *Much Ado about Nothing*, 1940
Note the use of perspective scenery in contrast to figure 18.
(Courtesy of the Maddermarket Theatre Trust, Ltd.)

for while Monck's artistry was wonderfully executed, the Norwich Players failed to match that standard in their acting.

After this production Monck decided to lessen some of his burden in running the Maddermarket by hiring a full-time scenic designer. Since Owen Paul Smyth left for the Old Vic in 1928 no regular designer had been employed at the Maddermarket, leaving most of the work to Monck and Andrew Stephenson, one of his most active and talented performers. Monck hired a young recent graduate of the Royal College of Art to fill the new post. Her name was Barbara Wilkes and she arrived just in time to design Shaw's *The Six of Calais* and Sheridan's *The Trip to Scarborough* in October 1934.

Monck's selection of Miss Wilkes was a significant one. She was a particularly gifted painter of perspective, a talent for which Monck's system of staging had little need. With his permanent architectural background and extensive use of curtains, perspective scenery was unnecessary. But Monck had no desire to become stagnant in his approach. He had staged all of Shakespeare's plays, adhering as closely as seemed reasonable to his system of Elizabethan staging. He now wanted to try new ideas and fresh approaches which would give added variety to his productions while still adhering to his basic principles of rapid and continuous action. As an artist without a background in theatre Miss Wilkes had no commitment to old approaches; as an artist of perspective she had a natural disinclination for a simple mimicry of Monck's ideas.

By 1934 Monck had fully exploited the beauty and variety his system of curtains made possible. With Miss Wilkes's arrival there began a gradual shift away from the use of the curtains toward a use of more pictorial scenery. The special two-sided flats Monck first employed in his London production of *The Machine Wreckers* in 1923 began to be employed with increased frequency. By the time he retired in 1952 painted scenery had completely displaced his system of curtains.

The two-sided flats proved to be nearly as adaptable as Monck's curtains and considerably less noisy. But such painted scenery, no matter how cleverly done, does not have the stamp of originality that Monck's curtains had. Scenery painted on flats also tends not to provide the same unbroken continuity of action that the system of curtains had given. With the painted scenery on reversible flats there came a growing tendency to use blackouts to cover the scene changes and the steady flow of Monck's early productions was lost.

It was not really until the March 1935 production of *The Second Brother* that Monck and the Players got back to the high standards they maintained in the early 1930s. After seeing this show David Garnett wrote for *The New Statesman and Nation,* on April 13, 1935,

It is to be hoped that Mr. Monck will bring his Norwich amateurs to London. Perhaps they could give a performance for the Phoenix Society which promises to revive from its ashes in the autumn. The old Phoenix had its success with Restoration plays and Elizabethan comedies. Mr. Monck could show them how to act tragedy and speak poetry.(p. 524)

At the end of this run Monck put Peter Taylor Smith, who had recently left the Old Vic, in charge of the final show of his Maddermarket season and went to Nottingham to produce another pageant, this one with a cast of 6,000.

Monck's major undertaking for the 1935–36 season was a production of *Timon of Athens* for the Group Theatre Company at the Westminster Theatre, London. The play opened November 18 and the cast featured Ernest Milton in the title role, with Trevor Howard as Lucullus, Torin Thatcher as Alcibiades and the former Old Vic producer Harcourt Williams as Apemantus. Incidental music for the play was composed and conducted by the young musician Benjamin Britten and the Group Theatre's usual director, Rupert Doone, served as choreographer.

The production received an unusual range of critical comment. Elizabeth Heaton, after writing a five-page article which was heavily critical of the state of Shakespearean production in London, criticism in which the Gielgud *Hamlet* received especially harsh treatment, wrote of Monck's production:

Since writing this essay, I have attended *Timon of Athens* at the Westminster Theatre, staged by Nugent Monck. I felt an astonished and deep respect. In this production one could look into and pore over every detail; it reminded me of embroidery "anglaise"; every word seemed like a hole perfectly stitched round and made to ornament. I would mention particularly the economy of gesture, in which indeed action was suited to the word,... I will add that the play was given a form in production which was a pleasure in itself.[2]

The *Evening News* reported on November 20, "Mr. Nugent Monck's production... is impressive and ingenious, with just sufficient originality of detail to give it style without affectation," and the *Morning Post*, the *Daily Mirror* and *The Times* echoed that assessment the same day. But most reviewers agreed with the *Glasgow Herald* that "this skilled presentation was worthy of a better vehicle."[3]

The play was not liked and in spite of Robert Speaight's declaration that the Timon of this play was "the last authoritative Shakespearian creation of an actor [Ernest Milton] who had something of Irving's hypnotic presence,"[4] Milton was not liked either. Una Ellis-Fermor's review in *English* was typical in expressing praise for the production but criticizing Milton as too restrained and dignified in this emotionally demanding role.[5] It was Monck's belief that "Timon's part could only be rendered by a man who could tear a subject to tatters or by a man who, by very subtle analysis, could make the subject live in the restrained manner by which we in these days expressed our emotions."[6] Milton was not able to move his audience with the subtle analysis and would perhaps have had greater success if he and Monck had chosen the more bombastic approach.

The set and costumes for this show came in for some especially severe comment.[7] Ivor Brown, writing for the *Observer* on November 24, said, "Mr. Monck had lit the stage cleverly, and it was not his fault, I suppose, that Robert Medley's decoration gave an air of miminy-piminy charade to the whole business. . . . " Such criticism was unusual for one of Monck's shows. And it is obvious that Monck did not exert full control over the elements of design. Why this should be so is not clear, but it represents a significant shift in Monck's approach to producing.

There were, however, two direct criticisms of Monck's work mentioned in the reviews of this production. Ivor Brown gave the clearest articulation to the first when he wrote in the article quoted above, "Lest we should nod, Mr. Nugent Monck suddenly discharges a cry of players to pursue each other round the stalls with much clashing and slashing of swords. *Timon* is only semi-Shakespeare, but it is not so feeble as to need this kind of antic on its side." The other scene which came in for much criticism was Timon's discovery of gold in Act IV, Scene iii. "The spectacle of the tragic man poking a spade into what had all the look of a stone staircase, and presently extracting a chest said to contain gold, seemed about as unconvincing a treatment of the incident as can be conceived."[8] The fight in the audience was not characteristic of Monck's approach, which was usually more reserved than this. The staging of Timon's discovery of gold was also unusual. Never at any time did Monck feel compelled to use realistic settings in Shakespeare's plays, but normally the required locality was suggested sufficiently for the audience to accept the events taking place before them. Clearly Monck's producing was becoming more relaxed and he was giving less attention to details.

The remainder of Monck's 1935–36 season was uneventful except for the production of another world premiere, *Last Voyage*. In June *The Shoemaker's Holiday* was produced in the gardens of the Strangers' Hall beside the Maddermarket in celebration of the twenty-fifth anniversary of the Norwich Players. The decline in standards was by now quite obvious. One critic noted, "To say that the work of the Norwich Players for twenty-five years was crowned with their silver jubilee programme last night would be to overweight a frolicsome piece. . . . It made sure that 'a good time was had by all,' good enough to overshadow for the time memories of finer as well as more difficult achievements."[9]

As with most such institutions, the Maddermarket reputation was out of step with its actual achievements. While its seasons were becoming progressively more uneven in terms of the quality of the performances its reputation was steadily increasing as reports of earlier achievements continued to spread. *The Times* heralded the Norwich Players' twenty-fifth anniversary as "the most shining achievement that any repertory outside London can at present show," and in America the *Christian Science Monitor* called it "a repertory theatre of practically unique significance."[10] Earlier *The Amateur Stage* had said, "The Maddermarket Theatre, under Mr. Monck's direction, stands for all that is best in the non-professional stage,"[11] and G. Wilson Knight had felt compelled to apologize in the 1936 preface to his *Principles of Shakespearian Production,* "I regret not knowing more of the Old Vic ... or of Mr. Nugent Monck's important work at the Maddermarket Theatre, Norwich."[12] Perhaps if he had known more about the Maddermarket he could have traced Monck's influence in his own work, for immediately before this statement he said, "What knowledge I have of the possibilities of significant grouping owes much to Mr. Bridges-Adams' productions." Such grouping was Monck's special artistic gift and it was his legacy to Bridges-Adams in the early years of the Norwich Players.

The reputation was based not only on the exceptionally high production standards Monck had maintained from the mid-1920s to the mid-1930s, but also on the remarkable diversity of the productions staged at the Maddermarket. Monck's record of premiere productions and first modern revivals of forgotten plays was one of the most impressive in England. By the end of the fifth season at the Maddermarket alone Harold Child was able to credit Monck with the first postwar revivals of 12 plays.[13] He should have credited him with 17 since Monck produced *The Merry Wives of Windsor, Love's Labour's Lost, Twelfth Night, A New Way to Pay Old Debts,* and *The Rivals* before the earliest postwar productions listed in Child's article. Only the Phoenix Society of London had a better record; the Old Vic ran a distant third place. No one else had revived as many medieval religious plays and only the Old Vic had revived as many of Shakespeare's. But Monck's greatest sweep was with the plays of Sheridan, all of which were first revived after World War I at Monck's theatre.

By the time of his retirement in 1952 Monck had had 42 plays licensed for production by the Lord Chamberlain. Eighteen of these were original scripts, while the rest ranged from never-before licensed plays, like Browning's *Pippa Passes,* to first performances of new translations of European scripts which were usually, as with Iwaszkiewics's *Summer at Nohant,* the first productions in England of these plays. "There are moments when even the most devoted supporters of the Norwich Players are inclined to wonder at their daring,"[14] wrote a local critic after one of these productions. At times this wonder was sufficient to keep those supporters away from the theatre. Monck was continuously disappointed by the lack of adventurousness in his audience, but still he found practical reasons for the continuation of his policy of producing such plays. "The little-known plays that we occasionally do are actually very good publicity in a wider sense," he pointed out. "For instance, in America they are quoted as an example of the Maddermarket's scope, and there is no doubt that they help a great deal in keeping its name known."[15]

Monck's March production of T. S. Eliot's *Murder in the Cathedral* was the one great success of the 1936-37 season, with the others ranging from average to poor. After this production Monck again left the remainder of his Maddermarket season to Peter Taylor Smith and went off for one of his "busman's holidays," this time producing a pageant at Chester just 30 miles from his birthplace. The most interesting features of Monck's next season, 1937-38, were the premiere of *The Queen's Pleasure* by Horace Horsnell, a former Norwich Player turned drama critic for the *Observer,* the second production of Auden and Isherwood's poetic drama, *The Ascent of F6,* and the only revival of Milton's *Samson Agonistes* since Poel's 1908 attempt.

As had now become his standard practice, Monck left the Maddermarket early that season as well to take up duties as a much sought after pageant producer. This 1938 pageant was Monck's most ambitious project to date, with over 8,000 performers presenting the history of Manchester. It was also Monck's last pageant. Europe was on the verge of its second great war of the century and the frivolities of the historical pageants would have to give way to the desperate struggle.

One of the crowning moments of Monck's career came on August 10, 1938, when Queen Mary attended his production of his own work, *The Masque of Anne Boleyn.* It was staged, as it had been twice previously, in the foreyard of the great Jacobean mansion Blickling Hall. Three hundred performers took part with the Norwich Players performing the speaking roles. On the day of the queen's visit over 1,200 audience members swelled the stands. Whether or not Monck's artistry was seen at its best in this production is difficult to assess, as the reviewers were understandably more interested in the queen's presence than in what was seen of the play. But her patronage remained a great tribute to Monck's reputation.

Monck's 1938-39 season opened under the shadow of ever-growing political tensions. On September 28, 1938, Monck received Shaw's rewritten script for *Geneva* upon which the author had added the note, "You understand, of course, that it will be a waste of paper if we go to war next Sunday."[16] This came only two days before the Munich conference. Monck's mind was obviously occupied by the political situation during this season. The only real artistic successes of this period were Shaw's *Geneva,* given in January 1939, and Elmer Rice's *Judgment Day* which ran in March. Both plays are staunchly anti-fascist.

During May Monck announced a new program for the Maddermarket.

By that time war seemed imminent and Monck was taking a hard look at his need to retire. He wanted both to produce certain plays he had as yet been unable to do and to ensure that the Maddermarket Theatre would continue to operate after his eventual retirement. To serve both ends he announced the formation of the Maddermarket Theatre Society. This was to be a private society so Monck could produce plays the censor would not license for public presentation. In addition this Society, which Monck believed would number about 1,000, was to provide the economic base to ensure continuation of the Maddermarket.

The first private production under the auspices of The Maddermarket Theatre Society was *The Norwich Passion Play*. This was a revival of *The Passion Play* for which Monck had nearly been arrested in 1909. It was Monck's own arrangement of a group of plays from the so-called "Ludus Coventriae" cycle, which dealt with the death and resurrection of Christ. The origin of this cycle is uncertain, its only connection with Coventry being that the manuscript was found there. But Monck argued that, as it was written in an East Anglian dialect and the prologue states that it was done in Nor-town, Norwich had a proper claim to it. (Modern scholarship gives Lincoln as the more likely origin.) Monck considered this production the greatest artistic achievement of his career,[17] but with Europe on the verge of war and this being a private production the reviewers contented themselves with a few comments on its striking beauty and power with little elaboration.

In August Monck further tried to ensure the continuation of the theatre he had worked so hard to establish by forming the Maddermarket Theatre Trust, Ltd. Its stated object was to promote and encourage dramatic art, to help establish a repertory theatre in Norwich and to produce, supply and assist stage plays, operas, concerts, public meetings, social functions, exhibitions and entertainments of all kinds. The Trust was composed of nine members who were to pay Monck a salary of £800 per year while running the Maddermarket as a nonprofit-making concern. This move was intended to take considerable financial burdens off Monck and off the Maddermarket. For the first time Monck would have a fixed income and some of the theatre's tax burden would be eased.

When war came the Maddermarket Theatre Society was terminated after sponsoring only its second production, but the Maddermarket Theatre Trust, Ltd. struggled on through the war. After the war it was restructured and among other changes it became "a recognized educational and cultural body."[18] This allowed it to build up reserves of cash while still remaining exempt from income tax, something the original organization did not allow. From that time to this it has been a most effective governing body which has conscientiously preserved Monck's ideals.

The Second World War

After a full year of ever-growing international tension, Germany invaded Poland on September 1, 1939 and the long-dreaded war was finally declared. As a hospital orderly during the last great war Monck had seen the most tragic consequences of such a conflict. Now, at the age of sixty-one, he had once again to prepare for a long struggle; and, as had happened in 1914, the government ordered the indefinite closure of all theatres, cutting Monck off from both his life's work and his sole source of income. It must have been a crushing blow to Monck but, like so many others, he joined the war effort, becoming an air raid warden and continuing on as best he could.

By November the government lifted its ban on theatres and Monck rushed Shaw's newest play, *In Good King Charles' Golden Days,* into production. To Monck this was a matter of both economic necessity and patriotism. The Maddermarket was his livelihood, but in his view theatre was an important social force and he felt compelled to use it to keep people's minds off the struggle when it was possible to do so and to strengthen their spirits when it was not. *In Good King Charles' Golden Days* played to full houses November 20 through 25. The next production, however, was not so successful. Monck produced the Nativity group of *The Wakefield Mysteries* on December 14 through 16 and the response was most disheartening. Norwich, like most cities in Britain, was maintaining a strict blackout and travel after dark had suddenly become something which was undertaken only when necessary. It was a costly lesson, but Monck learned from the experience. For the duration of the war he scheduled his productions to correspond to the full phases of the moon and starting times were gradually moved back to 6:45 p.m.

Monck's problems multiplied though the winter and spring of 1940. January and February brought the worst winter weather England had seen in a decade, cutting deeply into the attendance at the Maddermarket. Better weather arrived by March and April, but this served only to expose a previously unnoticed difficulty. Monck had been forced to cancel the Maddermarket Mondays subscription series when the war began and now it was realized that this audience had not been replaced. For years the Monday subscribers had filled the house on opening nights and the rest of the public had become accustomed to thinking of those nights as sold out. With the program cancelled few people thought of attending the Maddermarket on a Monday and the Norwich Players were opening their shows to nearly empty houses. The May production of Etherege's *She Would If She Could* coincided, unfortunately, with the capitulation of Belgium to the Nazis and the production of Priestley's *Music at Night* in June coincided with the capitulation of France, both of which strongly deterred people from attending the theatre. By July 1940 Monck's theatre, like Britain itself, was in desperate straits.

Monck made it known before the July opening of *Much Ado about Nothing* that the Maddermarket was in serious difficulty and needed greater support if it were to continue, and despite their more serious concerns an encouraging number of audience members turned out for this production. During the intervals Monck made a plea for a guaranteed audience to get the 1940–41 season under way. Guarantors, he explained, were to buy a stated number of tickets for each of the first four productions. (He hoped each regular audience member would buy at least six tickets per show.) They would be free to resell or dispose of these tickets in any way they pleased. It is doubtful whether Monck got the guarantee of 1,000 to 1,500 audience members per production that he desired. But with the help of Tyrone Guthrie he secured a guarantee for payment of the rates and expenses relating to the building's operation from the Council for the Encouragement of Music and the Arts (CEMA) and that assistance, combined with the response Monck received to his appeal, was sufficient to allow the Maddermarket to be reopened. The guarantee system proved successful and brought in adequate houses, but when the four guaranteed productions were finished attendance dropped sharply again. Shaw's *You Never Can Tell* in January and Romains's *Doctor Knock* in February were only sparsely attended, though they were the kind of light comedy it was thought would attract the public.

In March Monck resorted to a new tactic and invited his old friend, the well-known West End actor Esmé Percy, to come to Norwich and appear in a Maddermarket show. In spite of a busy schedule Percy came to Norwich to help out and appeared in the title role of Shaw's *Don Juan in Hell,* which was performed with what seems to have been the first English production in this century of Molière's *Don Juan.* Monck had managed to cast a large number of his most experienced players in these plays and while Percy was unquestionably the outstanding performer, the local press reported that the supporting cast held their own as well as most professionals might have done.

Following Percy's appearance the next three productions by Monck attracted meager houses. This was due in part to the plays Monck had chosen to produce. But another very important factor was that the ever-intensifying rationing now made it impossible for people to travel any significant distance for something as unnecessary as seeing a play. It soon became obvious that the bulk of the Maddermarket's regular audience was made up, not of local Norwich people, but of people from the outlying areas who had often driven 20 miles and more to see Monck's productions. So by July 1941 Monck's Maddermarket was once more in a state of crisis. For Monck this was not simply a matter of money. He had a grant to maintain the theatre and was used to having little income for himself. What he wanted was community support. He had built a world-famous theatre in Norwich, only to find that it was primarily supported by an audience from out of town. If the people of Norwich did not care enough to give their support, he felt the Maddermarket had failed and was willing to let it close.

Monck appealed once more for better audience attendance and once again his request attracted a sufficient response to convince him to undertake another season, this time with the reintroduction of the Maddermarket Mondays program. But this appeal also inspired an open debate on the Maddermarket in the letters column of the local press and the comments were not all favorable. E. G. Hamlin wrote in a letter to the *Eastern Daily Press,* "Too often at the Maddermarket the eye and the aesthetic sense are delighted, while the ear and the intellect are left discontented because the words of the play have been neglected," and a few weeks later a correspondent signing himself E. Veryman added, "Frankly, since the production of *The Beggar's Opera* about 1920 has it not relied too much on effects of production, beautiful grouping, museum pieces, and charming Dresden china plays?... The Theatre has been divorced from emotion and life, and has concentrated too much on aesthetic spectacle at the expense of real acting."[19] But this restraint on the part of Monck's actors was intentional and something for which they were often praised by out-of-town critics. In 1924 Raymond Mortimer wrote for an American journal that

> at the Maddermarket it is recognized that the play's the thing, that Shakespeare knew his job, and that the words are expressive enough in themselves without the muttering, screams, and general beastly overacting in which professional actors without exception indulge. The result is that Mr. Monk's [*sic*] productions of Shakespeare are much the best I have ever seen.[20]

The standards by which good acting is judged vary markedly from one period to the next. On the professional stage significant changes occurred during the 1930s when actors like John Gielgud, Laurence Olivier and Ralph Richardson were first becoming prominent. These changes had altered the basis on which judgments were made about what constituted good acting. It is certainly possible, then, that the exact same performance of *Hamlet* for which the Norwich Players were acclaimed in 1924 would have looked significantly less impressive if it could have been recreated in the 1940s. But change in taste alone did not account for the criticism the Norwich Players received. It seems that as a group they were not as good as they had been.

It is probably fair to say that during the First World War Monck gave up the kind of systematic training of actors he had used so effectively at the Abbey Theatre. After that war he depended more on his abilities to inspire those with talent to the best performances of which they were capable. When necessary he would correct specific acting problems, but in general players learned by experience, not by training. By 1929 Monck had a reasonably large group of talented Norwich Players who responded to the inspiration he provided and gave many outstanding performances. Gradually, however, this group began to shrink and Monck's ability to inspire new performers was also on the decline. By the 1938–39 season and thereafter the majority of reviews began reporting that casts were "at a satisfactory level throughout" or that they were "adequate," but only occasionally was the acting praised as outstanding as it had so often been in previous years. Monck's producing, too, began to be described more by such terms as "highly competent" than by the earlier superlatives which indicated a standard considerably above that.

With the outbreak of the war Monck's problems had multiplied tremendously. A large number of his Players were called into service. Many who were not called immediately were subject to call at any moment and the rest were not only coping with their regular employment but were involved with war work night and day. For many productions the actors were inexperienced, of necessity miscast and had only managed to rehearse as a group once before performance week. It was remarkable that Monck was able to produce any plays at all under such conditions. It is all the more remarkable considering that the Maddermarket staff were subject to the same call-ups and war duties. As a consequence, by 1943 Monck found himself running the box office, making the costumes, designing and building the sets, cleaning the theatre, and even spending nights sleeping in the Maddermarket office as part of the fire watch. This was a work load that many a younger producer would have had difficulty sustaining and Monck was well into his sixties.

The reviewers took these difficulties into account and were usually kind enough to give emphasis to the better points in a production while glossing over the failings. But the productions could not be considered representative of Monck's best abilities and those who attacked the Maddermarket during and after the war tended either to be unaware of, or to have forgotten, the work done there during the mid-1920s and early 1930s. But the reviewers who remembered the previous years of excellence considered it one of their highest compliments to say that a production was almost up to those earlier standards. Those standards had indeed been very high and when Monck was able to cast a significant number of his veteran Norwich Players, he could still produce outstanding drama in spite of the difficulties involved.

In December of 1941 the United States of America entered the war. The numerous airbases around Norwich soon swelled with large numbers of U.S. Air Force personnel. In later months these troops provided Monck's theatre with the new audience he so needed. But in the meantime Monck and his company struggled along. On April 27 through 29, 1942 Norwich was blitzed by the German Air Force and extensive damage was done to the city. Monck was forced to cancel his May production while all joined in the cleanup effort. The Maddermarket Theatre, however, remained undamaged and Monck continued his work in June and July.

Monck spent the month of August 1942 at the Prince of Wales Theatre, Cardiff, South Wales. There he directed Donald Wolfit and his company in a production of *King Lear* and helped with productions of *Twelfth Night* and *A Midsummer Night's Dream*. The following year Wolfit took his company to London where they opened *King Lear* at the St. James' Theatre in the winter of 1943. Its reception was not enthusiastic and it was not until the play reopened at the Scala Theatre on April 12, 1944 that it received any significant critical attention.[21] On the following Sunday (April 16) James Agate wrote a remarkably positive review of the production and London suddenly took notice. This production of *King Lear* soon became the most highly acclaimed performance of Wolfit's career. Speaight refers to it as a "definitive" production of the play and numerous others expressed similar evaluations.[22]

It is difficult to determine from the reviews to what extent Monck's influence on this production was responsible for its remarkable success. The beautiful staging and rapid action with a single interval were much admired (though erroneously assumed to be exclusively the ideas of Granville-Barker), but most of the other comments were directed toward the acting. Wolfit and his company were apparently very grateful to Monck for his assistance in this area. In 1946, the cast sent Monck a letter thanking him for his work with them.[23] In 1951, in a speech to the Arts Theatre Club in London, Wolfit expressed his own appreciation of Monck's assistance by referring to Norwich as "the luckiest city in England" because it possessed Nugent Monck and the Maddermarket Theatre. The Maddermarket he called "a unique national possession" and Monck he referred to as a genius who trained fine actors who were "too good to be classed with ordinary amateurs." Monck tackled plays few other producers would attempt, he added, and professionals were always glad to turn to Monck for advice. Finally he commented that he would never forget Monck's help with his own production of *King Lear*.[24] Wolfit revived this *Lear* production for many years and each revival carried the program note, "First produced for Donald Wolfit by Nugent Monck." In 1953 this note prompted the critic for *The Times* to comment on February 24, "It is time that Mr. Monck looked in to see what has been happening to his work."

Monck returned to Norwich in September 1942. Fewer experienced players were available to appear in the productions as the war dragged on and rehearsal periods suffered constant interruption and abridgment. Still, there were consolations for Monck. Theatrical designer Oliver Messel was stationed in Norwich with the Camouflage Corps and numerous well-known people of the stage visited the city as they passed through Norfolk entertaining the troops or just escaping from London. One not so well-known young actor of that period who found himself in the home city of the famous Maddermarket Theatre was Alec McCowan. He has written of the experience:

> I went to the Maddermarket Theatre and met the producer, Nugent Monck . . . already an almost legendary figure. . . . Eagerly I offered my services and for a few weeks became an amateur. Monck gave me board and lodging and ten shillings a week pocket money. I helped to run his theatre backstage and played in his production of *Major Barbara*. He was a sensitive humorous dictator, and I loved him and his theatre. I also loved his beautiful Elizabethan house which was always full of interesting people.[25]

But the biggest consolation for Monck was that, despite declining artistic standards, there was a steady increase in the size of the audiences. Monck's fame in America had not been imaginary and, once having settled into their bases, many of the U.S. military personnel in and around Norwich began to come to see the theatre they had read about before the war.

Postwar Recognition

It is a great irony that just at the time when Monck's productions were generally at their least successful artistically the Maddermarket box office began doing the best business it had ever done.

During the war the Second Air Division of the Eighth United States Army Air Force was stationed in some 40 camps and aerodromes in the vicinity of Norwich. The Maddermarket was hardly the only place of entertainment available in Norfolk; yet, beginning with the 1943–44 season, these American servicemen began attending Monck's productions in ever-growing numbers. Without this significant increase in audience the heroic efforts Monck and the Norwich Players had made to save their little theatre from bankruptcy could not have succeeded. When the war in Europe ended on May 8, 1945, there was concern that the withdrawal of these troops would once again leave the Maddermarket with an insufficient audience to support its operation. Surprisingly, it was found that the audience continued to grow even after the Americans had gone. While Monck's prewar audience had been composed mostly of people from outside Norwich, Norwich citizens themselves began making up the majority of the Maddermarket following in this postwar period. It was just in time and probably past time for them to do so.

The postwar period brought a renewed interest in the arts in England. As one of the most respected of the prewar producers, Monck's work was highly regarded during these years of rebuilding and the government honored his achievements by awarding him the O.B.E. (Order of the British Empire). In

1946 Barry Jackson had been given control of the Shakespeare Memorial Theatre at Stratford-upon-Avon and as one of his first official actions he invited Nugent Monck to produce *Cymbeline* as Shakespeare's birthday play for that year.

Monck went to Stratford-upon-Avon in February, leaving the Maddermarket to the guidance of Peter Taylor Smith and J. A. Mitchley. He was not overawed by the opportunity to work with professionals again. "When asked by Jackson how he found the actors, he replied, 'Not so bad; only nine of them lisp,'" reported Robert Speaight.[26] The professionals, however, had considerable respect for Monck. Paul Scofield was a young actor in his first season at Stratford when he took the role of Cloten in this production by Monck. He has recently recalled:

> I have a strong recollection of Nugent Monck directing an ensemble scene in *Cymbeline* and hissing his demand that we all lean forward in a "baroque" manner and utter a "love moan." He was tiny, waspish and formidable, and most of us were rather alarmed by him. Indeed Walter Hudd, an actor and director of great authority and experience, met him in Stratford Post Office and was so intimidated by the encounter, that, fumbling for words, he said "Good Nugent" instead of "good morning."
>
> His regard for the text was paramount, and I remember little of his direction except in that area. I don't think he cared much what we looked like or what the set looked like, so long as we expressed the words with clarity.... He had I think a healthy contempt for "professionalism"—he was truly academic in his approach.... He was not interested in the psychology of the plays or the characters.[27]

The production, which also featured Valerie Taylor as Imogen and a little-known actor named Donald Sinden as Arviragus, was very well received by the critics. *The Times* reported on April 24, "Mr. Nugent Monck is as careful as was Shakespeare himself to see that no touches of reality put to shame the hollow artificialities of the melodrama and the characters move as gaily coloured puppets in a swiftly unfolding pattern of brave speech and romantic flourish." To this the critic for the *Birmingham Post* added that same day, "Mr. Monck, the producer, is more than justified in his insistence on speed in playing. By swift propulsion of each theme, Mr. Monck gives urgency and importance to what, under less skilled directions, might easily become tedious. This is a good production, rippling with good performances."

The sheer size of the theatre made the usual impact of Monck's work less effective, however. As the *Daily Mail* of April 24 pointed out, "Mr. Monck has done his best to bridge the wide open spaces of the Stratford stage by bringing his actors down to the apron. He sacrifices picture and gains personal touch." Monck's lighting too was not as impressive as it usually was. In the large dimensions of the Shakespeare Memorial Theatre his effects appeared too dim.[28] (Interestingly, this production of *Cymbeline* by one of the oldest, most respected Shakespearean producers in England was followed by a production of *Love's Labour's Lost* by a twenty-one-year-old producer, Peter Brook.)

This *Cymbeline* production at Stratford-upon-Avon was a good, workmanlike production, but not one of Monck's best artistic efforts. From the start he seems to have been preoccupied with other things. The Norwich Players had let their own thirtieth anniversary and their twentieth year at the Maddermarket pass uncelebrated during the war. In September 1946, however, a special production of *A Midsummer Night's Dream* was planned to open their twenty-fifth season at the Maddermarket. The production was given a good reception; but again, it was noticeably below the standard of Monck's prewar endeavors.

The postwar era had brought great prosperity to the Maddermarket, but it had created special problems for the Norwich Players. Those experienced Players who were gradually being demobilized had a great deal to catch up on in their lives, including things which were more important than acting. Young actors had to be given major roles before they had sufficient experience to sustain them. Monck had always maintained that it took three years to make a good amateur actor, but in the aftermath of the war there were few male performers who were able to work at the Maddermarket continuously for so long a period. By the end of the 1946–47 season Monck was in the awkward position of finally being able to fill his theatre consistently while at the same time often having great difficulty in finding sufficient cast members to perform in it. This was the reverse of the situation in the 1930s when he could find a cast of 60 if necessary but was on occasion hard-pressed to get an audience of equal size to attend the performance.

The reviews of this period began to reflect a noticeable change in Monck's character. Prior to the war Monck's great successes, other than his Shakespeare plays, were usually with plays of wit like those of Shaw and of the Restoration dramatists.[29] After the war his productions of Chekhov became more admired than anything else he did. *The Seagull* was the best show of his 1943–44 season. *The Three Sisters* was the great success of 1946–47 and in 1951 *Uncle Vanya* received exceptional praise from *Punch.*[30]

It was also during this period that Monck's work first began to be referred to as "uneven." In 1947 Norman Marshall wrote of Monck in *The Other Theatre* (p. 95), "His weakness as a producer is that his work is extremely uneven. I have seen some of the best productions in England at the Maddermarket and also some of the worst." During these postwar years other writers made similar observations, but never prior to 1936 does any such indication of unevenness in Monck's work appear in print. In fact, his early work was quite remarkable for the consistently high quality of all elements of production excluding acting.

While Monck's work continued to grow more melancholy in tone and more uneven in quality, recognition of his work was becoming more widespread. On September 23, 1946 the BBC broadcasted a tribute to Monck's 25 years at the Maddermarket. In the program the Maddermarket was referred to as "one of the most remarkable theatre ventures of modern times."[31] The Maddermarket's January 1947 production of *Othello* was filmed for inclusion in the British film magazine *The World We Live In,* and in April of that year Monck was sent to Austria by the British Council to lecture on Shakespeare, the Elizabethan playhouses and modern British drama.

In August of 1947 Monck returned to Stratford-upon-Avon to produce *Pericles,* the final play of that season at the Memorial Theatre. With Paul Scofield in the title role Monck did as he had done in his 1929 production at Norwich, cutting the first act and converting the Gower chorus into song. The set design was by Barry Jackson, the last design he ever did for the stage, but the grouping, coloring and lighting remained characteristically Monck's own.[32] At the age of sixty-nine Monck seems to have been content to turn out once again a good solid production, taking no risks and making no attempt to recapture the outstanding quality of his earlier work. But in 1951, when Monck revived this play at the Maddermarket, he became experimental once more and produced the play complete with Act I and all other sections which he had cut in his previous productions.

All this outside activity had distracted Monck from the real problems of the Maddermarket. It was not until the 1947–48 season that he produced all the regular shows for his Norwich Players and not until the 1948–49 season that the reviews indicate any consistent quality in the Maddermarket performances. Monck began thinking about retirement again during this period. In order for him to be able to retire comfortably and to ensure the continuation of his life's work, he realized, the seating capacity of his theatre had to be expanded. Toward that end he purchased, on October 19, 1948, the group of buildings known as Farnell's Court which lay directly to the south of his theatre.

At the opening of his next season, 1949–50, Monck announced the beginning of a £25,000 appeal drive for his Maddermarket. He hoped to raise £10,000 to pay for extending the building to the south, thereby providing 100 additional seats without destroying the intimacy of his theatre or affecting his stage area. The project was also to include much-needed rehearsal and storage space. The additional £15,000 was intended as an endowment to ensure the theatre's continued operation. But the timing of this appeal proved most unfortunate. Almost immediately similar appeals were launched to raise funds for badly needed repairs to Norwich's great Cathedral and to its twelfth-century castle, which serves as one of the city's museums. As a consequence it took five years to raise sufficient funds to expand the Maddermarket, and even then the original plans had to be cut back significantly. Monck reacted to this disappointing turn of events with characteristic generosity. When he opened his next season the first performance was given to benefit the Cathedral appeal fund. In the spring of 1950 Monck turned his theatre over to a young producer, Lionel Dunn, for six months and embarked on a lecture tour in Jamaica and Mexico.

Monck returned to full-time producing at the Maddermarket for the 1950–51 season. He opened this season with the premiere of a new play by a local author, then went through Shaw, Ustinov, Shakespeare, a Restoration comedy, a new American play, a rarely-produced play by Lord Byron, a Victorian comedy, Maugham's *The Circle* and a full text production of *Pericles.* Monck's adventurousness and catholicity of taste seemed to be reviving after the struggles of the war, even though he was seventy-two. The productions attracted generally favorable reviews, although in April Monck and his Players received some rather harsh criticism in the letters column of the *Eastern Evening News.* A controversy began when Bernard Cooke wrote, in a letter dated April 10, 1951, that he was tired of hearing the Maddermarket referred to as unique. It was in no way unique, he declared, and the acting, especially in Shakespeare, was constantly underplayed. He then went on to compare the Norwich Players unfavorably with the best professional actors of the century. Monck's work and the acting standards of the Norwich Players were undoubtedly open to criticism during these postwar years, but Cooke's comments were unduly severe and his comparisons unfair. The criticism inspired a number of less censorious comments as well as numerous defenses of Monck and the Players. Still, it could not have been the most gratifying of milieux in which to embark on a thirtieth season at the Maddermarket for the aging Monck.

The 1951–52 program at the Maddermarket was as adventurous and wide-ranging as the previous one. On March 15–24 of that season Monck finally achieved his career-long dream of staging *The Passion Play* for a public performance. Since his near arrest in 1909 for an attempted production of this script, in which Christ appears as a character, he had staged it only for the private Maddermarket Theatre Society. This 1952 production was not of the same high quality that the 1939 private staging had been, but still it was something of a personal triumph for Monck that the religious plays he had worked on for so many years were at last becoming appreciated. After the final performance he said to the actor who had portrayed Christ, "I have done it, now I can retire."[33] On April 1 Monck announced that 1952 would be his last year as producer of the Norwich Players.

Monck was now seventy-four years old. Producing had been his life and he might easily have been excused for trying to run the Maddermarket right up to his death. But Monck was fully aware that his creative abilities were failing and that it was past time that a younger person with fresher ideas took over the Maddermarket. As he said in a retirement speech broadcast by the BBC,

> The Norwich Players have served their dictator loyally through some three hundred productions. But I feel if the place and the work is [*sic*] to continue, fresh minds and fresh ideas and younger bodies must be drawn into it. The danger is that producer, players and audience might all grow old. We might easily all fade out together, and that is why I am retiring.[34]

Between his announced retirement in April and his last official production in December 1952 Monck produced a medieval play, a Japanese Noh play, *Henry V*, Christopher Fry's *Venus Observed*, Thomas Otway's adaptation of Molière's *The Cheats of Scapin* and a modern European play translated by Granville-Barker. His last production as the full-time producer of the Norwich Players was of *The Beggar's Opera*, which was given in conjunction with Norwich's Amateur Opera Society, December 13 through 20, 1952. It was Monck's most successful production in several seasons and a fitting end to his career at the Maddermarket.

On December 30 of that year Monck turned over his theatre with its large collection of properties and extensive wardrobe to the Maddermarket Theatre Trust for a retirement payment of £700 and an agreed land rent of £500 per year, the land going to the Trust upon Monck's death. With this final act of generosity Monck retired from his post as producer for the Guild of the Norwich Players, a position he had held for over forty years.

Considerable recognition was given to Monck after his retirement. *The Times* honored him with a leader on December 9, 1952 and the BBC produced four programs in his honor over the next year. The Shakespeare Stage Society invited him to lecture in London on January 7, 1953 and in 1957 he was invited to speak at the Eighth Shakespeare Conference at Stratford-upon-Avon. The British government, too, showed its respect for Monck's achievements and appreciation for his contribution to theatre in Britain. Having awarded Monck the O.B.E. in 1946, the government made him a C.B.E. (Commander of the British Empire) in June 1958.

Meanwhile, Monck continued to produce plays. During the summer of 1953 the long-postponed extension of the Maddermarket was finally undertaken but delays in the project threatened to cause a cancellation of the autumn production. Monck realized that the loss of revenue this would cause, especially at that particular time, would be devastating to the Maddermarket. He therefore produced *A Midsummer Night's Dream* in the grounds of the Bishop's Palace. The production was surprisingly successful considering Monck's age and the immense difficulty of such a project. It was also an appropriate play with which to end his career as a producer of Shakespeare in Norfolk, for in 1910 an outdoor production of *A Midsummer Night's Dream* had been his first Shakespearean production in East Anglia.

In 1955 Monck produced a final revival of *Everyman,* based on Poel's original staging. Productions of his own works, *Osric Dear Osric* and *The Big Field,* were also done that year, as was a production of *The Wakefield Second Shepherd's Play* for the Alderburgh Festival. In 1957, at the age of seventy-nine, he organized a Jacobean Festival in Norwich for which he produced Ben Jonson's *The Masque of Cupid* at Blickling Hall and arranged the promptbook for a production of Webster's *The White Devil* at the Maddermarket. Finally, on June 6, 1958, he staged an interesting compilation of John Lyly's *Campaspe* and Marlowe's *Doctor Faustus* for the Maddermarket Theatre Association under the title *Elizabethan Patchwork.* This was the last production of his career, which had spanned fifty-eight years. On October 21, 1958 Walter Nugent Bligh Monck suffered a stroke and died immediately in his home at 6 Ninham's Court. After a funeral in Norwich Cathedral his remains were cremated and he was laid to rest in the north aisle of St. John's Maddermarket, where he had long been a church warden, just twenty yards from the famous theatre he had built and guided for more than thirty years.

Figure 20. *The Pilgrim's Progress*, 1949
(*Courtesy of the Maddermarket Theatre Trust, Ltd.*)

Figure 21. *The Passion Play,* 1952
(from, The Sphere, 5 April 1952)

7

Summary and Conclusion

There was a final irony in the production of *As You Like It* done at the Maddermarket in September 1952. A local critic wrote of it,

> The very bareness and simplicity of the setting resulted in some moments of great visual beauty.... The unlocalized stage, with its variety of exits and entrances, enabled the action to move rapidly... The virtual absence of scenery has the interesting effect of throwing more emphasis than usual on the text and giving more responsibility to the players. They take it by speaking all their lines clearly and directly.[1]

Such statements could have been taken almost verbatim from reviews of Monck's original production of the play 31 years before. The irony was that this production was staged on a bare, curtainless stage, not by Monck, but by his successor, Lionel Dunn.

The artistic simplicity which Monck had championed had now been superseded by scenery which was even simpler than his original experiments. Where Monck had used a richly dyed curtain of blue trees against a golden sky for a woodland scene, Dunn suggested the forest of Arden simply by lighting the stage posts to cast vertical shadows across the stage façade. Clearly the torch had been passed to a new generation of producers.

The Principles

Nugent Monck was born at the beginning of the period which is now referred to as the "modern" era in theatre. One of the most distinctive characteristics of this era had been the rise of the *régisseur,* the single individual responsible for all aspects of a production who brought a unity to the whole. In the United States this person was known as the director, but in England he was called the producer. During Monck's schooldays most producers were applying their energies towards the achievement of complete illusion on stage. But a few, like William Poel, were searching for a new, less garish artistic style for the theatre.

Poel found the inspiration for his own reaction against the excesses of "realism" in the Elizabethan Revival, the movement to discover what stage practice might have been in the age of Shakespeare.

The legitimacy of Poel's conclusions about Shakespeare's stagecraft has long been debated. But from Poel's work developed our entire approach to the staging of Shakespeare's plays in the twentieth century. That approach may be no closer to the actual practice of Shakespeare's Globe than were the lavish productions by Irving and Tree in the late Victorian and early Edwardian days; it may also have brought us to no better understanding of Shakespeare's plays than those producers had. But our approach and understanding are different from those of other times, and it was Poel and his followers who established the nature of that difference.

Under William Poel Monck served his apprenticeship for a career as a producer. Like Poel, Monck was dissatisfied with the interminable ponderousness of the Shakespearean productions he saw in the commercial theatre, where, he said, they hammered out each word as if it were inspired text, "however carelessly the author may have written it."[2] Long waits for scene changes, unnecessarily long and unnecessarily frequent intervals, painfully slow lighting effects which contributed nothing to the meaning of the work being performed, and the constant delays as leading performers made each exit and entrance pointlessly impressive, all sapped the vitality from drama.[3] This was especially true for classic plays like those of Shakespeare which were not written for such treatment. Monck therefore adopted those elements of Poel's theories which best served to combat the slow pace of generally practiced staging methods.

"I have no theories about production. I borrow anyone's ideas. But after they have gone through my mind the persons who gave birth to the ideas do not seem to recognize them," Monck said around the time of his retirement.[4] These borrowed ideas were undoubtedly unrecognizable to those who spawned them because Monck had made them distinctly his own. There was a definite style to a Nugent Monck production but it is not always easy to describe, and even harder to identify, the general principles upon which this style was based.

"To a producer, every production is a disappointment in that it is completely different from the thing of which he dreams: it may be better, it may be worse, but it is different," Monck once said.[5] It is therefore unwise merely to extrapolate theories from reviews of what Monck actually did. Yet no study of the man's work could be considered complete without some basic explanations of his general beliefs about his art.

For Monck, all drama was a three-part collaboration between dramatist, actor and audience. In his early years Monck considered the dramatist the most important of these, as "it is he who supplies the brains of the play, which the actor must translate into action."[6] Indeed the phrase "the play's the thing" was the most often quoted dictum in all the literature relating to Monck's work. Monck's respect for playwrights had caused him to begin his career in theatre as a dramatist but in this he met with little success. He gradually learned the importance of the producer as the interpreting mind of a playwright's work and found that this was the profession in which his real talent lay. By the time he retired he had entered the producer as a fourth partner in the collaboration he saw as basic to the theatre, saying, "The author has his interpreter in the producer, the actors are the instrument of interpretation, and the audience throw back the emotion to the actors who are thus stimulated."[7]

Conspicuously absent in this list of the fundamental components of theatre are the scenic arts. They are absent from Monck's list because they seemed to him to dominate the commercial theatre he saw around him and much of his career was spent experimenting with the extent to which these arts could be done without on the stage. When Monck left Poel and set out working on his own, his old schoolmate and longtime friend, Reginald F. Rynd, said, "The work Mr. Monck set himself to do was to break through the restrictions and artificialities of ordinary stage production and to endeavour to show that artistic results do not mainly depend upon a proscenium, a curtain, and footlights."[8] After five hard years, however, Monck learned that such work was not to be done in the commercial theatre of London. There he found that the imaginative producer

> works under the difficulties of haste. Time is money, the play must be rehearsed in the shortest possible period—there is not time for conference or experiment—ready made theories are used because the producer is too tired to create—has become insensible to the spirit of the play—or that spirit is too weak to make itself felt quickly. Too often the public cries out for "stunts," and for the sake of finances the producer deliberately perverts the author's motive.[9]

This was not the kind of producing which appealed to Monck and when he got the opportunity to take up residence in the ancient city of Norwich, he took it. "Norwich," wrote Reyner Banham, "is a great graveyard of promising careers, where people who might just have made the big-time with an effort relax and go small-time instead. It is quite a cushy ecology for a certain kind of intellectual. . . . But," he went on, "if, like Nugent Monck, he decides not to let the gracious living drag him down, the place can be quite an arena for a determined mind."[10] Monck entered into this arena with enormous zeal and absolute dedication. He founded the Guild of the Norwich Players, secured for them a theatre in which to work, and in the meantime produced whenever and wherever he could, including the Abbey Theatre, learning thoroughly the discipline of his chosen profession.

Monck took his job as a producer very seriously. At the height of his career he defined the producer's role, saying:

> That rather banal phrase—the art of the theatre—was invented by, or for, Gordon Craig, our one eminent English producer. . . . Play acting may be a very ancient amusement, but the art of the theatre is the very newest of arts. It means the bringing together of all those parts of the theatre to make an interpretive whole, roughly, that the author, actor, designer, electrician, etc., shall be expressing the same thing at the same time in the same key. This unity of effect can only be achieved by unity in control. . . . But to do this successfully the man who controls the whole must have some knowledge of the parts; he must be able to show his staff how to act, to design, to paint; he must have a working knowledge of music and architecture, of carpentry and electricity, a knowledge of periods and the cut of clothes: he must be able to answer his conservative expert's "Impossible, sir!" with "It is not impossible, you do it like this"—and do it. [11]

Monck practiced what he preached. "Helplessness is my stock-in-trade," [12] he used to say, but he was constantly teaching complete novices to act, dye the hessian curtains with aniline dye, make historically accurate costumes, create props out of the most unlikely objects, design sets, and do all the many strenuous jobs that go into running a theatre. [13] When necessary he did all this work himself and did it very well, distinguishing himself especially as a lighting designer.

During his early years in London, Dublin and Norwich, Monck achieved a remarkable mastery of all the technical skills needed for the staging of a play in a modern theatre. His career in Egypt during the war gave him extensive experience in how to improvise whatever was needed on a stage. With his technical abilities as a foundation Monck developed his art, which was perhaps best described by a critic for the *Leeds Mercury,* who wrote, in a review of *The Tempest* on October 23, 1928, "Mr. Monck, like the able producer that he is, regards himself as a story-teller first and foremost, and pays most attention to telling his story in the plainest and easiest way possible." Monck, he said, took "no more time over the changing of his scenes than we should take over the turning of a page in the book, and because he only allowed us one interval for rest, the magic of the story had full play and its beauty full flavour." The distinctive characteristics of Monck's productions were artistic simplicity, fast tempo, and clear, rapid articulation of lines.

To exploit fully these special qualities of his work, Monck built the Maddermarket Theatre, the first permanent non-picture-frame theatre in twentieth-century England. It was called an Elizabethan Playhouse but Monck was one of the first to admit, "We do not really know anything about the Elizabethan Playhouse. It is all very carefully worked out supposition." [14] Monck himself "would cheerfully refer to his stage as 'bogus,'" Muriel St.

Clare Byrne has pointed out, but she added, "Secure in the knowledge that the smallness of his theatre, seating just over two hundred, gave the necessary intimacy for quick, natural speech, and that his Elizabethan performances captured the essentials, he could afford his joke."[15] Whether the essentials Monck captured were truly Elizabethan cannot be said with any degree of certainty. What can be said with certainty is that regardless of any possible criticism of the Maddermarket as an Elizabethan theatre, it was ideally suited to Monck's style of producing and for over sixty-five years has proved itself admirably adaptable to every kind of drama.

The Practice

When Monck began his work at the Maddermarket, it was his belief that "there is really no necessity for changing scenery. It is quite true that the senses, as well as the brain, should be stimulated by a dramatic production, and that the eye yearned for some colour. This effect, however, can be obtained by costume and grouping."[16] Oddly, Monck did not add "lighting" to this, although it was always such an important factor in the visual effectiveness of his productions. With meticulously detailed costumes, light, and a few simple curtains, Monck created beautiful stage pictures which one audience member described as "something that affected one emotionally, almost a tangible thing."[17]

It was Monck's belief that at any great moment in a play the grouping was quite as important as the dialogue. But the groupings he created were not framed pictures upon which an act curtain slowly closed for effect. His stage had neither frame nor act curtain. Rather, Monck's stage pictures were fluid sculptures which were constantly changing but which, at any given time, were beautiful to look at. "Mr. Monck's strength lies in his feeling for beauty," wrote Julian Hall:

> It is the source and inspiration of his work as a producer. Beauty in words, in the form and style of a play, in the picture which a stage as a whole should present: for him, these things lie close to the heart of life, and his awareness of them, like that of all artists, is intensely individual and distinctive. . . . At least once in every play produced by him, an audience has suddenly been made aware of the remarkable visual significance of a situation. The scene attains a quality of poetry in its aspect. It is viewed through a poet's eye. It reflects a poet's mind.[18]

But to sustain the effectiveness of his beautiful staging over 500 and more productions, Monck gradually found it useful to increase his scenic adjuncts. "After six productions of *Twelfth Night* [using his Elizabethan mode of production], the audience got nearly as bored with it as I did," he later explained.[19] Monck did not, however, simply "go over" to realism and begin building cheap imitations of West End theatrical designs. The scenery he employed had always to fit in with his methods; and scene changes were not allowed to slow the rapid tempo of performance. As William A. Armstrong explained in 1952:

> Like those of William Poel, Monck's Shakespearean productions are distinguished by their rapid tempo and crisply modulated diction. He wastes no time on scene changes or slow lighting effects; his basic media are the words of the text and the body and voice of the actor... At the same time, Monck is too experimental to confine his methods as a Shakespearean producer to the limited knowledge of Elizabethan stagecraft made available by scholarly treatises. He does not scorn the aids of paint and canvas for the creation of emblematic or evocative settings so long as they do not slacken the texture of his production.[20]

Monck had an intuitive sense about exactly how to make the proper appeal to the imagination of his audience.

"Mr. Monck's genius for just the right setting, for the exact shade of colour in lighting or in curtains, has always been apparent even when handicapped by the—in parts—poor acting material at his disposal," wrote a local critic in 1933. He went on to add, "That material has been wonderfully strengthened and improved of recent years. Mr. Nugent Monck's present company is the best he has ever had."[21] But the statement indicates a paradox in Monck's career. Monck had originally developed his simple, evocative scene designs in order to give greater focus to the acting and thereby to the play. Yet financial realities prevented him from using professional actors who could have exploited the advantages of that focus most fully. As a consequence Monck began to depend increasingly on his own artistic abilities.

As early as 1931 a writer for the *Observer* said, "The Maddermarket Theatre is a producer's theatre and the Players are first and last the stuff of Mr. Monck's creation. The appeal is often to the eye and to the senses, and thus there is always something interesting even when the acting falls below what ought to be average."[22] In the late 1920s and early 30s the acting only occasionally fell that low. After the 1932–33 season however the quality of the acting seems to have declined in general, although there were various brief periods of outstanding work. It is probably not mere coincidence then that Monck hired an excellent perspective artist as his designer in the autumn of 1934. Perhaps he saw his own ability to inspire his players declining and hoped to compensate with new variety in setting. Perhaps he had simply become more interested in exploring the versatility of his Elizabethan stage in terms of its scenic possibilities and began to put less stress on the acting. For whatever reason, the drama critics who went to the Maddermarket in the late 1930s and after gave increasing praise to Monck's artistic taste but made noticeably fewer comments about the capabilities of the Norwich Players.

Although the Maddermarket Theatre was a producer's theatre, Monck avoided the all-too-common tendency on the part of producers to force their own unusual interpretations of a work onto the actors and audience. "Sincerity not peculiarity"[23] must be the keynote in a production, Monck said. In a program note to Auden and Isherwood's *The Ascent of F6* he wrote, "I have not touched upon the ascent of the spiritual F6 because each individual will interpret it differently for himself. All I can do is to produce the play simply and clearly and leave the audience to feel the emotion of the author." This was characteristic of every production he did, and if he usually depended more on the visual beauty of his staging than on the histrionic art of his players to communicate the author's feelings, he did not do it obtrusively. After seeing one of Monck's productions in 1927, a critic for the *Christian Science Monitor* wrote, "Behind it all, guiding and uniting it, is Mr. Monck's art, never obtrusive, always sustained. Anybody who has seen a performance at the Maddermarket must be struck by the skill in which the hand is so far withdrawn that the production seems to progress as if by its own impetus."[24]

The subtlety and reserve of Monck's directing, however, also limited somewhat the drama he could most successfully produce. The demonstration of great emotion seems always to have been a weak point in Monck's productions. Norman Marshall points out that Monck's realistic productions of Chekhov were excellent.

> The mood of these plays is perfectly in tune with the gentle melancholy of his own character. In his handling of other plays his streak of melancholy often leads him into a mere sentimentalism. His production of *From Morn to Midnight* [1931] was an astonishing example of this. He managed to transform this angry, noisy, violent play into something sad, gentle and pointless.[25]

This melancholy pervaded Monck's own plays, even his comedies, and it strongly influenced the new plays he chose to produce. In 1937 a Maddermarket follower wrote in exasperation, "Is it absolutely necessary for new work to be acceptable to the Players that it should invariably lack incident and any approach to passion? . . . They have been charming, sometimes witty and interesting pictures of everyday life, but not plays that called for great acting or could move an audience."[26] Working as he did with amateurs Monck was wise not to place great demands upon them, but the lack of passion in his work is a strange paradox considering the depth of his emotional commitment to the theatre.

The Purpose

The basis of Monck's work in the theatre was his belief that:

> There is nothing to be gained in the theatre at all by artistic settings; you can leave that to the
> kinema [*sic*]. The one great thing the kinema has done for the theatre is that it has stopped it
> attempting to compete with realism, and it is going to prevent it continuing on these lines.
> The theatre will have to come back and search for its success in spirituality—I don't mean
> something far away, searching and highbrow, but the kind of simple spirituality that can
> touch everybody.[27]

Though in his later years Monck was a church warden at St. John's
Maddermarket Parish Church, through most of his life he was a self-avowed
agnostic. But Monck believed that there was a basic sense in most people of
something beyond mere materialism and it was this sense, which he did not
define, that he recognized as being at the heart of all religious belief. For him,
theatre was potentially the most powerful spiritual force outside a definite
religion,[28] and he wished to develop it as an alternative to religion for those
who, like himself, were dissatisfied with what they saw in the established
churches around them. He once wrote in a lecture,

> The spirituality that we get from our churches is what we ourselves bring into them. So
> much has been killed by dogma, by argument, by all the various sects that hate each other
> for the love of God, that it surely would be a relief to find some spiritual movement that
> wasn't a little egotism, that had no doctrine, but did materialize the religious experience we
> feel in our hearts, for the mission of the theatre is not to preach but to reveal.[29]

It was this desire that first led Monck to the dramas of the medieval
Church. In the Middle Ages the Church had used the stage as a way to teach
the people and the drama produced during this period expressed the same joy
in life that Monck saw reflected in the architecture, carvings, paintings and
stained glass of the great cathedrals of Europe.[30] The Reformation, he
contended, had crushed this joy out of religious belief, forcing on Western
culture a dedication to "respectability," which, as he pointed out, "consists of
purely negative qualities, and having really no being itself naturally has much
to fear from vitality and the exhibition of vitality in others."[31] This is where the
real split between drama and religion had begun, he thought, and as a result
drama had ceased to be the vital social force it had once been.

"Loving the drama above all else in the world, he was fired with the
ambition of making the theatre of his day the intimate part of the lives of the
people that it was in the days of the guild-players," an interviewer had once
said of Monck.[32] But, unfortunately, Monck himself was too much of a

respectable Victorian to produce the medieval plays with the kind of joyous vitality he read in them and the rest of society around him could not have accepted it if he had.

What Monck did provide in his productions was color, ritual and discipline, the same elements that he found so attractive about the ceremony of the Anglican Church.[33] It was with these elements that Monck hoped to attract those young people who after the First World War had turned away from religion and become increasingly influenced by materialism.[34] "What can drama do?" Monck would later ask rhetorically.

> It is the easiest way to make people think about the beauty of life and to bring beauty into life. From Comedy, which is the criticism of life, people are led on to tragedy, which gives the realization of spiritual values. It teaches the younger generation that life is something more than mere money-getting, which possibly is all their fathers have been able to tell them.[35]

Monck thought that the educational value of drama was as important as its spiritual value and he chose all plays he produced according to both their intellectual and spiritual content. In the program to his September 1920 production of *The Comedy of Errors* Monck stated that the aim of the Norwich Players was to present good plays in an intelligent manner. "Their test of a play," a reviewer later wrote, "is not that it should be reputed a good draw, but that it should be a good, or—what is not always exactly the same thing—an interesting play, in which the dramatist has something to say."[36] To an extent these criteria invariably led to a certain highbrow quality in the seasons Monck produced, but Monck worked hard against letting his theatre become merely an "arty clique." He would certainly have been in full agreement with Mariette Soman, who wrote in a booklet on the Norwich Players:

> Art for art's sake has been proved an untenable theory. Art should not seek, primarily, to please, but if it does not please, then its existence is not justified. It has failed in its mission, which is to interpret man to himself. The art which is above the heads of the people is either unreal or born out of due time, and as unsatisfying as any anachronism. A dramatic work of art especially should be popular as well as aesthetic, since the audience is an essential factor in its composition.[37]

"Have nothing to do with the fallacy that intelligence need be dull," Monck would advise; "a brow can be high without being pretentiously puckered."[38]

Monck believed in doing theatre for the joy of it, and even in 1933 when he was on the verge of bankruptcy he did two evenings of medieval plays and a week of *Oedipus Rex* for his own amusement. "If you are doing plays for your own amusement," he had always taught, "do the best scripts you can find."[39] Bad plays are not worth the effort and besides, badly written scripts are the hardest to act.

Monck enjoyed experimenting with a wide variety of plays and his selection prompted one reviewer to comment,

> The list of plays the Norwich Players have produced since 1919 has infinite variety and a refreshing lack of balance. One is reminded of small children tasting all the kinds of goodies, one after another.... Some of these have been wonderfully done. Others, if the players' own very critical judgement is to be believed, have gone less well. But all of them, they agree, have given them great joy in the doing.[40]

Ten times a year for 36 years, Monck exposed his Players and his Norwich audience to some of the finest drama in world literature. "Consequently the use of a season ticket to the Maddermarket became—and remains to this day—the groundmark of a liberal education,"[41] wrote Eric Fowler in 1960.

"Once during the war [World War II] I found a young soldier lingering after a performance," Monck once said. " 'Do you want anything?' I asked. " 'No,' he replied, 'But I have never seen *Hamlet* before. I did not know that anybody by stringing words together could make so much beauty!' 'You are lucky,' I said, ... 'that is what we exist for.' "[42] This was the purpose of existence not only for the Maddermarket Theatre but for all the theatres that later followed it and became known as the Little Theatre Movement. But these theatres were not merely, or even primarily, intended for the benefit of their audiences; they were for the benefit of their numerous participants. The prolific author and playwright J. B. Priestley described it this way:

> These theatres are attracting to themselves the more eager, impressionable, intelligent younger people in these industrial towns, where depression has hung like a black cloud for the last few years. Some of them, in various places, have told me what this dramatic work has meant to them, and in many instances the persons in question have not been producing, designing scenery, playing big parts, but may only have been selling programmes, taking tickets, or doing the accounts.... In communities that have suffered the most from industrial depression, among the younger people who frequently cannot see what is to become of their jobs and their lives, these theatres have opened little windows into a world of ideas, colour, fine movement, exquisite drama, have kept going a stir of thought and imagination for actors, helpers, audiences.[43]

The opportunity to work with some of the world's greatest drama continuously over a period of several years gave those young people who became part of the Norwich Players the chance to develop intellectual qualities in themselves that might otherwise have simply lain dormant.[44] "Some of us who 'left school' in Norwich were lucky enough to have at hand the Maddermarket Theatre, ... where we could experience real thought and feeling formally expressed," explained the novelist and critic David Holbrook. "In later life we find this, and its consequent assistance in understanding our civilization, the envy of those who lived elsewhere."[45]

It was an astonishing faith that had prompted Monck to maintain the highest standards in the drama he chose to produce in the belief that, if the theatre refused to "play down to the audience," the audience would gradually learn to appreciate the more intelligent and cultured things in life. It was a long struggle through the most difficult and trying of times but in the postwar years of the late 1940s a significant portion of the general population of Norwich was finally won over, and for them the Maddermarket became a cultural and educational institution of enormous value.

Monck's cultural influence did not stop with the drama he produced. He had an enormous range of interests, was up to date and widely read, and his door was always open to those who were interested in art, culture, or education. He filled people's lives not only with the excitement and camaraderie of the theatre, but with all sorts of interests and hobbies they might not otherwise have ever discovered. By Monck (or "Moncklet," as he was often affectionately called) young men and women were introduced to lifelong interests in art, poetry, music, antiques, writing, printing, travel and numerous other cultural and intellectual activities that made their lives fuller and more interesting. "To many of us who went in our youths to act at the Maddermarket," wrote Donald FitzJohn upon Monck's death, "Moncklet showed the way to a different world. Our debt to him is enormous—artistically and personally."[46]

Figure 22.   Badge of the Norwich Players
            (Courtesy of the Maddermarket Theatre Trust, Ltd.)

Appendix A

Chronological List of Productions

The following is a list of all plays on which Monck worked in any capacity. For the purpose of clarity, productions done for the Norwich Players by producers other than Monck between 1910 and 1952 have been included in this list and marked with square brackets. After each title, or group of titles when several plays were performed together, is the date of performance. This is followed by an indication of the capacity in which Monck worked on the production (see symbols). When no indication is given, Monck served as producer. This information is followed by the name of the performing group if known, the theatre where the production occurred if known, the city of production, and any special note which seems of value. Appendices B and C are designed to serve as an index to this list.

Symbols:

?   the information which immediately follows this symbol is not verifiable, not known, or otherwise doubtful.

*   indicates productions on which Monck worked in a capacity other than that of producer, i.e.:

*d = Dramatist

*s.m. = Stage Manager, a capacity in which Monck served under William Poel only. All productions so marked were William Poel productions.

*actor = This symbol is followed by the name of the role Monck played in parentheses, when known. Monck often appeared anonymously in his own productions; his roles in these cases are given a special note.

[ ]   indicates a production done for the Norwich Players by a producer other than Monck between 1910 and 1952.

1900

The Angel Boy (Monck)   March 28   *d Royal Academy of Music, London.
                                  June 29   St. George's Hall, London.
                                    ?   ?Criterion Theatre, London.

1901

The Man in Rags (Monck)   July 12   *d Academy of Dramatic Art students,
                                            St. George's Hall, London.

Beyond Human Power (Bjørnson)   Nov. 7   *actor (Pastor Janson) Royalty Theatre,
                                        London. Mrs. Patrick Campbell producer.

1902

Everyman (15th century)   May 26   *actor (Fellowship) St. George's Hall,
                                      London. William Poel producer.
                                  ? June   Tour of cathedral cities including Manchester,
                                      Dublin and Edinburgh.
                                July ?1-10 Imperial Theatre, Westminster.

?The Alchemist (Jonson)   July 11-12   ?s.m. Imperial Theatre, Westminster.

1903

The Adversity of Advertisement (Monck) Jan. 26   *d Opera House, Yeovil
The Domestic Fowl (Monck)
The Primrose Way (Monck)

Everyman (15th century)   April ?   *actor (Fellowship) Opera House, Tunbridge
                                      Wells. William Poel producer.

?Twelfth Night (Shakespeare)   April 23   *s.m. Lecture Hall, Burlington Gardens,
                                      London.
                                  June 16-20 ?*s.m. Court Theatre, London.

1903 (cont.)

?Edward II (Marlowe)	Aug. 10	?*s.m. New Theatre, Oxford.
The Primrose Way (Monck)	Sept. 21	*d Empire Theatre, Balham.

1904

Much Ado about Nothing (Shakespeare)	Feb. 23	*actor (Balthasar) & s.m. Town Hall, Shoreditch.
	" 25	Town Hall, Bow and Bromley.
	" 26	Town Hall, New Cross.
	Mar. 1	Town Hall, Hammersmith.
	" 2	Town Hall, St. Pancras.
	" 3	Town Hall, Battersea.
	" 4	Town Hall, Bermondsey.
	" 19	Elizabethan Stage Society, Court Theatre, London.
	Apr. 22	London Shakespeare League, Burlington Gardens, London.
Doctor Faustus (Marlowe)	Oct. 29	*actor (Robin) & s.m. Court Theatre, London.
Doctor Faustus (Marlowe)	Oct. 31-Dec. 10	*actor (Robin, Pinch) & s.m. Plays done alternately on tour of Northern cities, ended at Terry's Theatre, London.
The Comedy of Errors (Shakespeare)		

1905

The First Franciscans (Poel)	Apr. 6, 7, 13, 14	*actor (Giovanni) & s.m. Elizabethan Stage Society, St. George's Hall, London.
Romeo and Juliet (Shakespeare)	May 5, 6, 9, 11	*s.m. Elizabethan Stage Society, Royalty Theatre, London.

The Elizabethan Stage Society was dissolved. Monck formed English Drama Society (Eng. D. S.)

1905 (cont.)

In a Balcony (Browning) Life's Measure (Monck)	June 8	Eng. D. S. Victoria Hall, London.
The Dialogue of D'Alcarmo (Rossetti)	? Sept.	Eng. D. S. One performance given, date and place unknown.
The Interlude of Youth (15th century)	Dec. 12-14	Eng. D. S. Bloomsbury Hall, London.

1906

The Vision (Norton) Ghosts (Ibsen)	? Feb.	Eng. D. S. National Sporting Club, Covent Garden. G. B. Shaw attended.
Love's Labour's Lost (Shakespeare)	Apr. ?27-29	Eng. D. S. Bloomsbury Hall, London.
The Two Gentlemen of Verona (Shakespeare)	?	Scenes from, one performance. Date and place unknown.
?The Good-Natur'd Man (Goldsmith)	Aug. 9-10	?*s.m. New Theatre, Cambridge.
The Sun's Darling (Ford & Dekker)	Oct. 31	Eng. D. S. Queen's Gate Hall, London.
The Chester Mysteries: (14th century) Salutation, Nativity, Shepherd's	Nov. 29	Eng. D. S. Old Music Hall, Chester.
Three Kings	Dec. 5-?	Eng. D. S. Bloomsbury Hall, London. 16 performances given.

1907

The Merchant of Venice (Shakespeare)	Jan. 31	Eng. D. S. People's Palace, Mile-end Road.
Twelfth Night (Shakespeare)	? Feb.	Eng. D. S. One performance, date and place unknown.
The Interlude of Youth (15th century)	Mar. 25	Eng. D. S. Coronet Theatre, Notting Hill.

1907 (cont.)

?The Redemption of Agnes (Poel)	Mar. 30	?s.m. Coronet Theatre, Notting Hill.
The Taming of the Shrew (Shakespeare)	? Apr.	Eng. D. S. Date and place unknown.
Cleopatra in Judea (Symons) The Hour (Monck)	May 6-?18	Eng. D. S. Bijou Theatre, Bayswater.
?The Merchant of Venice (Shakespeare)	June 11-15	?s.m. Fulham Theatre, London.

Monck toured the coastal cities of England with his own Shakespeare Company at some period. Summer and Autumn 1907 seem most likely, but uncertain.

The Chester Mysteries (14th century)	Dec. 20-21	Eng. D. S. University College, London. Slaughter of the Innocents added to original four plays.

1908

Peter the Fool (Monck) The Domestic Fowl (Monck) The Foiled Fiend (Coke)	Jan. 22	Eng. D. S. Queen's Gate Hall, London.
The Song of Songs (Monck) The Votaries (Monck)	Mar. 8	Eng. D. S. Queen's Gate Hall, London.
?Measure for Measure (Shakespeare)	Apr. 11-18 Apr. 21-22	?s.m. Gaiety Theatre, Manchester. Memorial Theatre, Stratford-upon-Avon.
The Mill (Monck)	June 23	Eng. D. S. Scala Theatre, London.
?The Bacchae (Euripides)	Nov. 10 & 17	?s.m. Court Theatre, London.
?Samson Agonistes (Milton)	Dec. 10, 18	?s.m. New Theatre, Cambridge.
	Dec. 14-15, 16	Burlington Gardens, London.
	Dec. 19	Manchester University.

1909

Play	Date	Notes
Historic Tableaux (Monck)	Jan. 7-9	St. Andrew's Hall, Norwich.
Pippa Passes (Browning)	Jan. 18-22	Eng. D. S. Fortune Playhouse, London.
The Magistrate (Pinero)	? Feb.	Richmond Thespians, Richmond-upon-Thames.
?Everyman (15th century)	Mar. 24-25	?*actor (Fellowship) Coronet Theatre, Notting Hill.
	Mar. 26-27	Fulham Theatre, London.
	Mar. 31	Kennington Theatre, Kennington.
	Apr. 7-8	Coronet Theatre, Notting Hill.
The Passion Play (15th century)	(Apr. 7-10)	Scheduled but banned from public performance.
	Apr. 15-18	Eng. D. S. Fortune Playhouse, London. Private performance.
Macbeth (Shakespeare)	June 22-26	*s.m. Fulham Theatre, London.
The Masque of Anne Boleyn (Monck)	Aug. 11-13	Blickling Hall, Norfolk.
In the Beginning (Monck)	?	Crowe Hall, Stutton, Suffolk.

1910

Play	Date	Notes
The Two Gentlemen of Verona (Shakespeare)	Apr. 20	*actor (The Host) & s.m. His Majesty's Theatre, London. W. Bridges-Adams assistant s.m.
	Apr. 25, 26 & 30	Gaiety Theatre, Manchester.
Everyman (15th century)	Apr. 27, 28 & 29	*actor (Fellowship) & s.m. Gaiety Theatre, Manchester.
Narcissus, a Water Frolic (Monck)	Aug. 9-10	Blickling Hall, Norfolk. Bridges-Adams designed.
A Midsummer Night's Dream (Shakespeare)	Sept. 6-8	Rectory gardens, Thorpe, Norfolk. ?Bridges-Adams assisted.
The World and the Child (16th century)	Nov. 3	Nugent Monck's Players, later to become the Norwich Players (N.P.). The Crypt (Monck's home), Norwich.

1910 (cont.)

The Peacemaker (Bryant) Rosemary (Parker)	Dec. 2-3	G. Gurney's Acting Troupe, Thatched Assembly Rooms, Norwich.
Paradyse (16th century) The Wakefield (14th century) Second Shepherd's Play The World and the Child (16th century)	Dec. 26	Nugent Monck's Players, Blackfriars' Hall, Norwich. Bridges-Adams assisted.

1911

Bethlehem Tableaux (Monck)	Jan. 5-7	Nugent Monck's Players, Blackfriars' Hall, Norwich.
The Countess Cathleen (Yeats)	Feb. 21-22	Old Girls' Assoc., Norwich High School. W. B. Yeats attended.
Job (Amherst)	Mar. 23	Nugent Monck's Players, Blackfriars' Hall, Norwich. W. B. Yeats attended.

Guild of Norwich Players (N.P.) organized but continued to be referred to (by press) as Nugent Monck's Players.

St. George and the Dragon (Traditional) The Holly and the Ivy (Monck and Kinder)	May 24 & 25	N.P., The Crypt (Monck's home), Norwich.
King Argimenes and the Unknown Warrior (Dunsany) The Well of the Saints (Synge)	June 26-28	Irish Players, Court Theatre, London.
The Death of Wallenstein (Schiller)	Aug. 11	*actor (Seni) New Theatre, Oxford, Poel producer.
Between the Showers (Monck)	? Sept.	N.P. Date and place unknown.

1911 (cont.)

The Golden Mean (Amherst)　　　　　　　　Oct. 4　　　　N.P.　　Thatched Assembly Rooms, Norwich.
The Votaries (Monck)

　　　　Monck went to Dublin to found school of acting at the Abbey Theatre,
　　　　and produced the following plays with students of the Abbey Theatre
　　　　School of Acting while the Irish Players were touring America,
　　　　　　　　　　　　　　Nov. 1911-Mar. 1912

The Interlude of Youth (15th century)　　　Nov. 16-19
The Marriage (Hyde)
The Shadow of the Glen (Synge)

The Interlude of Youth (15th century)　　　Nov. 23-25　　also *actor (Youth)
The Wakefield (14th century)
Second Shepherd's Play

The Marriage (Hyde)　　　　　　　　　　Nov. 30-Dec. 1
The Nativity Play (Hyde)
Dervorgilla (Gregory)
The Workhouse Ward (Gregory)

Red Turf (Mayne)　　　　　　　　　　　　Dec. 7-9
The Shadow of the Glen (Synge)
The Interlude of Youth (15th century)

MacDarragh's Wife (Gregory)　　　　　　　Dec. 15　　　Copyright performance.

The Countess Cathleen (Yeats)　　　　　　Dec. 14-16
The Interlude of Youth (15th century)

1912

Play	Date	Notes
The Wakefield Mysteries: (14th century) Annunciation, Second Shepherd's Play, Flight into Egypt The Nativity Play (Hyde)	Jan. 4-6	also *actor (St. Joseph)
MacDarragh's Wife (Gregory) Red Turf (Mayne) The Marriage (Hyde) The Workhouse Ward (Gregory)	Jan. 11-13	
The Building Fund (Boyle) Dervorgilla (Gregory) The Rising of the Moon (Gregory)	Jan. 18-20	
The Country Dressmaker (Fitzmaurice) The Gaol Gate (Gregory)	Feb. 1-3	
The Countess Cathleen (Yeats) Spreading the News (Gregory)	Feb. 7-9	also *actor (Aleel)
The Tinker and the Fairy (Hyde) The Canavans (Gregory)	Feb. 15-17	First play in Gaelic at Abbey Theatre. First use of Craig screens in full length play at Abbey Theatre.
The Land of Heart's Desire (Yeats) The Building Fund (Boyle) The Rising of the Moon (Gregory)	Feb. 22-24	
The World and the Child (16th century) The Gaol Gate (Gregory) Spreading the News (Gregory) The Tinker and the Fairy (Hyde)	Feb. 29- Mar. 2	Monck took over lead role moments before play opened.

1912 (cont.)

Monck left Dublin Mar. 3, returned to Norwich.

The Mancroft Pageant (Monck)
The Wakefield Abraham and Isaac
(14th century)

June 26-29,
July 1

N.P. and c. 500 extras, Spring Gardens, St. Faith's House, Norwich. N.P. performed Abraham and Isaac as part of pageant.

The Countess Cathleen (Yeats)

July 11

Irish Players, Court Theatre, London. London premiere.

St. George and the Dragon
(Traditional)
The World and the Child
(16th century)

Aug. 31

N.P., Thatched Assembly Rooms, Norwich. Flood Relief benefit. First printed reference to Norwich Players by that name.

Monck returned to Abbey Theatre Oct. 1 to head Second Company for tour of Ireland.

The Country Dressmaker (Fitzmaurice)
The Wakefield Second Shepherd's Play
(14th century)

Oct. 3-5

Abbey Theatre

Second Company tour of Irish cities

The Hour Glass (Yeats)
Damer's Gold (Gregory)

Nov. 21-23

Irish Players, Abbey Theatre, Dublin. Monck also played the Old Man in Hour Glass.

[Job (Amherst)]

Nov. 28

N.P. King's Hall, Covent Garden. Poel and Bridges-Adams producers.

1913

Monck headed Irish Players (Abbey Theatre's First Company)
for their second U.S.A. tour Dec. 28, 1912–May 1, 1913.

23 plays performed in repertory, including:

Cathleen ni Houlihan (Yeats)
The Countess Cathleen (Yeats)
Coats (Gregory)
Damer's Gold (Gregory)
Family Failing (Boyle)
The Galway Race (Gregory)
The Gaol Gate (Gregory)
The Hour Glass (Yeats)
The Land of Heart's Desire (Yeats)   Toured Chicago, Univ. of Notre Dame, New York,
The Magnanimous Lover (Ervine)   Pittsburg, Philadelphia, Montreal, Boston.
Maurice Harte (Murray)
The Mixed Marriage (Ervine)
The Patriots (Robinson)
The Playboy of the Western World (Synge)
The Rising of the Moon (Gregory)
The Shadow of the Glen (Synge)
Spreading the News (Gregory)
The Workhouse Ward (Gregory)

[Job (Amherst)]   Feb. 13-14   N.P. Blackfriars' Hall, Norwich.
                                                               Bridges–Adams producer.
                                           ? May 8   King's Hall, Covent Garden.
The Interlude of Youth (15th century)   June ?   N.P. Grammar School, Norwich.
The World and the Child (16th century)   July 3   N.P. Lambeth Palace, London.
The Interlude of Youth (15th century)   July 10   N.P. Lambeth Palace, London.

1913 (cont.)

Title	Date	Venue/Notes
A Midsummer Night's Dream (Shakespeare)	July 26	Students, Grammar School, Norwich, scenes only.
Everyman (15th century)	July ?	*actor (?) Crosby Hall, Chelsea. Monck purchased Poel's entire production, stage, costumes, props, etc., after this show.
Job (Amherst) The Interlude of Youth (15th century)	Aug. 15	N.P. Memorial Theatre, Stratford-upon-Avon. Bridges-Adams assisted.
The Pageant Play of King Arthur (Monck)	? Sept.	N.P. Winchester College, Winchester.
Everyman (15th century) Aucassin and Nicolette (Monck and Kinder)	Dec. 1-6	N.P. Theatre Royal, Norwich.

1914

Title	Date	Venue/Notes
The Holly and the Ivy (Monck and Kinder) The Interlude of Youth (15th century) The Chester Play of The Three Kings (14th century)	Jan. 7-8	N.P. Old Music House, King St., Norwich.
Twelfth Night (Shakespeare)	Feb. 18-21	N.P. Old Music House, Norwich.
Merchandise (Monck and Kinder) The Mock Doctor (Molière) Columbine (Arkell)	Apr. 29-30, May 1-2	N.P. Old Music House, Norwich.

1914 (cont.)

The Merchant of Venice (Shakespeare)   June 17-20   N.P. Old Music House, Norwich.

As You Like It (Shakespeare)   July 25   Students, Grammar School, Norwich, scenes only.

Germany invaded Belgium on Aug. 3, 1914, bringing Great Britain
into World War I. Monck joined the R.A.M.C. and was
sent to Aldershot for training.

1915

In Feb. Monck was sent to Alexandria, Egypt, where he joined
the 15th General Hospital. He did no productions from
July 1914-April 1916. This was the longest period
he spent away from producing during his career.

1916

The Clowns' Play (from A.M.N.D.)   Apr. 23   15th Gen. Hospital, Musical & Dramatic Soc.,
Alexandria, Egypt. Shakespeare Tercentenary
celebration.

All subsequent productions staged by Monck during World War I were done
for the 15th General Hospital, Musical & Dramatic Soc., at their
base in Alexandria, Egypt, unless otherwise noted.

The Taming of the Shrew (Shakespeare)   June ?
A Touch of Truth (Walbrook)

The Land of Heart's Desire (Yeats)   ?

The Workhouse Ward (Gregory)   ?

The Ghost of Jerry Bundler (Jacobs)   ?

1917

Columbine (Arkell) — ?

Twelfth Night (Shakespeare) — ?

The Importance of Being Earnest (Wilde) — Mar. 14 / Mar. 24 — 2nd anniversary of landing in Egypt. Monck also played Lady Bracknell. Special officers' performance.

The Merchant of Venice (Shakespeare) — Mar. 28 or 31

Candida (Shaw) — June 4
An Adventure (Milne)

Candida (Shaw) — July 4 — 15th Gen. Musical & Dramatic Soc. with Miss Ashwell's Y.M.C.A. Concert Party, Alhambra Theatre, Alexandria, Egypt. Monck also played Marchbanks. Miss Yvette Pienne and Miss M. (?Gwen) Ffrangcon Davies in cast.
Love the Doctor (Molière)

Macbeth (Shakespeare) — ?
Cinderella (Monck) — Dec. ?

Monck's unit was transferred to Salonika (now Thessaloniki), Greece and disbanded.

1918

The Cyclops (Shelley) — ? — 15th Gen. Musical and Dramatic Soc., Salonika, Greece.

Twelfth Night (Shakespeare) — Aug. 7-8 — 61st Gen. Hospital, Salonika, Greece. / Dec. ?18 — 52nd Gen. Hospital, Salonika, Greece.

1919

Play	Date	Venue / Notes
?Twelfth Night (Shakespeare)	?Jan.	?52nd Gen. Hospital, Salonika, Greece.
?The School for Scandal (Sheridan)	?	?52nd Gen. Hospital, Salonika, Greece.

Monck returned to Norwich in June 1919.

Play	Date	Venue / Notes
Twelfth Night (Shakespeare)	July 28	Students, Grammar School, Norwich, scenes only.
A Midsummer Night's Dream (Shakespeare)	Aug. 27-28	Nugent Monck's Players, Gardens of Blickling Hall, Norfolk.
Much Ado about Nothing (Shakespeare)	Sept. 24-27	The Norwich Players (N.P.) reorganized with new members. The Old Music House, Norwich.
The Land of Heart's Desire (Yeats) Nishikigi (Motokiyo) Omar Khayyam (Monck) The Comedy of Errors (Shakespeare)	Nov. 12-15	N.P. Old Music House, Norwich.
The Wakefield Mysteries (14th century) The Annunciation or Salutation of Elizabeth, The Second Shepherd's Play, The Offering of the Magi, The Flight to Egypt, Herod the Great	Dec. 15-20	N.P. Old Music House, Norwich.

1920

The Beggar's Opera was scheduled for Jan. but postponed.

Play	Date	Venue / Notes
Much Ado about Nothing (Shakespeare)	Jan. 8	N.P. Central Hall, Willow Lane and Beccles, Norfolk.
The School for Scandal (Sheridan)	Feb. 9-17	N.P. Old Music House, Norwich. Extended run.
Love's Labour's Lost (Shakespeare)	Apr. 26– May 1	N.P. Old Music House, Norwich.

1920 (cont.)

The Beggar's Opera (Gay) Three Mimes (Herodias)	June 14-19	N.P.	Old Music House, Norwich.
The Two Idylls (Theocritus)	?	N.P.	?Old Music House, Norwich.
A Midsummer Night's Dream (Shakespeare)	July 27	N.P.	Old Music House, Norwich.
The Comedy of Errors (Shakespeare)	Sept. 6	N.P.	St. Andrew's Hall, Norwich. Special performance for Library Assoc.
Romeo and Juliet (Shakespeare)	Sept. 20-25	N.P.	Old Music House, Norwich. Monck acted Romeo.
Candida (Shaw)	Oct. 11-16	N.P.	Old Music House, Norwich.
Hippolytus (Euripides)	Nov. 1-6	N.P.	Old Music House, Norwich.
The Rivals (Sheridan)	Nov. 29– Dec. 4	N.P.	Old Music House, Norwich.

1921

The Merry Wives of Windsor (Shakespeare)	Feb. 2-11	N.P.	Old Music House, Norwich. Extended run.
The Song of Songs (Monck) Daniel the Prophet (Amherst)	Mar. 22-27	N.P.	Old Music House, Norwich.
The Yorkshire Tragedy (Anon.) The Dark Lady of the Sonnets (Shaw)	Apr. 30	N.P.	Old Music House, Norwich. Poel lectured at interval.
The Tragedy of Nan (Masefield)	June 15-18	N.P.	Old Music House, Norwich.
Revelry (Monck)	July 26-29	N.P.	Gardens of St. Helen's House, Bishopsgate, Norwich.

1921 (cont.)

Monck purchased a former Roman Catholic Chapel in St. John's Maddermarket Alley, Norwich, on March 24, 1921. During Aug. and Sept. it was converted into the Maddermarket Theatre. All productions done by Monck during 1921-1952 were done for the N.P. at this theatre unless otherwise noted.

As You Like It (Shakespeare)	Sept. 26–Oct. 1	Inaugural production of the Maddermarket Theatre. W. B. Yeats spoke at interval Sept. 26.
The Chester Mysteries (14th century)	Oct. 26-29	Benefit for Nursing Sisters of the Poor.
She Stoops to Conquer (Goldsmith)	Nov. 21-26	
A New Way to Pay Old Debts (Massinger)	Dec. 12-17	
The Merchant of Venice (Shakespeare)	Dec. 19	Special mat. and eve. production given for Grammar School students.
Fête Galante (Dobson)	Dec. 29-31	Benefit for Girl Guides

1922

Columbine (Arkell)		
The Affected Ladies (Molière)	Jan. 23-28	Molière Tercentenary celebration.
The Mock Doctor (Molière)		
The Taming of the Shrew (Shakespeare)	Feb. 27–Mar. 4	
King Monmouth (Presland)	Mar. 27–Apr. 1	Premiere production.
Twelfth Night (Shakespeare)	Apr. 24–May 2	
Electra (Euripides)	May 17-20	

1922 (cont.)

The Winter's Tale (Shakespeare)	June 19-24	
The Duchess of Malfi (Webster)	July 10-15	
Between the Showers (Monck) Fête Galante (Monck)	Aug. 225	N.P. Gardens of Ranworth Hall, Norfolk.
The Merchant of Venice (Shakespeare)	Sept. 25-30 & Oct. 2-3	
The Duenna (Sheridan/Linley) The Dark Lady of the Sonnets (Shaw)	Oct. 30- Nov. 4	Barry Jackson attended Nov. 3. Latter copied production at Birmingham Rep. Theatre.
The Shipboy (Monck) The Wakefield Abraham and Isaac (14th century)	Nov. ?	N.P. League of Nations Arts Exhibition, St. Albans.
Henry IV, Part I (Shakespeare)	Dec. 11-16	

1923

The School for Scandal (Sheridan)	Jan. 8-13	
Othello (Shakespeare)	Feb. 19-24	
The Way of the World (Congreve)	Mar. 19-24	Program contained unusual note "There will be a slight pause after each act."
Doctor Faustus (Marlowe)	Apr. 23-28	
The Machine Wreckers (Toller)	May 6, 7, 13, 14	The Stage Society, Kingsway Theatre, London. Herbert Marshall in cast.
A Midsummer Night's Dream (Shakespeare)	May 28- June 2	
The Two Gentlemen of Verona (Shakespeare) The Duenna (Sheridan/Linley)	June 25-30	

1923 (cont.)

Paradyse (16th century)	Sept. 8	N.P. Miss Pym's garden, also St. Mary Croft's
The Wakefield Abraham and Isaac (14th century)		churchyard. Plays staged on pageant wagon.
Cymbeline (Shakespeare)	Sept. 24–29	
Śakuntalā (Kālidāsa)	Oct. 18	Lecture/Performance series (L/P).
The Rivals (Sheridan)	Oct. 30–Nov. 3	
Kantan (Seami) Nishikigi (Motokiyo)	Nov. 22	L/P No. 2.
Henry IV, Part II (Shakespeare)	Dec. 10–15	

1924

Paphnutius (Hroswitha)	Jan. 3	L/P No. 3.
Antony and Cleopatra (Shakespeare)	Jan. 21–26	
The Magic Casement (Monck)	Feb. 7	L/P No. 4.
Pastoral Mimes (Theocritus) The May Lady (Sidney)	Mar. 6	L/P No. 5.
Hamlet (Shakespeare)	Mar. 31–Apr. 5	
Everyman (15th century)	Apr. 14–19	Replaced L/P No. 6.
Getting Married (Shaw)	May 5–10	George Bernard Shaw attended May 5.
Philip II (Alfieri)	May 22	L/P No. 7, end of series.
The Merry Wives of Windsor (Shakespeare)	June 16–21	

1924 (cont.)

Alcestis (Euripides)   Aug. 21   N.P.   Sheringham.
                                   Aug. 23   N.P.   Maddermarket Theatre, Norwich.
                                   Aug. 28   N.P.   Stoke Holy Cross.

All's Well that Ends Well   Sept. 22-27   First use of special hinged flats.
(Shakespeare)

The Critic (Sheridan)   Oct. 20-25

The Red King (Wheldon)   Nov. 17-22   Premiere production of The Red King.
The Dumb Wife (France)

The Gentleman Dancing-Master   Dec. 15-20
(Wycherley)

1925

Romeo and Juliet (Shakespeare)   Jan. 5-10

The Greatest Show on Earth (Cervantes)   Jan. 31   Special performance for M.L.A.

Mary Stuart (Drinkwater)   Feb. 2-7
The Greatest Show on Earth (Cervantes)

The Tempest (Shakespeare)   Mar. 16-21

Macbeth (Shakespeare)   May 11-16

Pippa Passes (Browning)   June 11-12   Benefit to clear theatre's debt. Lennox
The Scheming Lieutenant (Sheridan)   Robinson attended June ?11.

The Masque of Anne Boleyn (Monck)   Aug. 6-8   N.P. with extras. Garden of Blickling Hall,
                                          Norfolk.

Shakespearian Scenes   Sept. 14   N.P.   Blickling Hall, Norfolk.

1925 (cont.)

Measure for Measure (Shakespeare)	Sept. 21-26	
Hedda Gabler (Ibsen)	Oct. 26-31	
The Duchess of Malfi (Webster)	Nov. 24-26, 28, 30 Dec. 2	Everyman Theatre Co. The Guild Hall, York.
[The Trojan Women (Euripides) The Magic Casement (Monck)]	Nov. 30- Dec. 5	?Isabel Roland, producer.
Orfeo (Monteverdi)	Dec. 7-9	Oxford Univ. Opera Club. Oxford Playhouse, Oxford. Performed in English as Orpheus. Translation by Robert Stuart.

1926 [x]

Julius Caesar (Shakespeare)	Jan. 4-9	
Marriage à la Mode (Dryden)	Feb. 8-13	Nigel Playfair and Phoenix Soc. director. Montague Summers attended one evening. Playfair later copied production at Lyric Theatre, Hammersmith.
Androcles and the Lion (Shaw) The Farce of the Master Peter Pathelin (17th century)	Mar. 15-20	
The Cherry Orchard (Chekhov)	Apr. 19-24	
Twelfth Night (Shakespeare)	May 28- June 5	

[x]All productions 1921-1952 were done for N.P. at Maddermarket Theatre unless otherwise noted.

1926 (cont.)

The Norwich Pageant (Monck) The Wakefield Abraham and Isaac (14th century)	July 21-24	N.P. with 1000 extras. Newmarket Rd. Sporting Ground, Norwich. N.P. performed Abraham and Isaac as part of Act IV of Pageant.
King Lear (Shakespeare)	Sept. 27-Oct. 2	Granville-Barker attended Sept. 27 or 28.
The Beaux' Stratagem (Farquhar)	Nov. 1-6	
Alceste (Gluck)	Dec. 6-8	Oxford Univ. Opera Club, Oxford Playhouse, Oxford.
The Man with a Load of Mischief (Dukes)	Dec. 13-18	Ashley Dukes attended one or more performances.

1927

The Chester Mysteries (14th century) The Annunciation, The Three Kings, The Shepherds	Jan. 5-6 Jan. 8	N.P. Mrs. Caroe's home, London, private performance.
Much Ado about Nothing (Shakespeare)	Jan. 17-22	
The Chinese Lantern (Housman)	Feb. 14-19	Laurence Housman attended one or more performances.
King John (Shakespeare)	Mar. 21-26	
The Three Sisters (Chekhov)	Apr. 25-30	
Doctor Knock (Romains)	May 23-28	
The Man with a Load of Mischief (Dukes)	June 16-18	Special program for Builders' and Merchants' Federation Conference.

1927 (cont.)

Robert, King of Sicily (Monck)	July 5-17	Leeds Civic Playhouse Company with 1000 extras. Kirkstall Abbey, Leeds.
The Taming of the Shrew (Shakespeare)	Sept. 26–Oct. 1	
The Provoked Wife (Vanbrugh)	Nov. 7-12	
The Sea Gull (Chekhov)	Dec. 5-10	

1928

Mr. Pepys (Bax and M. Shaw) An Episode (Schnitzler)	Jan. 9-14	Clifford Bax attended Jan. 13.
Coriolanus (Shakespeare)	Feb. 6-11	
The Lady from the Sea (Ibsen)	Mar. 12-17 Mar. 24	N.P. Arts Theatre Club, London.
Heartbreak House (Shaw)	Apr. 16-21	
Troilus and Cressida (Shakespeare)	May 14-19	
The Pleasure Garden (Mayor)	June 11-16	
Henry V (Shakespeare)	Sept. 24-29	
The Tempest (Shakespeare)	Oct. 22–Nov. 3	Leeds Civic Playhouse Company, Albert Hall, Leeds.
Minna von Barnhelm (Lessing) The Man of Destiny (Shaw)	Oct. 22-27	

1928 (cont.)

Waterloo Leave (Bax and M. Shaw) The Parable of the Industrious Wife (Monck)	Nov. 12-17	Premiere productions. Clifford Bax, Martin Shaw, and Nigel Playfair attended Nov. 12.
Rosamunde (Schubert)	Nov. 26	Maddermarket Mondays performance.
Uncle Vanya (Chekhov)	Dec. 10-15	

1929

The Merchant of Venice (Shakespeare)	Jan. 14, 16, 18, 19	
The Lady of Belmont (Ervine)	Jan. 15, 17, 19 mat.	
The Twelve Thousand (Frank) E and OE (Crawshay-Williams)	Feb. 11-16	
All for Love (Dryden)	Mar. 18-23	
Everyman (15th century)	Mar. 25-26	
Six Characters in Search of an Author (Pirandello)	Apr. 22-27	
The Fountain Head (Dukes)	June 3-8	First public performances.
Henry VIII (Shakespeare)	July 8-13	N.P. with 300 extras. Gardens of Bishop's Palace, Norwich. Bridges-Adams attended July 12.
Everyman (15th century)	Aug. 19, 21, 22 mat., 23	N.P. In front of west door of Canterbury Cathedral. Inaugural production of Canterbury Festival.

1929 (cont.)

Play	Date	Notes
Doctor Faustus (Marlowe)	Aug. 20, 22, 24	N.P. Chapter House of Canterbury Cathedral. Part of first Canterbury Festival.
The Critic (Sheridan)	Sept. 23-28	
Anatol (Schnitzler)	Oct. 21-26	
Doctor Faustus (Marlowe)	Nov. 4	Maddermarket Mondays performance.
Pericles (Shakespeare)	Nov. 18-23	
The Marquise (Coward)	Dec. 16-21	

1930

Play	Date	Notes
La Finta Giardiniera (Mozart)	Jan. 8, 10, 12	London Festival of Opera Co. New Scala Theatre, London. Robert Stuart translated.
Othello (Shakespeare)	Jan. 20-25	Christopher Fry attended several rehearsals.
The Chester Mysteries (14th century)	Feb. 21-22	N.P. Bishop's Palace, Norwich.
The Devil's Disciple (Shaw) The Maid of the Oaks (Burgoyne)	Feb. 24- Mar. 1	
Richard II (Shakespeare)	Mar. 31- Apr. 5	
The Shadows of Strife (Davidson)	May 5-10	
The Northampton Pageant (?)	May 27-31	c. 2000 performers, Abington Park, Northampton.

1930 (cont.)

The Ipswich Pageant (Monck) The Chester Shepherd's Play (14th century)	June 23–28	c. 3000 performers, Christ Church Mansion, Ipswich. Also called Cardinal Wolsey Pageant, this was Monck's adaptation of Shakespeare's Henry VIII. Prince of Wales attended June 26 mat. The Chester Shepherd's Play included in Pageant.
Love's Labour's Lost (Shakespeare)	July 14–19	N.P. Gardens of Strangers' Hall, and Madder-market Theatre, Norwich. Andrew Leigh as Sir Nathaniel. Tyrone Guthrie attended and later copied production at the Westminster Theatre, London.
The Chester Shepherd's Play (14th century)	July 24	Lecture/performance for British Drama League (BDL) School of Drama.
	July 28	Lecture/performance for BDL School. Tyrone Guthrie attended.
Love's Labour's Lost (Shakespeare)	July 31	Lecture/performance for BDL School.
The Wakefield Abraham and Isaac (14th century)	Aug. ?	N.P., ?, Bournemouth, Dorset. Inaugural pro-duction for First School of Religious Drama.

Aug. Monck visited Festivals at Salzburg and Oberammergau.

Hamlet (Shakespeare)	Sept. 24– Oct. 4
Amphitryon (Dryden)	Oct. 25, 27– Nov. 1
A Month in the Country (Turgenev)	Nov. 17–22
Saint Joan (Shaw)	Dec. 15–20

1931[x]

Hassan (Flecker)	Jan. 20-25	
The Force of Circumstance (McCreery)	Feb. 16-21,	Professional Co. with some N.P., Grafton Theatre, London.
	Feb. 23-28	Professional Co. with some N.P., Maddermarket Theatre, Norwich.
Macbeth (Shakespeare)	Mar. 23-28	
The Clandestine Marriage (Colman and Garrick)	Apr. 27-May 2	
Timon of Athens (Shakespeare)	June 1-6	
The Mayor of Zalamea (Calderón) Georges Dandin (Molière)	July 27, 30, Aug. 1 mat.	Part of Monck's Little Festival of 17th Century Music and Drama. Done in conjunction with BDL Drama School.
[The Duchess of Malfi (Webster)]	July 28, Aug. 1 eve.	Part of Monck's Little Festival. Peter Taylor Smith producer.
As You Like It (Shakespeare)	Sept. 21-26	
From Morn to Midnight (Kaiser)	Oct. 19-24	
Arms and the Man (Shaw)	Nov. 16-21	
Titus Andronicus (Shakespeare) The Magic Casement (Monck)	Dec. 14-19	

1932

The Importance of Being Earnest (Wilde)	Jan. 18-23	

[x]All productions 1921-1952 were done for N.P. at Maddermarket Theatre unless otherwise noted.

1933 (cont.)

The Wakefield Noah's Flood (14th century)	Mar. 20–21	
Death in the Tree (Sachs) Śakuntalā (Kālidāsa)		
The Pilgrim's Progress (Monck)	Mar. 22–25	
Oedipus Rex (Sophocles)	Apr. 10–15	
Too True to Be Good (Shaw)	May 1–6	
2/6 and 3/6 (Gardner) The Doll Dance (Edgar)	May 22–27	Premiere productions.
Henry VI, Part I; Part II, Acts I–III	June 19, 21, 23, 24 mat.	With these productions Monck became first pro-
Henry VI, Part II, Acts IV and V; Part III (Shakespeare)	June 20, 22, 24 eve.	ducer to stage all of Shakespeare's plays. G. B. Shaw attended June 19 and 20.
Romeo and Juliet (Shakespeare)	Sept. 18–23	Hugh Hunt as s.m. and chorus.
Gloriana (John)	Oct. 16–21	Hugh Hunt s.m.
Kantan (Seami)	Oct. 30	Maddermarket Mondays production.
A Doll's House (Ibsen)	Nov. 13–18	Hugh Hunt s.m.
The School for Scandal (Sheridan)	Dec. 11–16	Hugh Hunt s.m.

1934

All on a Summer's Day (Stephenson and Beckwith)	Jan. 4–6	Premiere, special children's production.

1934 (cont.)

The Winter's Tale (Shakespeare)　　　Jan. 22-27　　　Hugh Hunt s.m.

Monck left Norwich for holiday in Europe, c. Jan. 28.

Hugh Hunt leased Maddermarket producing End and Beginning (Masefield) and The Forced Marriage (Molière), Feb. 19-24; Much Ado about Nothing (Shakespeare), Mar. 19-24; Gammer Gurton's Needle (Anon.) and The Parting (Boltomley), Apr. 14; Strife (Galsworthy), Apr. 23-28; Macbeth (Shakespeare), May 14-19; On the Rocks (Shaw), June 11-16; Children in Uniform (Winsloe), July 9-14. (Hunt also produced The Kettering Water Mask July 25 and 26 but this was not an N.P. show.) Masefield attended Feb. 19.

The Ramsgate Pageant (?)　　　July 16-21　　　4000 performers, Ellington Park, Ramsgate. Lord Mayor of London attended Sept. 24.

Antony and Cleopatra (Shakespeare)　　　Sept. 24-29

The Six of Calais (Shaw)　　　Oct. 22-27　　　First production designed for N.P. by Barbara
A Trip to Scarborough (Sheridan)　　　Wilkes.

The Devil's in the News (Linklater)　　　Nov. 19-24　　　Linklater attended Nov. 19.

The Marvellous History of St. Bernard　　　Dec. 12-19　　　First Wed. to Wed. run.
(15th century)

1935

The Merry Wives of Windsor　　　Jan. 14-19
(Shakespeare)

The Three Sisters (Chekhov)　　　Feb. 11-16

1935 (cont.)

Title	Date	Notes
The Wakefield Mysteries (14th century) Noah's Flood, The Sacrifice of Isaac, The Annunciation, The Second Shepherd's Play	Mar. 4	N.P. Peter Hungate Church Museum, Norwich.
The Marriage of Hamlet (Sarment)	Mar. 11-16	
The Second Brother (Beddoes) The Comedy of Errors (Shakespeare)	Mar. 30, Apr. 1-6	
[The Mask and the Face (Chiarelli)]	May 13-18	Peter Taylor Smith producer.
The Nottingham and Notts Pageant (McIntire)	June 10-15	6000 performers, grounds of Wollaton Hall, Nottingham.
Twelfth Night (Shakespeare)	Aug. ?	N.P. Date and place unknown.
The Comedy of Errors (Shakespeare)	Aug. ?	N.P. Date and place unknown.
Twelfth Night (Shakespeare)	Sept. 6— Sept. 9-14	Special production for British Assoc.
Within the Gates (O'Casey)	Oct. 14-19	
Viceroy Sarah (Ginsberg)	Nov. 11-16	
Timon of Athens (Shakespeare)	Nov. 19	The Group Theatre, Westminster Theatre, London. Ernest Milton as Timon, Harcourt Williams as Apemantus, Torin Thatcher as Alcibiades.
Lady Precious Stream (Hsiung)	Dec. 9-14	

1936[x]

The Tempest (Shakespeare)	Jan. 20-25	
The Simpleton of the Unexpected Isles (Shaw)	Feb. 17-22	
Tobias and the Angel (Bridie)	Mar. 16-21	
The Last Voyage (E. and T. Thompson)	Apr. 20-25	Premiere production. Edward and Theo Thompson attended Apr. 20.
All's Well That Ends Well (Shakespeare)	May 18-23	
The Shoemaker's Holiday (Dekker)	June 22-27	N.P. Garden of Strangers' Hall, Norwich. 25th Anniv. of N.P.
The Merchant of Venice (Shakespeare)	Sept. 28-Oct. 3	
Fortune My Friend (Edgar)	Oct. 26-31	Premiere production.
Youth at the Helm (Volpius)	Nov. 16-21	
Rosamunde (Schubert)		
The Rape of the Lock (Wood)	Dec. 14-19	Premiere of The Rape of the Lock. Adaptation of Pope's poem.

1937

King Lear (Shakespeare)	Jan. 18-30	
The Millionairess (Shaw)	Feb. 15-20	
Murder in the Cathedral (Eliot)	Mar. 15-20	
[Henry V (Shakespeare)]	Apr. 19-24	Peter Taylor Smith producer.

[x]All productions 1921-1952 were done for N.P. at Maddermarket Theatre unless otherwise noted.

1937 (cont.)

[The Black Eye (Bridie)]	May 24-29	Peter Taylor Smith producer.
[Candida (Shaw)]	June 21-26	Peter Taylor Smith producer.
The Chester Pageant (?)	July 5-10	6000 performers, Chester College grounds, Chester.
Julius Caesar (Shakespeare)	Sept. 20-25	
The Queen's Pleasure (Horsnell)	Oct. 16-23	Premiere production.
The Ascent of F6 (Auden and Isherwood)	Nov. 15-20	
Miss Elizabeth Bennett (Milne)	Dec. 11-18	Adaptation of Pride and Prejudice.

1938

Measure for Measure (Shakespeare)	Jan. 24-29	
The Road to Rome (Sherwood)	Feb. 21-26	
Ah, Wilderness! (O'Neill)	Mar. 21-26	
Samson Agonistes (Milton)	Apr. 9-13	
[Richard II (Shakespeare)]	May 9-14	Peter Taylor Smith producer.
[Martine (Bernard) One Can But Try (France)]	June 13-18	Owen Paul Smyth producer.
The Manchester Pageant (?)	June 27- July 2	8000 performers, ? , Manchester.
The Masque of Anne Boleyn (Monck)	Aug. 8-10	N.P. with 300 extras, gardens of Blickling Hall, Norfolk. Queen Mary attended Aug. 10 mat.
Hamlet (Shakespeare)	Sept. 26- Oct. 1	

1938 (cont.)

Cranford (Lindsey and Russell)	Oct. 24-29	Adaptation of Gaskell's novel.
Wuthering Heights (Davidson)	Nov. 14-19	Adaptation of the Brontës' novel.
The Critic (Sheridan)	Dec. 12-17	

1939

Geneva (Shaw)	Jan. 23-28	
As You Like It (Shakespeare)	Feb. 20-25	
Judgment Day (Rice)	Mar. 20-25	
Othello (Shakespeare)	Apr. 24-29	
The Cherry Orchard (Chekhov)	May 15-20	
Caesar and Cleopatra (Shaw)	June 12-17	
The Norwich Passion Play (15th century)	July 24-29	First private production of the Maddermarket Theatre Soc.

On Aug. 11, 1939, the Maddermarket Theatre Trust Ltd. was established. Germany invaded Poland on Sept. 1, bringing Great Britain into World War II. Monck's Sept. production of Much Ado about Nothing cancelled.

In Good King Charles' Golden Days (Shaw)	Nov. 20-25	
The Wakefield Mysteries (14th century) The Annunciation, The Second Shepherd's Play, Herod and the Wise Men, The Flight into Egypt	Dec. 14-16	Last private production for the Maddermarket Theatre Soc.

1940

Title	Date	Note
The Game of Poem Cards (Chikamatsu)	Jan. 22-27	English premiere production.
Asmodee or The Intruder (Mauriac)	Feb. 19-24	
Easter (Strindberg)	Mar. 16-20	
The Highway to Heaven (Mérimée)		
[The Importance of Being Earnest (Wilde)]	Apr. 15-20	Peter Taylor Smith producer.
She Would if She Could (Etherege)	May 20-25	
Music at Night (Priestley)	June 17-22	
Much Ado about Nothing (Shakespeare)	July 15-20	
The Man with a Load of Mischief (Dukes)	Sept. 23-28	
She Had to Do Something (O'Faolain)	Nov. 18-23	English premiere production.
Twelfth Night (Shakespeare)	Dec. 14-21	Modern dress production.

1941[x]

Title	Date	Note
You Never Can Tell (Shaw)	Jan. 13-18	
Doctor Knock (Romains)	Feb. 10-15	
Don Juan in Hell (Shaw)	Mar. 10-15	Esmé Percy as Don Juan.
Don Juan (Molière)		?First English production of Molière's play.

[x]All productions 1921-1952 were done for N.P. at Maddermarket Theatre unless otherwise noted.

1941 (cont.)

The Family Reunion (Eliot)	Apr. 5-9
Amphitryon 38 (Giraudoux)	May 12-17
The Star-Crossed Lovers (Scenes from Romeo and Juliet)	May 30 — Special war charities production.
Romeo and Juliet (Shakespeare)	June 9-14
The Quiet Wedding (McCracken)	July 7-12
Spring Meeting (Farrell and Perry)	Sept. 22-27
Lavengro (Monck)	Oct. 20-25 — Adaptation of Borrow's novel.
Squaring the Circle (Kataev) Great Catherine (Shaw)	Nov. 17-22

United States enters war Dec. 7, 1941.

A Midsummer Night's Dream (Shakespeare)	Dec. 15-20

1942

She Stoops to Conquer (Goldsmith)	Jan. 19-24
Distant Point (Afinogenov)	Feb. 16-21
An Ideal Husband (Wilde)	Mar. 16-21
Everyman (15th century)	Mar. 28-31
Helen of Troy (Euripides)	Apr. 20-25

Norwich blitzed Apr. 27-29. May production cancelled.

1942 (cont.)

Play	Date	Notes
The Tempest (Shakespeare)	June 8-13	
The Philanderer (Shaw)	July 6-11	
King Lear (Shakespeare)	Sept.	Donald Wolfit Co., Prince of Wales, Cardiff. Monck also helped with Twelfth Night and A Midsummer Night's Dream.
The Winter's Tale (Shakespeare)	Sept. 21-26	
Summer at Nohant (Iwaszkiewics)	Oct. 31-Nov. 7	Premiere production.
A Farewell Supper (Schnitzler) / Magic (Chesterton)	Dec. 12-19	

1943

Play	Date	Notes
Hamlet (Shakespeare)	Jan. 30-Feb. 6	
Village Wooing (Shaw) / The Shewing-up of Blanco Posnet (Shaw)	Mar. 6-13	
House of Regrets (Ustinov)	Apr. 10-17	Curtain time 6:45.
The Rivals (Sheridan)	May 15-21	
The Western Chamber (Hsiung)	June 19-26	
Cymbeline (Shakespeare)	July 17-24	Staged with Shaw's rewriting of Act V.
The Apple Cart (Shaw)	Sept. 20-25	
Rosmersholm (Ibsen)	Oct. 18-23	
The Silver Cord (Howard)	Nov. 15-20	
The Merchant of Venice (Shakespeare)	Dec. 11-18	

1944

The School for Scandal (Sheridan)	Jan. 24–29	Premiere production.
Essex and Elizabeth (Thompson)	Feb. 21–26	
The Seagull (Chekhov)	Mar. 20–25	
The Merry Wives of Windsor (Shakespeare)	Apr. 24–29	
Misalliance (Shaw)	May 22–27	
The Taming of the Shrew (Shakespeare)	June 19–24	
Mandragola (Machiavelli)	Sept. 18–23	
The Silent Woman (Jonson)	Oct. 16–21	
The Way of the World (Congreve)	Nov. 13–18	
The Duenna (Sheridan and Linley)	Dec. 11–16	

1945

The Italian Straw Hat (Labiche)	Jan. 22–27	
Lady Windermere's Fan (Wilde)	Feb. 19–24	
Major Barbara (Shaw)	Mar. 19–24	Alec McCowan in cast.
Uncle Vanya (Chekhov)	Apr. 23–28	

War in Europe ends May 8, 1945.

The Playboy of the Western World (Synge)	May 28–June 2

1945 (cont.)

Tobacco Evil (Chekhov)
An Invitation to a Voyage (Bernard) — June 25-30

The Time of Your Life (Saroyan) — July 23-28

[The Arbitration (Menander)] — Sept. 17-22 — Owen Paul Smyth producer.

[As You Like It (Shakespeare)] — Oct. 15-20 — Owen Paul Smyth producer.

The Imaginary Invalid (Molière) — Nov. 12-17

The Good-Natur'd Man (Goldsmith) — Dec. 10-15

1946^x

The Government Inspector (Gogol) — Jan. 14-19

[King John (Shakespeare)] — Feb. 11-16 — Peter Taylor Smith producer.

[A Woman of No Importance (Wilde)] — Mar. 11-16 — Peter Taylor Smith producer.

[La Locandiera or The Innkeeper (Goldoni)] — Apr. 8-13 — J. A. Mitchley producer.

Cymbeline (Shakespeare) — Apr. 20-Sept. 28 — Shakespeare Memorial Theatre Co. Stratford-upon-Avon. Paul Scofield as Cloten, Valerie Taylor as Imogen, Donald Sinden as Arviragus.

When We Dead Awaken (Ibsen) — May 13-18

John Bull's Other Island (Shaw) — June 17-22

The Ephesian Matron (Dibden)
Marriage (Gogol) — July 15-20

A Midsummer Night's Dream (Shakespeare) — Sept. 23-28

^xAll productions 1921-1952 were done for N.P. at Maddermarket Theatre unless otherwise noted.

1946 (cont.)

The Three Sisters (Chekhov)	Oct. 21-26	
The Frogs (Aristophanes)	Nov. 18-23	
Monsieur Perrichon Takes a Holiday (Labiche)	Dec. 16-21	

1947

Othello (Shakespeare)	Jan. 20-25	
Tomorrow Will Be Different (Magno)	Feb. 17-22	
The Country Wife (Wycherley)	Mar. 17-22	
[Captain Brassbound's Conversion (Shaw)]	Apr. 14-19	Owen Paul Smyth producer.
Much Ado about Nothing (Shakespeare)	May 12-17	
Monck sent by British Council on lecture tour of Austria.		
[In Good King Charles' Golden Days (Shaw)]	June 9-14	Peter Taylor Smyth producer.
The Dark Shadow (Gardner)	July 7-12	Premiere production.
Pericles (Shakespeare)	Aug. 18-?	Shakespeare Memorial Theatre Co. Stratford-upon-Avon. Paul Scofield as Pericles. Set designs by Barry Jackson.
Everyman (15th century)	Sept. 13	N.P. Dennington Church, Dennington.
	Sept. 27	N.P. Maddermarket Theatre, Norwich.

1947 (cont.)

Production	Date	Note
Twelfth Night (Shakespeare)	Sept. 15–22	Production runs extended from 7 to 8 perfor-mances from this production on.
The Thracian Horses (Valency)	Oct. 13–20	
A Month in the Country (Turgenev)	Nov. 10–17	
Evelina (Masefield)	Dec. 8–15	Adaptation of Burney's novel.

1948

Production	Date	Note
On the Rocks (Shaw)	Jan. 12–19	
Comus (Milton)	Feb. 9–16	
The Magic Casement (Monck)		
And He Did Hide Himself (Silone)	Mar. 8–15	
Macbeth (Shakespeare)	Apr. 5–12	
Less than Kind (Mauriac)	May 3–10	
Troilus and Cressida (Shakespeare)	June 7–14	
[The Unattainable (Maugham)]	July 5–12	
Two Gentlemen of Verona (Shakespeare)	Sept. 13–20	Owen Paul Smyth producer.
Happy as Larry (MacDonagh)	Oct. 18–25	
John Gabriel Borkman (Ibsen)	Nov. 12–22	
The Beaux' Stratagem (Farquhar)	Dec. 13–20	

1949

Production	Date	Note
[Quality Street (Barrie)]	Jan. 10–17	Lionel Dunn producer.

1949 (cont.)

Richard II (Shakespeare)   Feb. 7-14

The Cherry Orchard (Chekhov)   Mar. 7-14

The Pilgrim's Progress (Monck)   Apr. 4-11

The Shadow of the Glen (Synge)   May 9-16
The Padlock (Dibden)

The Tempest (Shakespeare)   June 13-20

Jonathan Wilde (Jackson)   July 11-18   Barry Jackson's adaptation of Fielding's novel.

Romeo and Juliet (Shakespeare)   Sept. 19-26   Barry Jackson lectured at interval.

Buoyant Billions (Shaw)   Oct. 17-24

Wealth (Aristophanes)   Nov. 14-21
The Votaries (Monck)

Wives and Daughters (Macnamara)   Dec. 12-19   Adaptation of Gaskell's novel.

1950

Monck was sent by Foreign Office to lecture in Jamaica and Mexico.
Lionel Dunn produced for the N.P., The School for Scandal (Sheridan), Jan. 16-23;
The Winter's Tale (Shakespeare), Feb. 13-20; Max (Cannan), Mar. 13-20;
Coriolanus (Shakespeare), Apr. 17-24; La Parisienne (Becque), May 15-22;
Fading Mansions (MacDonagh), June 19-26; Love for Love (Congreve), July 17-24.

The Merchant of Venice (Shakespeare)   Mar. 25, 29   Little Theatre Co. Ward Theatre, Kingston,
                                            Apr. 1, 5   Jamaica.

The Fighting Bishop (Edwards)   Sept. 18-23   Premiere production.

The Doctor's Dilemma (Shaw)   Oct. 16-25

1950 (cont.)

The Indifferent Shepherd (Ustinov)	Nov. 13-20
The Merchant of Venice (Shakespeare)	Dec. 11-20

1951[x]

The Confederacy (Vanbrugh)	Jan. 22-29	
The Glass Menagerie (Williams)	Feb. 19-26	
The Two Foscari (Byron)	Mar. 12-17	
The Importance of Being Earnest (Wilde)	Apr. 9-14	
The Circle (Maugham)	May 7-12	
Pericles (Shakespeare)	June 18, 20, 22, 26, 28, 30	Part of Maddermarket Theatre Festival. Performed uncut. Arthur Colby Sprague attended one evening.
[The Taming of the Shrew (Shakespeare)]	June 19, 21, 23, 25, 27, 29	Cecily Smyth producer. Part of Maddermarket Theatre Festival.
[Captain Carvallo (Cannan)]	July 23-28	Lionel Dunn producer.
The Critic (Sheridan)	Sept. 17-26 Sept. 30	N.P. Guild Hall, King's Lynn.
Celestina (Dukes)	Oct. 15-22	
Uncle Vanya (Chekhov)	Nov. 12-19	
Love's Labour's Lost (Shakespeare)	Dec. 10-19	

[x]All productions 1921-1952 were done for N.P. at Maddermarket Theatre unless otherwise noted.

1952

Fanny's First Play (Shaw) — Jan. 21-30

[Hedda Gabler (Ibsen)] — Feb. 18-25 — Patrick Bullen producer.

The Norwich Passion Play (15th century) — Mar. 15-24

Noah Gives Thanks (Crozier) / Nishikigi (Motokiyo) — Apr. 19-28

Henry V (Shakespeare) — May 19-26

Venus Observed (Fry) — June 14-23

[The Highway to Heaven (Mérimée)] / The Cheats of Scapin (Molière) — June 12-21 — Patrick Bullen producer for Highway, Monck producer for Scapin.

June 20 mat. — N.P. Guild Hall, King's Lynn. Part of King's Lynn Festival.

[As You Like It (Shakespeare)] — Sept. 20-29 — Lionel Dunn producer.

By Candlelight (Geyer) — Oct. 20-27

[The Moment of Truth (Ustinov)] — Nov. 15-22 — Lionel Dunn producer.

The Beggar's Opera (Gay) — Dec. 15-22 — N.P. with The Amateur Opera Soc. Maddermarket Theatre, Norwich.

Nugent Monck retired Dec. 30, 1952.

1953

A Midsummer Night's Dream (Shakespeare) — Sept. 7-12 — N.P. Gardens of Bishop's Palace, Norwich.

1955

Everyman (15th century)   Jan. 7-15   N.P. Maddermarket Theatre, Norwich. Revival of Poel's 1902 touring production, using 10 of the original costumes.

Osric Dear Osric (Monck)   Feb. 2   N.P. Maddermarket Theatre, Norwich. Special production for Maddermarket Assoc.

The Wakefield Second Shepherd's Play (14th century)   June 22, 24   N.P., ? , Alderburgh. Alderburgh Festival.

The Big Field (Monck)   Sept. 30– Oct. 12   N.P. Maddermarket Theatre, Norwich. Adaptation of the 1912 Mancroft Pageant.

1957

The Masque of Cupid (Jonson)   May 24– June 4   N.P. Gardens of Blickling Hall, Norfolk. Part of Jacobean Festival organized by Monck.

*[The White Devil (Webster)]   May 24– June 4   *Monck prepared promptbook only. N.P. Maddermarket Theatre, Norwich. Frank Harwood producer. Part of Jacobean Festival.

1958

*The Magic Casement (Monck)   Feb. 1-8   *d. N.P. Maddermarket Theatre, Norwich. Frank Harwood producer.

Elizabethan Patchwork (Monck)   July 6   N.P. Maddermarket Theatre, Norwich. Special production for Maddermarket Assoc.

Nugent Monck died Oct. 21, 1958.

Appendix B

Alphabetical List of Shakespearean Productions

The following is a list of all productions of Shakespeare's plays on which Monck worked in any capacity. For the purpose of clarity, Shakespearean productions done for the Norwich Players by producers other than Monck between 1910 and 1952 have been included in this list and marked with square brackets. Each title is followed by a number indicating the order in which Monck produced it as part of the Shakespeare canon and by a complete list of years in which it was produced by Monck. For exact dates and further details, see appendix A by year.

Symbols:

[ ]   indicates productions done for the Norwich Players by producers other than Monck before Monck's retirement

+   indicates productions done by Monck for groups other than the Norwich Players

*   indicates productions on which Monck worked in a capacity other than producer, i.e., as actor or stage manager. All such Shakespearean productions were produced by William Poel.

( )   the number in parentheses immediately following each title indicates the order in which Monck completed the Shakespeare canon

+*   two symbols before a date indicate that Monck was involved in more than one production of the play in that year. Revivals of productions done earlier in any given year with the same cast appearing both times are indicated only if significant.

All's Well That Ends Well (19),
1924, 1936

Antony and Cleopatra (17), 1924,
1934

As You Like It (8), 1921, 1931,
1939, [1945], [1952]

Comedy of Errors, The (4), *1904,
1919, 1920, 1935

Coriolanus (26), 1928, [1950]

Cymbeline (15), 1923, 1943, +1946

Hamlet (18), 1924, 1930, 1938,
1943

Henry IV, Pt. I (11), 1922

Henry IV, Pt. II (16), 1923

Henry V (27), 1928, 1952, [1937]

Henry VI, Pts. I, II, & III
(35-37), 1933

Henry VIII (29), 1929

Julius Caesar (24), 1926, 1937

King John (25), 1927, [1946]

King Lear (24), 1926, 1937, +1942

Love's Labour's Lost (5), +1906
1920, 1930, 1951

Macbeth (21), *1909, +1917, 1925,
1931, 1948, [1934]

Measure for Measure (22), ?*1908,
1925, 1938

Merchant of Venice, The (2),
+1907, ?*1907, 1914, +1917,
1921, 1922, 1929, 1936, 1943,
+1950, 1950

Merry Wives of Windsor, The (7),
1921, 1924, 1935, 1944

Midsummer Night's Dream, A (13),
+1910, +1916, +1919, 1920,
1923, 1933, 1941, 1946, 1953

Much Ado about Nothing (3), *1904,
1919, 1920, 1927, 1940, 1947,
[1934]

Othello (12), 1923, 1930, 1939,
1947

Pericles (30), 1929, +1947, 1951

Richard II (31), 1930, 1949, [1938]

Richard III (34), 1932

Romeo and Juliet (6), *1905, 1920,
1925, 1933, 1941, 1949

Taming of the Shrew, The (9), +1907,
+1916, 1922, 1927, 1944, [1951]

Tempest, The (20), 1925, +1928,
1936, 1942, 1949

Timon of Athens (32), 1931, +1935

Titus Andronicus (33), 1931

Troilus and Cressida (27), 1928,
1948

Twelfth Night (1), ?*1903, +1907,
1914, +1917, ++1918, ?1919, 1922,
1926, 1935, 1940, 1947

Two Gentlemen of Verona, The (14),
+1906, *1910, 1923, 1948

Winter's Tale, The (10), 1922, 1934,
1942, [1950]

Appendix C

Alphabetical List of Productions, Excluding Shakespeare

The following is a list of all plays, excluding those by Shakespeare, on which Monck worked in any capacity. For the purpose of clarity, all non-Shakespearean productions done for the Norwich Players by producers other than Monck between 1910 and 1952 have been included in this list and marked with square brackets. Each title is followed by the author's surname and, if applicable, the name of the translator (–t) or adaptor (–a) when known, and by a complete list of years in which the play was produced by Monck. For exact dates and further details see appendix A.

Symbols:

[ ]   indicates productions done for the Norwich Players by producers other than Monck before Monck's retirement

+   indicates productions done by Monck for groups other than the Norwich Players

*   indicates productions on which Monck worked in a capacity other than producer, i.e., as playwright, actor or stage manager.

2–
+*   a number and hyphen or two symbols before a date indicate that Monck was involved in more than one production of the play in that year. Revivals of productions done earlier in any given year with the same cast appearing both times are indicated only if significant.

Abraham and Isaac
  See The Wakefield Mysteries

Adventure, An, +1917
  Milne

Adversity of Advertisement, The
  *1903
  Monck

Affected Ladies, The, 1922
  Molière

Ah, Wilderness!, 1938
  O'Neill

Alceste (opera), +1926
  Gluck

Alcestis, 1924
  Euripides

Alchemist, The, ?*1902
  Jonson

All for Love, 1929
  Dryden

All on a Summer's Day, 1934
  Stephenson & Beckwith

Amphitryon, 1930
  Dryden

Amphitryon 38, 1941
  Giraudoux

Anatol, 1929
  Schnitzler/Granville-Barker-t

And He Did Hide Himself, 1948
  Silone

And So to Bed, 1933
  Fagan

Androcles and the Lion, 1926
  Shaw

Angel Boy, The, *1900
  Monck

Apple Cart, The, 1932, 1943
  Shaw

Arbitration, The, [1945]
  Menander/Murray-t

Arms and the Man, 1931
  Shaw

Ascent of F6, The, 1937
  Isherwood & Auden

Asmodée (The Intruder), 1940
  Mauriac/Barttelt-t

Aucassin and Nicolette, 1913
  Monck & Kinder

Bacchae, The, ?*1908
  Euripides/Murray-t

Bear, The, 1932
  Chekhov

Beaux' Stratagem, The, 1926, 1948
  Farquhar

Beggar's Opera, The, 1920, 1952
  Gay/Monck-a

Bethlehem Tableaux, +1911
  Monck

Between the Showers, 1911, 1922
  Monck

Beyond Human Power, *1901
  Bjørnson

Big Field, The, 1955
  Monck

Black Eye, The, [1937]
  Bridie

Building Fund, The, ++1912
  Boyle

Buoyant Billions, 1949
  Shaw

By Candlelight, 1952
  Geyer

Caesar and Cleopatra, 1939
  Shaw

Canavans, The, +1912
   Gregory

Candida, +1917, 1920, [1937]
   Shaw

Captain Brassbound's Conversion,
   [1947]
   Shaw

Captain Carvallo, [1951]
   Cannan

Cathleen ni Houlihan, +1913
   Yeats

Celestina, 1951
   15th century Spanish/Dukes-a

Cheats of Scapin, The, 1952
   Molière/Otway-a

Cherry Orchard, The, 1926, 1939,
   1949
   Chekhov

Chester Mysteries, The (5 plays
   in various combinations),
   +1906, +1907, 1921, 1927,
   1930
   14th century
   Play of the Three Kings (only),
   1914
   The Shepherds' Play (only),
   1930

Chester Pageant, The
   See Pageants

Children in Uniform, [1934]
   Winsloe

Chinese Lantern, The, 1927
   Housman

Cinderella, +1917
   Monck

Circle, The, 1951
   Maugham

Clandestine Marriage, The, 1931
   Colman & Garrick

Cleopatra in Judea, +1907
   Symons

Coats, +1913
   Gregory

Columbine, 1914, +1917, 1922
   Arkell

Comus, 1948
   Milton

Confederacy, The, 1951
   Vanbrugh

Constant Wife, The, 1940
   Maugham

Countess Cathleen, The, ++1911,
   ++1912, +1913
   Yeats

Country Dressmaker, The, ++1912
   Fitzmaurice

Country Wife, The, 1947
   Wycherley

Coventry (or Lincoln) Mysteries,
   The
   See The Passion Play

Cradle Song, The, 1932
   Sierra

Cranford, 1938
   Gaskell/Lindsey & Russell-a

Critic, The, 1924, 1929, 1938,
   1951
   Sheridan

Cyclops, The, +1918
   Shelley

Damer's Gold, +1912, +1913
   Gregory

Daniel the Prophet, 1921
   Amherst

Dark Lady of the Sonnets, The,
   1921, 1922
   Shaw

Dark Shadow, The, 1947
   Gardner

Death in the Tree, 1933
   Sachs/Oules-a, Jackson-t

Death of Wallenstein, The, *1910
   Schiller/Coleridge-t

Dervorgilla, +1911, +1912
   Gregory

Devil's Disciple, The, 1930
   Shaw

Devil's in the News, The, 1934
   Linklater

Dialogue of D'Alcarmo, The, +1905
   Rossetti

Distant Point, 1942
   Afinogenov

Doctor Faustus, *1904, 1923, 2-1929,
   1934
   Marlowe

Doctor Knock, 1927, 1941
   Romains

Doctor's Dilemma, The, 1950
   Shaw

Doll Dance, The, 1933
   Edgar

Doll's House, A, 1933
   Ibsen

Domestic Fowl, The, *1903, +1908
   Monck

Don Juan, 1941
   Molière

Don Juan in Hell, 1941
   Shaw

Duchess of Malfi, The, 1922,
   +1925, [1931]
   Webster

Duenna, The, 1922, 1923, 1944
   Sheridan/Linley

Dumb Wife, The, 1924
   France

E and OE, 1929
   Crawshay-Williams

Easter, 1940
   Strindberg

Edward II, ?*1903
   Marlowe

Electra, 1922
   Euripides/Murray-t

Elizabethan Patchwork, 1958
   Monck

End and Beginning, [1934]
   Masefield

Ephesian Matron, The, 1946
   Dibden

Episode, An, 1928
   Schnitzler

Essex and Elizabeth, 1944
   Thompson

Evelina, 1947
   Burney

Everyman, *1902, *1903, ?*1909,
   *1910, *1913, 1913, 1924,
   2-1929, 1942, 1947, 1955
   15th century/Poel-a

Fading Mansions,[1] [1950]
   MacDonagh

Family Failing, +1913
   Boyle

---

[1] Adaptation of Romeo and Jeannette by Anouilh.

Family Reunion, The, 1941
  Eliot

Fanny's First Play, 1952
  Shaw

Farce of the Master Peter Pathelin,
  The, 1926
  17th century

Farewell Supper, A, 1942
  Schnitzler

Fête Galante, 1921, 1922
  Dobson/Monck-a

Fighting Bishop, The, 1950
  Edwards

Finta Giardiniera, La (opera),
  +1930
  Mozart/Stuart-t

First Franciscans, The, *1905
  Poel

Foiled Fiend, The, +1908
  Coke

Force of Circumstance, The, 1931
  McCreery

Forced Marriage, The, [1934]
  Molière

Fortunato, 1932
  S. & J. Quintero/Granville-
  Barker-t

Fortune My Friend, 1936
  Edgar

Fountain Head, The, 1929
  Dukes

Frogs, The, 1946
  Aristophanes/Murray-t

From Morn to Midnight, 1931
  Kaiser/Dukes-t

Galway Race, The, +1913
  Gregory

Game of Poem Cards, The, 1940
  Chikamatsu

Gammer Gurton's Needle, [1934]
  Anonymous

Gaol Gate, The, +1912, +1913
  Gregory

Geneva, 1939
  Shaw

Gentleman Dancing-Master, The, 1924
  Wycherley

Georges Dandin, 1931
  Molière

Getting Married, 1924
  Shaw

Ghost of Jerry Bundler, The, +1916
  Jacobs

Ghosts, +1906
  Ibsen/Archer-t

Glass Menagerie, The, 1951
  Williams

Gloriana, 1933
  John

Golden Mean, The, 1911
  Amherst

Good-Natur'd Man, The, ?*1906, 1945
  Goldsmith

Government Inspector, The, 1946
  Gogol

Great Catherine, 1941
  Shaw

Greatest Show on Earth, The, 1925
  Cervantes/Trend-t

Happy as Larry, 1948
  MacDonagh

Hassan, 1931
  Flecker/Dean-a

Heartbreak House, 1928
  Shaw

Heavens Shall Laugh, The, 1932
  Monck

Hedda Gabler, 1925, [1952]
  Ibsen

Helen of Troy, 1942
  Euripides

Highway to Heaven, The, 1940, [1952]
  Mérimée/Kent-t

Hippolytus, 1920
  Euripides/Murray-t

Historic Tableaux, +1909
  Monck

Holly and the Ivy, The, 1911, 1914
  Monck & Kinder

Hour, The, +1907
  Monck

Hour Glass, The, +1912, +1913
  Yeats

House of Regrets, 1943
  Ustinov

Ideal Husband, An, 1942
  Wilde

Imaginary Invalid, The, 1945
  Molière

Importance of Being Earnest, The
  +1917, 1932, 1951, [1940]
  Wilde

In a Balcony, +1905
  Browning

In Good King Charles' Golden Days,
  1939, [1947]
  Shaw

In the Beginning, ?+1909
  Monck

Indifferent Shepherd, The, 1950
  Ustinov

Interlude of Youth, The, +1905,
  +1907, +1911, 1913, 1914
  15th century

Intruder, The
  See Asmodée

Invitation to a Voyage, An, 1945
  Bernard

Ipswich Pageant, The
  See Pageants

Italian Straw Hat, The, 1945
  Labiche/Kent-t

Job, 1911, 1913, [1912], [1913]
  Biblical/Amherst-a

John Bull's Other Island, 1946
  Shaw

John Gabriel Borkman, 1948
  Ibsen

Jonathan Wilde, 1949
  Fielding/Jackson-a

Judgment Day, 1939
  Rice

Kantan, 1923, 1933
  Seami

King Argimenes and the Unknown
  Warrior, +1911
  Dunsany

King Monmouth, 1922
  Presland

Ladies' Game of Poem Cards, The
  See Game of Poem Cards

Lady from the Sea, The, 1928
  Ibsen

Lady of Belmont, The, 1929
  Ervine

Lady Precious Stream, 1935
  Hsiung

Lady Windermere's Fan, 1945
  Wilde

Land of Heart's Desire, The, +1912
  +1913, +1916, 1919
  Yeats

Last Voyage, The, 1936
  E. & T. Thompson

Lavengro, 1941
  Borrow/Monck-a

Leeds Pageant, The
  See Pageants

Less than Kind, 1948
  Mauriac

Life's Measure, +1905
  Monck

Locandiera, La (The Innkeeper),
  [1946]
  Goldoni

Love for Love, [1950]
  Congreve

Love the Doctor
  +1917
  Molière/Greene-t

Ludus Coventriae
  See Passion Play

MacDarragh's Wife, +1911, +1912
  Gregory

Machine Wreckers, The, +1923
  Toller/Dukes-t

Magic, 1942
  Chesterton

Magic Casement, The, 1924, [1925],
  1931, 1948, *1958
  Monck

Magistrate, The, +1909
  Pinero

Magnanimous Lover, The, +1913
  Ervine

Maid of the Oaks, The, 1930
  Burgoyne

Major Barbara, 1945
  Shaw

Man in Rags, The, *1901
  Monck

Man of Destiny, The, 1928
  Shaw

Man with a Load of Mischief, The,
  1926, 1927, 1940
  Dukes

Manchester Pageant, The
  See Pageants

Mancroft Pageant, The
  See Pageants

Mandragola, 1944
  Machiavelli/Dukes-a

Marquise, The, 1929
  Coward

Marriage, 1932, 1946
  Gogol/Monck-a

Marriage, The, ++1911, +1912
  Hyde

Marriage à la Mode, 1926
  Dryden

Marriage of Hamlet, The, 1935
  Sarment/Morland-t

Martine, [1938]
   Bernard

Marvellous History of St. Bernard,
   The, 1934
   15th century/Ghèon-a, Jackson-t

Mary Stuart, 1925
   Drinkwater

Mask and the Face, The, [1935]
   Chiarelli

Masque of Anne Boleyn, The, +1909,
   1925, 1938
   Monck

Masque of Cupid, The, 1957
   Jonson

Maurice Hart, +1913
   Murray

Max, [1950]
   Cannan

May Lady, The, 1924
   Sidney

Mayor of Zalamea, The, 1931
   Calderón

Merchandise, 1914
   Monck & Kinder

Mill, The, +1908
   Monck

Millionairess, The, 1937
   Shaw

Mimes of Herodias, The
   See Three Mimes

Minna von Barnhelm, 1928
   Lessing

Misalliance, 1944
   Shaw

Miss Elizabeth Bennett, 1937
   Milne

Mixed Marriage, The, +1913
   Ervine

Mock Doctor, The, 1914, 1922
   Molière

Moment of Truth, The, [1952]
   Ustinov

Monsieur Perrichon Takes a Holiday,
   1946
   Labiche

Month in the Country, A, 1930, 1947
   Turgenev

Mr. Pepys, 1928
   Bax & M. Shaw

Murder in the Cathedral, 1937
   Eliot

Music at Night, 1940
   Priestley

Narcissus, +1910
   Monck

Nativity Play, The, +1911, +1912
   Hyde

New Way to Pay Old Debts, A, 1921
   Massinger

Nishikigi (Love Wand), 1919, 1923,
   1952
   Motokiyo

Noah Gives Thanks, 1952
   Crozier

Noah's Flood
   See The Wakefield Mysteries

Northampton Pageant, The
   See Pageants

Norwich Mysteries, The
   See Paradyse

Norwich Pageant, The
   See Pageants

Quiet Wedding, The, 1941
  McCracken

Ramsgate Pageant, The
  See Pageants

Rape of the Lock, The, 1936
  Pope/Wood and Marillier-a

Red King, The, 1924
  Wheldon

Red Turf, +1911, +1912
  Mayne

Redemption of Agnes, The, ?*1907
  Poel

Revelry, 1921
  Monck

Rising of the Moon, The, ++1912,
  +1913
  Gregory

Rivals, The, 1920, 1923, 1943
  Sheridan

Road to Rome, The, 1938
  Sherwood

Robert King of Sicily
  See Pageants, Leeds

Rosamunde, 1928, 1936
  Schubert & Chezy/Monck-a

Rosemary, +1910
  Parker

Rosmersholm, 1943
  Ibsen

Saint George and the Dragon, 1911,
  1912
  Traditional/Monck-a

Saint Joan, 1930
  Shaw

Saint Patrick's Day or the Scheming
  Lieutenant
  See The Scheming Lieutenant

Śakuntalā, 1923, 1933
  Kālidāsa

Samson Agonistes, ?*1908, 1938
  Milton

Scheming Lieutenant, The, 1925
  Sheridan

School for Scandal, The, ?+1919,
  1920, 1923, 1933, 1944, [1950]
  Sheridan

Seagull, The, 1927, 1944
  Chekhov

Second Brother, The, 1935
  Beddoes

Second Shepherd's Play, The
  See The Wakefield Mysteries

Servant of Two Masters, The, 1932
  Goldoni

Shadow of the Glen, The, ++1911,
  +1913, 1949
  Synge

Shadows of Strife, The, 1930
  Davison

She Had to Do Something, 1940
  O'Faolain

She Stoops to Conquer, 1921, 1942
  Goldsmith

She Would if She Could, 1940
  Etherege

Shewing-up of Blanco Posnet, The
  1943
  Shaw

Shipboy, The, 1922
  Monck

Shoemaker's Holiday, The, 1936
  Dekker

Silent Woman, The, 1944
  Jonson

Silver Cord, The, 1943
Jonson

Simpleton of the Unexpected Isles,
The, 1936
Shaw

Six Characters in Search of an
Author, 1929
Pirandello

Six of Calais, The, 1934
Shaw

Song of Songs, The, +1908, 1921
Biblical/Monck-a

Spreading the News, ++1912, +1913
Gregory

Spring Meeting, 1941
Farrell & Perry

Squaring the Circle, 1941
Kataev/Dukes-t

Strife, [1934]
Galsworthy

Summer at Nohant, 1942
Iwaszkiewics

Sun's Darling, The, +1906
Ford & Dekker

Thracian Horses, The, 1947
Valency

Three Mimes, 1920
Herodias

Three Sisters, The, 1927, 1935,
1946
Chekhov

Time of Your Life, The, 1945
Saroyan

Tincear agus an T-Sidheog, An
See next entry

Tinker and the Fairy, The, ++1912
Hyde

Tobacco Evil, 1945
Chekhov

Tobias and the Angel, 1936
Bridie

Tomorrow Will Be Different, 1947
Magno

Too True to Be Good, 1933
Shaw

Touch of Truth, A, +1916
Walbrook

Towneley Mysteries, The
See The Wakefield Mysteries

Tragedy of Nan, The, 1921
Masefield

Trip to Scarborough, A, 1934
Sheridan

Trojan Women, The, [1925]
Euripides

Twelve Thousand, The, 1929
Frank

2/6 and 3/6, 1933
Gardner

Two Foscari, The, 1951
Byron

Two Idylls, The, 1920
Theocritus

Unattainable, The, [1948]
Maugham

Uncle Vanya, 1928, 1945, 1951
Chekhov

Venus Observed, 1952
Fry

Viceroy Sarah, 1935
    Ginsbury

Village Wooing, 1943
    Shaw

Vision, The, +1906
    Norton

Votaries, The, +1908, 1911, 1949
    Monck

Wakefield Mysteries, The (8 plays
    in various combinations), +1912,
    1919, 1935, 1939
    14th century/Monck-a
    Abraham and Isaac (only), 1912,
    1922, 1923, 1926, 1930
    Noah's Flood (only), 1933
    The Second Shepherd's Play
    (only), 1910, +1911, +1912,
    1955

Waterloo Leave, 1928
    Bax & M. Shaw

Way of the World, The, 1923, 1944
    Congreve

Wealth, 1949
    Aristophanes

Well of the Saints, The, +1911
    Synge

Western Chamber, The, 1943
    Hsiung

When We Dead Awaken, 1946
    Ibsen

White Devil, The, *1957
    Webster

Witch, The, 1932
    Wiers-Jennsen/Masefield-a

Within the Gates, 1935
    O'Casey

Wives and Daughters, 1949
    Gaskell/Macnamara-a

Wolsey Pageant, The
    See Pageants, Ipswich

Woman of No Importance, A, [1946]
    Wilde

Women Have Their Way, The, 1932
    S. & J. Quintero/Granville-
    Barker-t

Workhouse Ward, The, +1911, +1912,
    +1913, +1916
    Gregory

World and the Child, The, 2-1910,
    ++1912, 1913
    16th century/Monck-a

World of Light, The, 1932
    Huxley

Worship No More, 1932
    Gardner

Wuthering Heights, 1938
    Brontë/Davidson-a

Yorkshire Tragedy, The, 1921
    Anonymous

You Never Can Tell, 1941
    Shaw

Youth
    See The Interlude of Youth

Youth at the Helm, 1936
    Volpius/Griffith-a

Notes

Introduction

1. George Bernard Shaw, Letter to Nugent Monck, 22 May 1940. Property of Jack Hall, Pulham Market, Norfolk, England. Partially reproduced in Andrew Stephenson, *The Maddermarket Theatre* (Norwich: Soman-Wherry Press for the Maddermarket Theatre Trust, 1971), front.

2. Allardyce Nicoll, *English Drama 1900–1930* (Cambridge: At the Univ. Press, 1973), pp. 1–25.

3. Norman Marshall, *The Other Theatre* (London: John Lehmann, 1947).

4. Gerald Clifford Weales, *Religion in Modern English Drama* (Philadelphia: Univ. of Pennsylvania Press, 1961), pp. 96–97.

5. Marshall, *Other Theatre,* p. 95.

6. Oscar G. Brockett and Robert R. Findlay, *Century of Innovation* (Englewood Cliffs, N.J.: Prentice-Hall, 1973), p.470.

Chapter 1

1. *"One Man in His Time,"* Reminiscent Talk by Nugent Monck, Pt. I, BBC radio, 30 Dec. 1952. TS of pp. 4–6 in Monck Collection, Norfolk Record Office, Central Library, Norwich, Eng., p. 4.

2. Nugent Monck, Unfinished Autobiography MS, Monck Collection, Norfolk Record Office, Central Library, Norwich, England, p. 40. Pages are numbered 35–50, the first 8 pages being TS. There is some duplication of material among the pages.

3. Laurence Henry Forster Irving, *Henry Irving* (London: Faber & Faber, 1951), pp. 109–10 and 460–61.

4. Autobiography MS, p. 41.

5. *Eastern Evening News,* 3 Nov. 1937.

6. Letter received from Miss M. J. Harington, 1 Aug. 1979.

7. Alan Dent, *Mrs. Patrick Campbell* (London: Museum Press, 1961), p. 186.

8. Ibid., p. 188.

9. See Robert Speaight's highly regarded work, *William Poel and the Elizabethan Revival* (London: Society for Theatre Research), 1954, p. 126.

10. William Poel, *Monthly Letters* (London: T. Werner Laurie, 1929), p. 44.

11. William Poel, *Shakespeare in the Theatre* (London: Sedgwick and Jackson, 1913), pp. 120–21.

12. Brockett and Findlay, p. 188.

13. Speaight, *Poel,* p. 103.

14. Sir Lewis Casson, "William Poel and the Modern Theatre," *The Listener,* 10 Jan. 1952, p. 56.

15. *One Man,* I, p. 5.

16. Cast lists for 1905 for these two Societies are not available for comparison, but Esmé Percy, Clare Greet, Lucy Wilson, and Courtenay Thorpe acted for both Poel and Monck over the next few years, and Miss Jennie Moore designed and made costumes for both producers.

17. *Freeman's Journal* [Dublin], 24 Nov. 1911.

18. Speaight, *Poel,* p. 68.

19. *"The Scene wherein We Play In,"* BBC radio, 11 Jan. 1953, TS, in Monck Collection, p. 2. [This title is a quotation from *As You Like It,* II, vii, 137–38].

20. Speaight, *Poel,* p. 81.

21. M. St. Clare Byrne, "Stage Lighting," *The Oxford Companion to the Theatre,* ed. Phyllis Hartnoll, 3rd. ed. (London: Oxford Univ. Press, 1967), p. 569.

22. Speaight, *Poel,* p. 68.

23. Ibid., p. 100.

24. Ibid., p. 70.

25. Ibid., pp. 68–69.

26. Ibid., p. 178.

27. Ibid., p. 156.

28. Ibid., p.105.

29. Ibid., p. 235.

30. See *Eastern Daily Press,* 7 Sept. 1910 and 19 June 1936.

31. *Eastern Daily Press,* 26 March 1930.

32. R. W. Cook, "The Norwich Players," *John O'London's Weekly,* 20 May 1922, p. 1.

33. Peter Kavanagh, *The Story of the Abbey Theatre* (New York: Devin Adair, 1950), p. 83.

34. Eleven letters written by W. B. Yeats to Nugent Monck between 4 Feb. 1911 and 13 Feb. 1922 are in the possession of Mr. Monck's heir, Jack Hall, Pulham Market, Norfolk, Eng.

35. Edward Hale Bierstadt, in his book *Dunsany the Dramatist* (Boston: Little Brown, 1920), confuses this production with the earlier one done by Robinson at the Abbey on January 26, 1911. Monck was busy in Norwich in January 1911 and could not have done a production at the Abbey as Bierstadt claims.

36. Three letters written by Lady Gregory to Nugent Monck, dated 15, 17, and 19 Sept. 1911, are in the possession of Jack Hall, Pulham Market, Norfolk, Eng.

37. A more detailed account of the activities of the Abbey Theatre School of Acting can be found in Robert Hogan et al., *The Modern Irish Drama, A Documentary History*, vol. 4, *The Rise of the Realists 1910–1915*, (Dublin: Dolmen Press, 1979), pp. 132–79, and in Franklin Joseph Hildy, *Reviving Shakespeare's Stagecraft: Nugent Monck and the Maddermarket Theatre, Norwich, England* (Ann Arbor: UMI, 1980) pp. 77–110.

38. Andrew P. Wilson, "Dublin Days—and Nights—II," *The Scottish Stage*, Nov. 1933, p. 184.

39. Letter, 15 Dec. 1911. All quotes from the letters of W. B. Yeats to Lady Gregory are taken from Xerox copies (originals in possession of Michael B. Yeats, 1970) in the Irish National Library, MSS. 18,718–18,724.

40. Yeats, Letter to Lady Gregory, 18 Nov. 1911. See also undated letter [late Feb. 1912], Irish National Library MS 18,720 and letter dated 14 April 1912.

41. *Freeman's Journal* [Dublin], 17 Nov. 1911, p. 9b.

42. Edward Martyn was a highly respected Catholic who was also a playwright and one of the founding directors of the Irish Literary Theatre.

43. *Freeman's Journal*, 24 Nov. 1911, p. 8b.

44. Yeats, Letter to Lady Gregory, 7 Jan. 1912.

45. Yeats, Letter to Lady Gregory, 29 Nov. 1911.

46. Yeats, Letter to Lady Gregory, 7 Dec. 1911.

47. *Irish Independent*, 15 Dec. 1911, cutting appended to Yeats's letter to Lady Gregory, 15 Dec. 1911.

48. Yeats, Letter to Lady Gregory, 2 Jan. 1912.

49. *Freeman's Journal*, 30 Dec. 1911, p. 5f.

50. *Freeman's Journal*, 5 Jan. 1912, p. 8g.

51. Yeats, Letter to Lady Gregory, 11 Jan. 1912.

52. *Freeman's Journal*, 20 Jan. 1912, p. 8f.

53. *Irish Times*, 19 Jan. 1912, in "Joseph Holloway Collection of Newscuttings on Theatre and the Arts," Jan. 1912, National Library of Ireland MS. 23,125. All subsequent citations of Irish newspapers given without page numbers are in this collection.

54. Yeats, Letter to Lady Gregory, 21 Jan. 1912.

55. Denis Bablet, *Edward Gordon Craig*, trans. Daphne Woodward (New York: Theatre Arts Books, 1966), p. 125.

56. Edward Craig, *Gordon Craig* (New York: Knopf, 1968), p. 254.

57. Hugh Hunt, *The Abbey* (Dublin: Gill and Macmillan, 1979), p. 97.

58. Yeats, Letter to Lady Gregory, 16 Feb. 1912.

59. *Evening Telegraph*, 23 Feb. 1912.

60. "Holloway Newscuttings," March 1912, National Library of Ireland MS. 23,127.

61. Cast lists for the first productions can be found in Lennox Robinson, *Ireland's Abbey Theatre* (London: Sedgwick, 1951), pp. 106–07, and in Hogan et al., *The Modern Irish Drama*, vol. 4, pp. 449–59.

62. James W. Flannery, *W. B. Yeats and the Idea of a Theatre* (New Haven: Yale Univ. Press, 1976), p. 275.

63. Hunt, *The Abbey*, p. 77.

64. Joseph Holloway, *Joseph Holloway's Abbey Theatre*, ed. Robert Hogan and Michael J. O'Neill (Carbondale: Univ. of Southern Illinois Press, 1967), p. 156.

65. Letter received from Andrew Stephenson, 5 Feb. 1980.

66. Kavanagh, p. 98.

67. Yeats, Letter to Lady Gregory, 17 Feb. 1913.

68. *One Man*, II.

69. *Joseph Holloway's Abbey Theatre*, p. 160.

70. *Eastern Daily Press*, 22 Sept. 1953.

71. Letter to Nugent Monck, 22 Dec. 1932, in Monck Collection.

72. *One Man*, II.

73. Poel, *Monthly Letters*, p. 84.

Chapter 2

1. Maurice Browne, *Too Late to Lament* (London: Victor Gollancz, 1955), p. 116.

2. Browne, p. 124.

3. *Eastern Daily Press*, 29 Nov. 1912.

4. *Eastern Evening News*, 2 Nov. 1937.

5. *Eastern Daily Press*, 9 Jan. 1955.

6. "An Elizabethan Playhouse: The Norwich Enterprise," *Manchester Guardian*, 2 Nov. 1921.

7. Personal interview with William Hewett, 3 May 1979. Mr. Hewett served as the Norwich Players' electrician, 1919–73.

8. E. J. Wood, "An Interesting Experiment," *The Gong*, May 1922, p. 247.

9. John Ruskin, *The Stones of Venice*, Vol. II (London: Smith, Elder, 1853), op. p. 138.

10. Autobiography outline, TS, Monck Collection, p. 4.

11. For a more detailed description of Monck's WWI experience see Hildy, *Reviving Shakespeare's Stagecraft*, pp. 126–38.

12. *Eastern Daily Press*, 25 Sept. 1919, p. 7b.

13. William Poel, *What Is Wrong with Our Stage* (London: Allen and Unwin, 1920), p. 25.

14. Mariette Soman and F. W. Wheldon, *The Norwich Players* (Norwich: Mariette Soman, 1920), p. 29.

15. *Eastern Daily Press,* 3 Feb. 1921, p. 8d.

16. Soman and Wheldon, p. 29.

17. Personal interview with Betty Stephenson, 23 Apr. 1979. Mrs. Stephenson began acting with the Norwich Players in the late 1920s and was elected a Player in 1937.

18. *Eastern Daily Press,* 15 June 1920, p. 7g.

19. Sir Nigel Playfair, *Hammersmith Hoy* (London: Faber & Faber, 1930), pp. 221-23.

20. Letter to Nugent Monck [c. May 1923], Monck Collection.

21. (Sir) Nigel Playfair, ed., *The Duenna by Richard Brinsley Sheridan* (London: Constable, 1925), p. xviii.

22. Personal interview with Mrs. Owen Paul (Cecily) Smyth, 19 Sept. 1979. Mrs. Smyth began acting with the Norwich Players in 1921, was elected a Player in 1926, and produced *The Taming of the Shrew* for them in 1951.

23. *Eastern Daily Press,* 18 Jan. 1927.

24. Norman Marshall lists these nine plays as the major Lyric productions in *The Other Theatre,* p. 36. Information on first revivals is taken from Harold Child, "Revivals of English Dramatic Works, 1919-1925," *Review of English Studies,* Apr. 1926, pp. 7-12.

25. *Eastern Daily Press,* 12 Nov. 1928.

26. *Eastern Daily Press,* 2 Nov. 1920, p. 6b.

27. A more detailed description of the Maddermarket Theatre property and conversion can be found in Hildy, *Reviving Shakespeare's Stagecraft,* pp. 152-84.

28. W. J. Lawrence, *The Elizabethan Playhouse and Other Studies,* 2 vols. (Stratford-upon-Avon: Shakespeare Head Press, 1912-13). Copy dated Apr. 1921 is in Monck's library, property of Jack Hall. [E. K. Chambers's definitive study on *The Elizabethan Stage* did not appear until 1923.]

29. Nugent Monck, "The Maddermarket Theatre and the Playing of Shakespeare," *Shakespeare Survey* 12 (1958), 72.

30. C. Walter Hodges, *The Globe Restored* (1953; rpt. New York: Norton, 1973), pp. 19-21.

31. R. H., "The Maddermarket Theatre, Norwich," *The Garrick Magazine* 10, No. 1 (1926), 5.

32. A discussion of several of these objections is taken up in chapter 3. For an analysis of some of the more dubious features of the models upon which the Maddermarket was based, see Richard Hosley, "The Origins of the So-called Elizabethan Multiple Stage," *The Drama Review* 12 (Winter 1968), 28-50. For an indication of the most modern view of the Elizabethan stage, see C. Walter Hodges, *Shakespeare's Second Globe* (London: Oxford Univ. Press, 1973). For an indication of the most modern view of the Globe Playhouse itself see John Orrell, *The Quest for Shakespeare's Globe* (Cambridge: Cambridge Univ. Press, 1983).

33. Yeats, Letter to Nugent Monck, 6 Sept. 1921, property of Jack Hall.

34. Yeats, Letter, 20 Oct. 1921, property of Jack Hall.

35. *Eastern Evening News,* 22 Sept. 1944.

36. *The Times,* 27 Sept. 1921.

37. *The Times,* 8 Jan. 1953, p. 9b.

38. *Manchester Guardian,* 1 Oct. 1921.

39. *Sunday Herald,* 2 Oct. 1921.

40. Nugent Monck, *On Retiring from the Maddermarket Theatre,* BBC radio, 16 Nov. 1952, London, Broadcast House Recording Library, No. 17,955 back.

41. *Italian Mail and Tribune,* 31 Oct. 1931.

42. *Scrutiny,* Dec. 1935, p. 258.

43. G. Wilson Knight, *Shakespearian Production* (Evanston: Northwestern Univ. Press, 1964), p. 79. Section quoted rpt. 1936.

44. *Yorkshire Post* [Leeds], 8 April 1930.

45. Brockett and Findlay, p. 223.

46. These alterations are detailed in *Eastern Daily Press,* 21 Sept. 1926, *Eastern Daily Press,* 25 Oct. 1927, and *Eastern Evening News,* 25 Feb. 1930.

Chapter 3

1. Monck, "Playing of Shakespeare," p. 72.

2. *Eastern Daily Press,* 27 Sept. 1921.

3. *Norfolk Chronicle,* 30 Sept. 1921.

4. Quoted in J. L. Styan, *The Shakespeare Revolution* (Cambridge: Cambridge Univ. Press, 1977), p. 28.

5. Monck, "Dramatic Art and Mysticism in Modern Life," TS in Monck Collection, p. 9.

6. Board of Education, Adult Education Committee, *The Drama in Adult Education* (London: His Majesty's Stationery Office, 1926), p. 191.

7. James Stinson, "Reconstructions of Elizabethan Public Playhouses," in *Studies in the Elizabethan Theatre,* ed. Charles T. Prouty (Hamden, Conn.: The Shoe String Press, 1961), pp. 60 and 112, fn. 6.

8. Hunt, *The Live Theatre* (London: Oxford Univ. Press, 1962), p. 76.

9. Hugh Hunt appeared in the role of the Chorus in Monck's 1934 production of *Romeo and Juliet.*

10. *The Nation,* 17 Jan. 1925.

11. *Vogue,* 1 Feb. 1925.

12. This solution may represent Monck's first major contribution to modern notions of Shakespeare's stagecraft. Lawrence proposed the use of exactly such staircases three years later in *Pre-Restoration Stage Studies* (Cambridge, Mass.: Harvard Univ. Press, 1927, pp. 16–23). Adams refutes Lawrence in "Appendix D" of his *The Globe Playhouse,* but his argument rests primarily on the notion that the staircases were permanent fixtures. As recently as 1971 T. J. King has again proposed the existence of such staircases in *Shakespearean Staging, 1599–1642* (Cambridge, Mass.: Harvard Univ. Press, 1971), p. 37.

13. Nugent Monck, "Shakespeare and the Amateur," *The Listener,* 17 Feb. 1937, p. 322.

14. Reynolds, p. 161.

15. Norman Marshall, "The Production of Shakespeare's Plays To-day," *The Bookman,* Apr. 1932, p. 63.

16. This was the curtain location used by Poel. See Speaight, *Poel,* p. 114.

17. Marshall, "Production of Shakespeare," p. 64.

18. "Diary," *The Scots Observer,* 2 Apr. 1931, p. 7.

19. R. H., "The Maddermarket," *The Garrick Magazine,* No. 2 (1926), 21.

20. "Shakespeare, His Life and Times," TS in Monck Collection, p. 7.

21. *Morning Post,* 25 Sept. 1924.

22. Norman Marshall, *The Producer and the Play,* 2nd ed. (London: Macdonald, 1962), p. 147.

23. *Eastern Daily Press,* 4 Nov. 1950.

24. *Eastern Daily Press,* 8 May 1924, report on Monck's lecture "The Work of The Maddermarket Theatre."

25. Speaight, *Poel,* p. 104.

26. Program to *Julius Caesar,* 20–25 Sept. 1937, in Monck Collection.

27. Poel, *Manchester Guardian,* 1 Oct. 1921.

28. "Balance sheets," income and expenditures for the Maddermarket Theatre, 1926–52, in Monck Collection. Thirteen years are missing; these figures are based on averages of available figures.

29. *"The Scene wherein We Play In,"* p. 30.

30. *Eastern Daily Press,* 1 Apr. 1924.

31. *Eastern Daily Press,* 1 Dec. 1925.

32. *Eastern Daily Press,* 1 Apr. 1924.

33. Monck, "Stage Setting, Costumes and Lighting," TS synopsis of lecture, in Monck Collection.

34. *Eastern Daily Press,* 13 Oct. 1931, report on Monck's lecture, "Expressionism."

35. *Eastern Daily Press,* 31 Aug. 1943.

36. *Morning Post,* 21 Aug. 1929.

37. *Eastern Daily Press,* 13 Oct. 1931.

38. *Eastern Evening News,* 12 June 1925.

39. Personal interview with William Hewett, 3 May 1979.

40. Personal interview with William Hewett, 3 May 1979.

41. *Eastern Daily Press,* 16 Nov. 1925.

42. Speaight, *Poel,* p. 119.

43. Poel, *Monthly Letters,* p. 88.

44. *Daily Chronicle,* 9 Jan. 1913.

45. Quoted in Board of Education, *Drama in Adult Education,* p. 162.

46. *Eastern Daily Press,* 24 Jan. 1933.

47. Fowler, *Eastern Daily Press,* 23 Oct. 1958, p. 4fg.

48. Marshall, *Other Theatre,* pp. 27, 51, 92, 167.

49. *The Bookman,* Feb. 1931, p. 326.

50. Marshall letter to Monck in Monck Collection.

51. "Personalities and Power," *Time and Tide,* 8 Oct. 1926, p. 901.

52. *Eastern Daily Press,* 22 Nov. 1921.

53. *Eastern Daily Press,* 13 Dec. 1921.

54. *Eastern Daily Press,* 29 May 1923.

55. *Daily Film Review* [London], 11 Feb. 1928.

56. *Eastern Daily Press,* 22 Jan. 1924.

57. *Daily Telegraph,* 3 Dec. 1925.

58. *Daily News,* 26 March 1928, and *Daily Telegraph,* 26 March 1928.

59. *Christian Science Monitor,* 9 Jan. 1928.

60. *"Six Characters in Search of an Author* at the Maddermarket Theatre, Norwich," *Festival Theatre Review,* 4 May 1929.

61. R. H. Mottram, "The Maddermarket," *War Time Drama,* Nov. 1942, p. 6.

62. Whiffler, "Over the Tea Table," *Eastern Daily Press,* 2 Sept. 1940.

63. *"The Scene wherein We Play In,"* p. 24.

64. Ibid., p. 26.

65. *The Garrick Magazine* 10, no. 1 (1926), 2.

66. *The Maddermarket Theatre Norwich: Programme to Mark Its Golden Jubilee and the Memory of Nugent Monck,* BBC radio, 17 Nov. 1960, London, Broadcast House Recording Library, No. 26,625 front.

67. Soman and Wheldon, pp. 21–22.

68. Nugent Monck, "The Producer and His Place in the Theatre," *Yorkshire Post,* 11 Feb. 1930, p. 6.

69. Personal interview with Beryl Starling, 19 Sept. 1979.

70. *Eastern Daily Press,* 3 Oct. 1934.

71. *Eastern Daily Press,* 13 Oct. 1931, report on Monck's lecture, "Expressionism."

72. Personal interview with Jack Hall, 7 Oct. 1979.

73. Stephenson, *Maddermarket* 1971, n. pag. [5].

74. *Eastern Daily Press,* 4 Nov. 1960.

75. Marshall, "The Production of Shakespeare's Plays To-day," p. 64.

76. *Eastern Daily Press*, 3 Sept. 1934.

76. Monck, "Shakespeare and the Amateur," p. 323.

77. *The Nation*, 9 Apr. 1927.

79. Board of Education, p. 163.

80. *Birmingham Post*, 4 March 1958.

Chapter 4

1. Editorial leader to Ross Hills, "The Maddermarket Theatre, Norwich," *Tabs* 19 (Dec. 1961), 17.

2. Eric Fowler, "Maddermarket Centenary," *East Anglia Magazine*, p. 350.

3. Herbert Farjeon, *The Shakespeare Scene* (London: Hutchinson, 1949), pp. 60–61.

4. Marshall, *Other Theatre*, p. 13.

5. *Yarmouth Independent*, 30 Nov. 1928. See also *Eastern Daily Press*, 2 May 1929.

6. Nicoll, p. 53.

7. *"The Scene wherein We Play In,"* p. 20.

8. Marshall, *Other Theatre*, pp. 165–67.

9. *Eastern Daily Press*, 20 Sept. 1949.

10. All records of the 1946 broadcast have been lost. The TS of the 1953 program, *"The Scene wherein We Play In,"* exists, but in the spot where Jackson's contribution appeared, there is merely the note "to be recorded." The same note is given where Sybil Thorndike's tribute to Monck's work was to occur in the broadcast.

11. *Eastern Daily Press*, 23 Oct. 1958, p. 6ab.

12. *Pall Mall Gazette*, 8 May 1923.

13. *Herald*, 8 May 1923; *Express*, 8 May 1923; *The London Mercury*, June 1923.

14. *"The Scene wherein We Play In,"* p. 21.

15. Shaw's letter to Nugent Monck, 25 Jan. 1923, property of Jack Hall.

16. *Norwich Mercury*, 5 Apr. 1924.

17. Francis Birrell, "The Drama: On Acting Shakespeare," *The Nation and The Athenaeum*, 12 Apr. 1924, p. 50.

18. "Romeo and Juliet at Norwich," *Vogue*, 1 Feb. 1925, n. pag., in Monck Collection.

19. *Observer*, 17 May 1931.

20. *Eastern Daily Press*, 17 Apr. 1928.

21. *Eastern Daily Press*, 28 Aug. 1956.

22. *Morning Post*, 23 and 25 Sept. 1924.

23. *Eastern Daily Press,* 24 Oct. 1924. Twenty-five letters written by George Bernard Shaw to Nugent Monck between 18 July 1906 and 24 Apr. 1950 are in the possession of Jack Hall, Pulham Market, Norfolk, Eng.

24. *Eastern Daily Press,* 18 Nov. 1924.

25. *Vogue,* 1 Feb. 1925; and *The Nation,* 17 Jan. 1925, n. pag., in Monck Collection.

26. *Eastern Daily Press,* 14 Aug. 1925.

27. Huntley Carter, *The New Spirit in the European Theatre, 1914-*1925 (London: Ernest Bonn, 1925), p. 267.

28. H. Watson Vince, "The British Repertory Theatres, No. X; The Maddermarket Theatre, Norwich," *Theatre World,* March 1928, pp. 26–27.

29. Board of Education, p. 4.

30. *Eastern Evening News,* 7 Feb. 1928.

31. Personal interview with Andrew Stephenson, 23 Jan. 1979.

32. *Eastern Evening News,* n.d. [Aug. 1928?], in Monck Collection.

33. Marshall, *Other Theatre,* p. 95.

34. The production was given in a translation by Stuart, under the title *Orpheus.*

35. *Eastern Daily Press,* 21 Sept. 1926. *The Norwich Pageant* was filmed by J. H. Willis for the Haymarket and Regent Picture Houses. After a private showing on July 24, 1926, the film was turned over to the Norwich Publicity Committee. No copy of the film is now available.

36. Six letters from Harley Granville-Barker to Nugent Monck written between August 1926 and June 1931 are in the Monck Collection.

37. *Eastern Evening News,* 31 Aug. 1943.

38. *The Times,* 23 June 1927.

39. *Toronto Globe,* 23 Nov. 1926.

40. Harley Granville-Barker, *Prefaces to Shakespeare,* Vol. 2, ed. M. St. Clare Byrne (Princeton: Princeton Univ. Press, 1963), p. 11, fn.4

41. Speaight, *Poel,* p. 268. See also pp. 100, 102, 130, 255 and 258.

42. Monck, "Shakespeare and the Amateur," p. 323.

43. *Eastern Daily Press,* 9 May 1924.

44. *Eastern Evening News,* 21 Jan. 1947.

45. An examination of Monck's existing promptbooks does not clear up the matter of how much he cut the plays. Cuts indicated in them are often compilations from several productions and Monck did not feel obliged to adhere to what was in these books when he was producing. His recorded cuts can be seen in relation to those of numerous other producers in William P. Halstead, *Shakespeare as Spoken,* 12 vol. (Ann Arbor, Mich.: Monograph Publishing, Univ. Microfilms International, 1978–80).

46. Edward Gordon Craig, "The Chances For And Against Good Theatres," *The Mask,* July 1926, p. 113. Article is continued in Nov. 1926, pp. 142– 45.

47. *Eastern Daily Press,* 20 June 1936.

Chapter 5

1. *Madras Mail* [India], 4 Aug. 1928.

2. *Eastern Daily Press,* 9 Feb. 1926 and 21 Oct. 1927. All information on these tours came from Monck. There are no existing documents to indicate the sources of these offers or to substantiate that they were actually made.

3. *Eastern Evening News,* 18 Dec. 1928. Interestingly, when Charles Rigby published a collection of his own reviews five years later, he used for its title *Maddermarket Mondays* (Norwich: Roberts, 1933).

4. *"Six Characters* at Maddermarket," *The Festival Theatre Review,* 4 May 1929, pp. 7–8.

5. *London Reference,* 15 July 1930; *Shanghai Times,* 11 Aug. 1929; *Christian Science Monitor,* 6 Aug. 1926; *Argus,* 24 Aug. 1929.

6. *Daily Chronicle,* 20 Aug. 1929.

7. James Dixon, *The Canterbury Festival Plays in Production 1928–1958,* Diss. Northwestern Univ. (Ann Arbor: UMI, 1977).

8. This enthusiasm was due primarily to the highly favorable reviews which ran in *The Times* on Aug. 21 and the *Sunday Times* on Aug. 28, 1929.

9. *Eastern Evening News,* 9 Sept. 1929.

10. *Madras Mail,* 12 Oct. 1929.

11. Tyrone Guthrie, *Theatre Prospects,* (London: Wishart, 1932), p. 49.

12. Harold Ridge, *Stage Lighting* (Cambridge: Heffer, 1930), p. 176.

13. Ibid., p. 106.

14. *Eastern Daily Press,* 31 Oct. 1931.

15. *Eastern Evening News,* 19 Nov. 1929.

16. *The Times,* 19 Nov. 1929, *Times of Bombay,* n.d., (1929), in Monck Collection.

17. Hotspur (pseud.), *"Pericles* at Norwich," *The Shakespeare Pictorial,* Jan. 1930, p. 15.

18. *Eastern Evening News,* 19 Nov. 1929.

19. *Sunday Pictorial,* 12 Jan. 1930.

20. Letter received from Christopher Fry, 13 Apr. 1979.

21. Nugent Monck, "Review of *Pageants* by Anthony Parker," TS, 1954, in Monck Collection.

22. *Kettering Leader,* 9 May 1930.

23. *East Anglian Daily Times* [Ipswich], 30 June 1930.

24. Horace Shipp, "Theatre Art and Theatre Artists," *Artwork* (Spring 1929), 62.

25. Letter received from Andrew Stephenson, 9 Apr. 1979.

26. Harcourt Williams, *Old Vic Saga* (London: Winchester, 1949), p. 84.

27. Williams, p. 97.

28. Personal interview with Mrs. Owen P. Smyth, 19 Sept. 1979.

29. Three letters from Lilian Baylis to Nugent Monck are now in the Monck Collection. One dated 17 May 1928 reads, "I should like your opinion on King Lear and hope if you are in town you will make time to see it."

30. In Harley Granville-Barker, *Prefaces to Shakespeare,* Vol. 2, pp. xxiv-xxv.

31. Tyrone Guthrie, *A Life in the Theatre* (London: McGraw-Hill Paperbacks, 1959) p. 84.

32. Letter, n.d. [c. 1953], in Monck Collection.

33. *Eastern Evening News,* 31 July 1946.

34. *The Times,* 18 Feb. 1931; *Evening News,* 17 Feb. 1931; *Era,* 18 Feb. 1931.

35. Geoffrey Whitworth, "Where Amateurs Beat Professionals," *Daily News and Chronicle,* 7 Jan. 1931, p. 4; Geoffrey Whitworth, "The Amateur Movement in England," *Theatre Arts Monthly,* July 1931, p. 577.

36. Burgoyne Miller, "Theatres to Remember," *The Bookman,* Feb. 1931, p. 326.

37. *Eastern Daily Press,* 17 May 1932.

38. *Eastern Daily Press,* 1 Oct. 1936, report on Monck's lecture, "Drama in Education."

39. *Eastern Daily Press,* 8 Jan. 1914.

40. *Yarmouth Independent,* 15 Dec. 1926.

41. *Morning Post,* 27 Sept. 1921.

42. *Norwich Mercury,* 21 Jan. 1922.

43. *Eastern Daily Press,* 19 July 1922.

44. *Eastern Daily Press,* 8 Feb. 1924.

45. George Bernard Shaw, Letter to Nugent Monck, 25 Jan. 1923, property of Jack Hall.

46. Vince, *Theatre World,* March 1928, p. 26.

47. *Eastern Daily Press,* 5 Feb. 1926, report on Monck's lecture, "John Dryden."

48. *Yarmouth Independent,* 30 Nov. 1928.

49. George Bernard Shaw, Letter to Nugent Monck, 25 Jan. 1923. Property of Jack Hall.

50. Nevill Truman, "The Norwich Maddermarket Theatre," *Amateur Stage,* May 1929, p. 144.

51. *Eastern Evening News,* 10 Jan. 1928.

52. Letter, *Eastern Daily Press,* 17 Jan. 1933.

53. *Eastern Evening News,* 23 Jan. 1934, and *Eastern Daily Press,* 23 June 1936.

54. Hugh Hunt, "The Maddermarket, Norwich," *Theatre World,* Jan. 1934, p. 48.

55. *Shakespeare Newsletter,* Feb. 1953, p. 1.

56. *Norwich Mercury,* 24 June 1933.

57. Basil Maine, "The Norwich Players: Mr. Nugent Monck's Achievement," *Observer,* 24 June 1933.

58. *Eastern Evening News,* 20 June 1933.

59. Poel, *Manchester Guardian,* 1 Oct. 1921.

60. *Eastern Daily Press*, 16 Apr. 1924.

61. Letter received from Hugh Hunt, 31 Aug. 1979.

62. *Norwich Mercury*, 18 Nov. 1933.

63. Hunt, "The Maddermarket," *Theatre World*, Jan. 1934, p. 48.

64. *Eastern Daily Press*, 8 May 1950.

65. *East Anglian Daily Times* [Ipswich], 31 Dec. 1952.

Chapter 6

1. *Eastern Daily Press*, 3 Sept. 1934.

2. Elizabeth Heaton, "Remarks on the Production of Shakespeare," *London Mercury*, Feb. 1935, p. 402.

3. *Glasgow Harold*, 21 Nov. 1935.

4. Robert Speaight, *Shakespeare on the Stage* (London: Collins, 1973), p. 165.

5. Una Ellis-Fermor, "Timon of Athens," *English* 1, No. 1 (1936), 64. For an overview of this production see: Gary Jay Williams, "Stage History of Timon of Athens" in Rolf Soellner, *Timon of Athens: Shakespeare's Pessimistic Tragedy* (Columbus, Ohio: Ohio State Univ. Press, 1979), pp. 174–75.

6. *Eastern Daily Press*, 3 March 1931, report on Monck's lecture, "Timon of Athens."

7. *Punch*, 27 Nov. 1935, p. 608, is representative.

8. *The Stage*, 21 Nov. 1935.

9. *Eastern Evening News*, 25 June 1936.

10. *The Times*, 23 June 1936 and *Christian Science Monitor*, 1 July 1931.

11. *The Amateur Stage*, 24 Apr. 1936, p. 11.

12. Knight, *Shakespearian Production*, p. 22.

13. Child, *Review of English Studies* 2 (Apr. 1926), 7–12.

14. *Eastern Daily Press*, 12 June 1925.

15. Whiffler, "Over the Tea Table," *Eastern Evening News*, 14 May 1940.

16. Script now in the possession of Jack Hall.

17. Andrew Stephenson, "The Norwich Passion Play," *Theatre Arts Monthly* 24, No. 11 (1940), 296–98 and Whiffler, "Over the Tea Table," *Eastern Evening News*, 6 Feb. 1942.

18. See "Articles of Association" for the Maddermarket Theatre Trust, Ltd., 11 Aug. 1939, in Monck Collection and Maddermarket Theatre Trust, Ltd. subcommittee report, 15 July 1954, in Monck Collection.

19. *Eastern Daily Press*, 5 and 27 July 1941.

20. "London Letter," *The Dial* [New York], July 1924, p. 5.

21. See *Eastern Daily Press*, 7 Sept. 1942; and Ronald Harwood, *Sir Donald Wolfit* (London: Secker & Warburg, 1971), p. 158.

22. Speaight, *Shakespeare on Stage,* p. 229; also Gordon Crosse, *Shakespearian Playgoing 1890-1952* (London: Mowbray, 1953), p. 148.

23. The Donald Wolfit Company, Letter to Nugent Monck, n.d. 1946, in Monck Collection.

24. *Eastern Evening News,* n.d. 1951, in Monck Collection.

25. Alec McCowan, *Young Gemini* (London: Elm Tree, 1979), p. 75.

26. Speaight, *Shakespeare on Stage,* p. 242.

27. Letter received from Paul Scofield, 12 March 1979.

28. Some detailed description of this production can be found in Crosse, pp. 85-86, and T. C. Kemp and J. C. Trewin, *The Stratford Festival* (Birmingham: Cornish, 1953), pp. 215-16.

29. Marshall, *Other Theatre,* p. 95.

30. *Drama,* Oct. 1944, p. 4; *Eastern Daily Press,* 22 Oct. 1946; Eric Keown, "At the Play," *Punch,* 28 Nov. 1951, p. 618.

31. *Eastern Evening News,* 24 Sept. 1946.

32. See J. C. Trewin, *The Birmingham Repertory Theatre, 1913-1963* (London: Barrie and Rockliff, 1963), p. 154. fn., and *Eastern Daily Press,* 19 Aug. 1947.

33. *"The Scene wherein We Play In,"* p. 36.

34. Monck, *On Retiring.*

Chapter 7

1. *Eastern Evening News,* 22 Sept. 1952.

2. *Yarmouth Independent,* 15 Dec. 1926.

3. Nugent Monck, "Elizabethan Acting," *Theatre Newsletter,* 24 Nov. 1951, p. 5.

4. *East Anglian Daily Times* [Ipswich], 31 Dec. 1952.

5. *Eastern Daily Press,* 23 Sept. 1946.

6. Truman, *Amateur Stage,* May 1929, p. 144.

7. *East Anglian Daily Times,* 31 Dec. 1952.

8. *Eastern Daily Press,* 19 Dec. 1920.

9. Nugent Monck, "The Producer and His Place in the Theatre, II," *Yorkshire Post,* 11 Feb. 1930, p. 6.

10. Reyner Banham, "How I Learnt to Live with the Norwich Union," *The New Statesman,* 6 March 1964, p. 372.

11. Monck, *Yorkshire Post,* 11 Feb. 1930, p. 6.

12. Donald FitzJohn, "Nugent Monck, Obituary," *Drama* 51 (Winter 1958), 39.

13. Andrew Stephenson, "Monck: The Man," *Eastern Daily Press,* 2 Feb. 1978.

14. *The Times,* 8 Jan. 1953, p. 9b.

15. In Granville-Barker, Vol. 2, p. xxxiii.

16. Board of Education, p. 191.

17. *Maddermarket,* BBC radio, 17 Nov. 1960, Broadcast House Recording, No 26,625 front.

18. Julian Hall, "Nugent Monck," *Truth,* 2 Jan. 1953, p. 7.

19. *The Times,* 8 Jan. 1953, p. 9b.

20. William A. Armstrong, "Nugent Monck and the Maddermarket Theatre," *Theatre,* 13 Sept. 1952, p. 20.

21. *Eastern Evening News,* 10 Jan. 1933.

22. *Observer,* 15 May 1931.

23. Nugent Monck, "The Director as Artist," TS outline, in Monck Collection.

24. *Christian Science Monitor,* 8 Jan. 1928.

25. Marshall, *Other Theatre,* p. 95.

26. E. Veryman, Letter, *Eastern Daily Press,* 22 Oct. 1937.

27. Nugent Monck, "The Elizabethan Playhouse and Its Adaptability to Modern Use," lecture to the Colchester Stage Society. Reported in unidentified article, Monck Collection (brown scrapbook), p. 1, bottom, center.

28. Board of Education, p. 9.

29. Monck, "Dramatic Art and Mysticism," p. 13, lecture TS in Monck Collection.

30. *Eastern Daily Press,* 26 May 1939, report on Monck's lecture, "The Passion Play."

31. Monck, "Theatre," p. 63, lecture TS in Monck Collection.

32. "Personalities and Powers, Nugent Monck," *Time and Tide,* 8 Oct. 1926, p. 901.

33. Board of Education, p. 65.

34. *Eastern Daily Press,* 2 May 1924.

35. *"The Scene wherein We Play In,"* p. 35; see also *Yarmouth Independent,* 15 Dec. 1926.

36. *Eastern Daily Press,* 27 Dec. 1952.

37. Soman and Wheldon, p. 17.

38. Rodney Bennett, "Centres of Repertory, II. The Maddermarket Theatre, Norwich," *Musical News and Herald,* June 1927, p. 257.

39. *Irish Independent* [Dublin], 26 Aug. 1928.

40. Alice Wildey, "Play's The Thing At Maddermarket" *Springfield Sunday Union* [Mass.], 4 Aug. 1929.

41. Eric Fowler [Jonathan Mardle], "The Maddermarket," *Eastern Daily Press,* 23 Jan. 1960.

42. *Eastern Daily Press,* 23 Sept. 1946.

43. J[ohn] B[oynton] Priestley, *English Journey* (London: William Heineman and Victor Gollancz, 1934), pp. 198–99.

44. *Eastern Daily Press,* 6 Jan. 1952.

45. David Holbrook, Letter, *Eastern Daily Press,* 9 May 1951.

46. FitzJohn, "Monck Obituary," *Drama* 51, p. 38.

Bibliography

The Works of Nugent Monck
(All materials in this section are in the Monck Collection, County Local Studies Library, Norwich, England, unless otherwise noted)

BBC Radio Broadcasts

The Founding of the Norwich Players. 27 Dec. 1934 [not available].
On Retiring from the Maddermarket Theatre. 16 Nov. 1952. London, Broadcast House Recording Library, No. 17,955 back [Time 3' 37"].
"One Man in His Time," Reminiscent Talk by Nugent Monck on Retiring from Management of the Norwich Players, Part I (1878–1910), 3 Dec. 1952. TS of pp. 4–6 in Monck Collection. County Local Studies Library, Norwich, Eng. Part II (1910–21). 6 Jan. 1953. London, Broadcast House Recording Library, No. 19,670 sides 1 and 3, and No. 19,671 side 2 [Time 13' 34"].
Nugent Monck, Talk on the Maddermarket Theatre, Norwich. Interview with James Roose Evans. 8 Dec. 1954. TS in Monck Collection. County Local Studies Library, Norwich, Eng.
Contributor to: *Entertainment at St. George's Hall, 1867–1937.* 1 Nov. 1937 [summary in *EEN.* 2 Nov. 1937].
Contributor to: *"The Scene wherein We Play In."* See Other Sources.

Articles

"Elizabethan Acting." *Theatre Newsletter,* 24 Nov. 1951, p. 6.
"Maddermarket Jubilee." *Eastern Daily Press,* 23 Sept. 1946, p. 2ce.
"The Maddermarket Theatre." *Drama,* Oct. 1944, pp. 3–4.
"The Maddermarket Theatre." *Drama* NS 12 (Winter 1949), 19–21.
"The Maddermarket Theatre." *The Half Wheel* [Norwich, Magazine of Barnards, Ltd.], July 1952. Synopsis in *Eastern Daily Press,* 17 July 1952.
"The Maddermarket Theatre." *Theatre Arts* 15, No. 7 (1931), 581–82.
"The Maddermarket Theatre and the Playing of Shakespeare." *Shakespeare Survey* 12 (1959), 71–75.
"Nugent Monck Worked with William Poel." *Plays and Players,* March 1954, p. 8.
"Preface to *Pericles.*" *Penguin Parade.* 2nd ser., No. 1. Ed. J.E. Morpurgo. West Drayton, Eng.: Penguin Books, 1947, pp. 35–41.
"The Producer and His Place in the Theatre: II—Meeting the Needs of the Modern Stage." *The Yorkshire Post,* 11 Feb. 1930, p. 6. [Part I of this series was not by Monck.]
"Shakespeare and the Amateur." *The Listener,* 17 Feb. 1937, pp. 321–24.

Manuscripts

Autobiography outline. TS, n.d., 8 pp.
"From Hum to Hah: An Autobiography." TS (unfinished), n.d. [c. 1955], pp. 35–50.
"On Producing *Antony and Cleopatra*." Letter to Calvin Smith, 1956, 2 pp.
"Review of *Pageants* by Anthony Parker." TS, 1954, 5 pp. Review written for *Drama*.
"The Theatre." TS (unfinished), n.d., pp. 1–70.

Accessible Lectures by Nugent Monck; Typescripts, Outlines, Synopses

"The Development of the Elizabethan Stage, Being Four Lectures at Stratford-upon-Avon." TS
    outline, 1953, 80 words.
"The Director as Artist." TS outline, n.d., 3 pp.
"Dramatic Art and Mysticism in Modern Life." TS synopsis, n.d., 11 pp.
"Elizabethan Music." Synopsis in *Eastern Daily Press* [Norwich], 8 Nov. 1924.
"The Elizabethan Stage." TS, 1910, 23 pp.
"The Elizabethan Stage." TS synopsis, n.d., 10 pp.
"English Comedy." Synopsis in *Eastern Daily Press*, 3 Nov. 1926.
"English Drama from the Religious Cycles to Shakespeare's Life." TS outline, n.d., 2 pp.
"The First Theatre." TS, n.d., 4 pp.
"From the Restoration to Beerbohm Tree." TS, incomplete, n.d., 3 pp.
"The Greek Drama." TS, n.d., 5 pp.
"How to Produce a Pageant." Synopsis in *Lynn News*, 19 Mar. 1929.
"The Maddermarket Theatre." Synopsis in *Eastern Daily Press*, 9 May 1924.
"The Maddermarket Theatre." TS, n.d., 2 pp.
"The Maddermarket Theatre, Norwich." TS, n.d., 2 pp.
"Medieval Drama." Synopsis in *Eastern Daily Press*, 10 Sept. 1923.
"Modern Drama." TS synopsis, n.d., 6 pp.
"Modern Verse Drama." TS synopsis, n.d., 11 pp.
"The Norwich Experiment." Synopsis in *Norfolk Mercury*, 18 Dec. 1926.
"The Norwich Players." Synopsis in *Eastern Daily Press*, 5 Dec. 1922.
"The Norwich Players and Their Theatre." TS. synopsis, n.d., 2 pp.
"On Puppets." TS synopsis, 1953, 3 pp.
"The Rise of the Mystery Play." TS, n.d., 24 pp.
"The Roman Theatre." TS, n.d., 5 pp.
"Shakespeare and the Amateur." TS, 1929, 11 pp. Reprinted in *The Listener*, 17 Feb. 1937, pp.
    321–24.
"Shakespeare at the Maddermarket." Synopsis in *The Times*, 8 Jan. 1953.
"Shakespeare, His Life and Times." TS, n.d., 11 pp.
"Shakespeare's Characters." TS, n.d., 10 pp.
"Shakespeare's *Richard II*." TS outline, n.d., 1 p.
"Shakespearian Comedy." Synopsis in *Eastern Evening News* [Norwich], 18 Jan. 1933.
"Shaw's Later Plays." Synopsis in *Eastern Evening News*. 28 March 1933.
"Studies for the Production of *Troilus and Cressida*." TS outline, n.d., 60 words.
"The Theatre and the Amateur." TS outline, 1958, 3 pp.
"The Work of the Norwich Players." Summary in *Eastern Daily Press*, 8 May 1924.
Untitled lecture on drama between the two wars. TS outline, 5 pp.

Published Plays

The Big Field. Norwich: Mansfield, for Maddermarket Theatre Trust, 1955.

The Interlude of Holly and Ivy Made by Nugent Monck from Fifteenth Century Sources. Norwich: The Saint William Hand-Press, 1913. 150 copies printed.

Life's Measure: A Morality Play. London: Women's Printing Society, 1905.

The Mancroft Pageant. Norwich: Fletcher & Son, 1912.

Masque of Anne Boleyn. Norwich: Jarrold & Sons, 1909.

Narcissus: A Water Frolic in One Act. Plymouth, Eng.: William Brendon & Son, 1910.

The Norwich Mystery Play of Paradise. Prepared for Modern Representation. Norwich: Jarrold & Sons, 1910.

The Norwich Passion Play. Norwich: The Wherry Press, 1939.

The Pageant Play of King Arthur. Introd. Caroline A. Cannon. London: Women's Printing Society, 1913.

The Pilgrim's Progress. Adaptation of Bunyan. Norwich: Soman-Wherry Press, 1949.

Revelry: A Pageant Masque. Norwich: A. E. Soman & Co., 1921.

Wolsey Pageant: An Adaptation of Shakespeare's Henry VIII. Ipswich, Eng.: East Anglian Daily Times Co., 1930.

Ed. *The Interlude of Youth.* London: The Blackfriars Printers, for the English Drama Society, 1905.

With Martin Kinder. *Aucassin and Nicolette.* Norwich: Saint William Press, 1913.

Unpublished Plays

"Between the Showers." 2 parts. TS, 1910.

"Cinderella: A Pantomime." TS, 1917.

"Dragonflies: A Pastoral Play." TS, c. 1902.

"A Farce." MS. Unfinished.

"The Heavens Shall Laugh." TS, 1932.

"King John Comes to Wisbech 1215." TS, n.d.

"The Kingdom of Heaven." TS, c. 1907.

"A Little Light." TS, n.d.

"Love—the Pedlar." TS, 1908.

"Love's Litany: A Drama in One Act, in Rhythmic Prose." TS, c. 1902.

"The Mill." MS, 1907.

"The Pagan Heart." TS, 1909.

"Peter—the Fool." TS, 1908.

"The Primrose Way." TS, 1903.

"Robert, King of Sicily." Privately printed, 1924.

"The Ship Boy." TS, 1912. Rewritten with Martin Kinder as "Merchandise." TS, 1912.

"The Votaries." TS, 1908.

"The Cobbler, a Miracle Play." With Martin Kinder. MS, 1913.

"In the Beginning, a Garden Play." With Martin Kinder. TS, 1909.

"Merchandise." With Martin Kinder. TS, 1912.

Adaptations

"Gogol's Marriage." Trans. Constance Garnett. Lyrics by Nugent Monck. Music by G. F. Smyly. TS, 1932.

"Malvolio, Scenes from *Twelfth Night.*" TS, n.d.

"The Magic Casement: Arranged from Florentine Commedia dell'Arte." TS, 1924.
"Omar Khayyam: Stage Pictures." TS, 1919.
"Rosamunde: A Play to Schubert's Music, from Synopsis by Helmina von Cheay." TS, 1928.

Lost Scripts

"The Adversity of Advertisement." Produced 1903.
"The Angel Boy." Produced 1900.
"The Domestic Fowl." Produced 1903.
"The Hour." Produced 1907. Written c. 1905.
"The Man in Rags." Produced 1901.
"The Song of Songs." Produced 1908 and 1921.

Works on Nugent Monck and the Maddermarket Theatre

Books and Booklets

Hildy, Franklin Joseph. *Reviving Shakespeare's Stagecraft: Nugent Monck and the Maddermarket Theatre. Norwich, England.* Diss. Northwestern Univ. Ann Arbor: UMI, 1980.
Mottram, R[alph] H[ale]. *The Maddermarket Theatre.* Norwich: A. E. Soman Co., 1928.
_____. *The Norwich Players.* Norwich: A. E. Soman Co., 1936. [Rpt. of above work with expanded Introd. by Nugent Monck and updated list of plays.]
Rigby, Charles. *Maddermarket Mondays: Press Articles Dealing with the Famous Norwich Players.* Forward by Basil Maine. Norwich: Roberts and Co., 1933.
S[oman], M[ariette], and F. W. W[heldon]. *The Norwich Players: A History, an Appreciation, and a Criticism.* Norwich: Mariette Soman, 1920.
Stephenson, Andrew. *The Maddermarket Theatre, Norwich.* Norwich: Soman-Wherry Press for the Maddermarket Theatre Trust, 1971.

Periodical Articles

Armstrong, William A. "Nugent Monck and the Maddermarket Theatre." *Theatre* [formerly *Theatre Newsletter*], 13 Sept. 1952, pp. 19–20.
Barnes, T. R. "The Maddermarket Theatre." *Scrutiny* 4 (Dec. 1935), 255–62.
Bennett, Rodney. "Centres of Repertory, II. The Maddermarket Theatre, Norwich." *Musical News and Herald,* June 1927, pp. 256–57.
Birrell, Francis. "The Madder Market [*sic*] Theatre at Norwich." *New Statesman,* 7 Apr. 1923, p. 774.
_____. "The Drama: On Acting Shakespeare." *The Nation and the Athenaeum,* 12 Apr. 1824, pp. 49–50.
Blythe, Richard. "An Elizabethan Theatre." TS [c. 1945]. Nugent Monck Collection. County Local Studies Library, Norwich, Eng.
_____. "Nugent Monck and the Maddermarket Theatre." TS [c. 1945]. Nugent Monck Collection. County Local Studies Library, Norwich, Eng.
Burley, Theodore Le Gay. "The Norwich Players." In *Playhouses and Players of East Anglia.* Norwich: Jarrold and Sons, 1928, pp. 94–103.
Cheston, Forbes. "Walter Nugent Monck: A Memoir." TS, 1963. Property of Jack Hall, Pulham Market, Norfolk, Eng.
Christie, Diana. "The Maddermarket Theatre, an Appreciation." *Drama,* Oct. 1931, pp. 12–13.

Craig, Edward Gordon. "The Chances for and against Good Theatres, in Provincial Centres in England, with Special Reference to the Maddermarket Theatre of Norwich." *The Mask* 12, No. 3 (1926), 113–14, and 12, No. 4 (1926), 142–45.

Danvers-Walker, Bob. "Norwich—'As You Like It.'" *In Britain*, May 1964, pp. 34–35.

Eastman, Fred. "Religious Drama in England." *The Christian Century* [Chicago], 2 Oct. 1929, pp. 1212–14.

Ellis-Fermor, Una. *"Timon of Athens." English* 1, No. 1 (1936), 64.

Emerson, Ian. "The Maddermarket Theatre." *Norfolk Drama Bulletin,* No. 5 (Summer 1963), 5–11.

F. J. D. "The Norwich Players' Anniversary." *Theatre World* 17, No 89 (1932), 306.

FitzJohn, Donald. "The Theatre with an Ideal." *Country Life,* 13 Sept. 1946, p. 450.

————. "Nugent Monck, Obituary." *Drama* 51 (Winter 1958), 39.

Fowler, Eric. "A Maddermarket Centenary." *East Anglian Magazine* 37 (May 1978), 348–50.

Fox, R. M. "The Theatre Goes On: In England [Report by Ashley Dukes]." *Theatre Arts* 24, No 11 (1940), 786–90.

Gardner, H. Vernon. "Where the Play's the Thing: The Maddermarket Theatre." *The Scottish Stage,* June 1932, p. 94.

————. "The Maddermarket Theatre and its Shakespeare Record." *Drama,* July 1933, pp. 171–72.

Gargáno, G. S. "Per una Societá Drammatica." Il Marzocco [Florence], Abbonamento straordinario dal l* marzo al 31* dicembre 1907, 12 (3 marzo 1907), 1. [Trans. for the author by Roy Dehn.]

Guest, L. Haden. "Drama: An Orgy of Frohman and the Bijou Theatre." *The New Age,* 16 May 1907, p. 49.

————. "Mr. Nugent Monck's *Mill.*" *The New Age,* 8 July 1908, p. 58.

Hall, Julian. "Nugent Monck and 'The Maddermarket.'" *Truth,* 2 Jan. 1953, p. 7.

Hill, Ronald. "Norfolk No-Man's-Land." *Theatre World,* Sept. 1963, pp. 15–17.

Hills, Ross. "The Maddermarket Theatre, Norwich." *Tabs* 19 (Dec. 1961), 17–24.

Horsnell, Horace. "The Drama, Three Ibsen Heroines." *Outlook,* 31 March 1928, p. 410.

Hotspur (pseud.). "*Pericles* at Norwich." *The Shakespeare Pictorial* [Stratford-upon-Avon], Jan. 1930, p. 15.

Hunt, Hugh. "The Maddermarket, Norwich." *Theatre World,* Jan. 1934, p. 48.

J. M. "Review, 'Norwich Passion Play,' March 15–24, 1952." *Theatre Newsletter,* 29 March 1952, pp. 21–22.

Lorraine, Philip L. "The Maddermarket Theatre, Norwich." *Drama,* June 1936, pp. 18–19.

Maine, Basil. "For My Part." *Musical Opinion,* June 1932, p. 749.

Massingham, H. W. "Love's Labour's Lost." *The Speaker,* 28 Apr. 1906, p. 91.

Miller, Burgoyne. "Theatre to Remember: The Maddermarket, Norwich." *The Bookman* 79 (Feb. 1931), 326.

Mortimer, Raymond. "London Letter." *The Dial* [New York], July 1924, p. 5.

Mottram, Ralph Hale. "The Maddermarket." *War Time Drama,* Nov. 1942, pp. 5–6.

————. "The Norwich Players: Their Rise, Their Home, Their Career and Achievement." TS, 1956. Nugent Monck Collection. County Local Studies Library, Norwich, Eng.

"News and Topics." *The Amateur Stage,* Feb. 1934, p. 99.

Olland, Doremy. "The Maddermarket." *The Queen,* 15 Aug. 1928, p. 34.

Ottaway, June. "Nugent Monck of Norwich." *Christian Drama* 2 (Spring 1953), 21–23.

"Personalities and Powers, Nugent Monck." *Time and Tide,* 8 Oct. 1926, pp. 900–901.

Randall, Brett. "Little Theatres . . . No. 6, the Maddermarket, Norwich." *Foyer,* Sept.-Oct. 1946, p. 15.

R. H. "The Maddermarket Theatre, Norwich." *The Garrick Magazine* 10, No. 1, (1926), 1–5, and 10, No. 2 (1926), 19–22.

"Six Characters in Search of an Author at the Maddermarket Theatre, Norwich." *Festival Theatre Review,* 4 May 1929, pp. 7–8.

Solt, A. R. "The Maddermarket Theatre." *East Anglian Magazine* 16 (Nov. 1956), 38–39.

Stephens, Jan. "Monck of Maddermarket: A Model for a Southern Theatre." *Mainly Musical Magazine,* Feb. 1936, p. 213.

Stephenson, Andrew. Letter. *Norfolk Life* 1 (Feb. 1962), 50.

———. "The Maddermarket Theatre." *Norfolk Fair* 7 (July 1974), 36–38.

———. "The Maddermarket Theatre." *Norfolk Life* 1 (Nov. 1961), 22–23.

———. "The Maddermarket Theatre." *Theatre Arts* 7, No. 3 (1923), 203–12.

———. "The Maddermarket Theatre." *Theatre Arts* 12, No. 4 (1928), 288–90.

———. "The Maddermarket Theatre, Norwich: Official Opening of the New Extension." Programme. 19 Nov. 1966. Nugent Monck Collection. County Local Studies Library, Norwich, Eng.

———. "The Maddermarket Theatre: The Third Season (The Faithful Five Hundred)." Author's TS, 1924.

———. "The Norwich Passion Play." *Theatre Arts* 24, No. 11 (1940), 296–98.

———. "Players Anonymous." Author's MS, 1960.

———. *"Samson Agonistes."* *Theatre Arts* 22, No. 12 (1938), 914–16.

———. "Speech in Honour of Nugent Monck upon His Retirement." Author's MS, 1952.

———. "Walter Nugent Bligh Monck." Speech delivered to the Norwich Players and Associates. Author's MS, 1961.

Tenent, Rose. "Monck of Maddermarket." *Theatre World,* May 1948, pp. 34, 36–37.

"Theatricals in Alexandria." *The Near East,* 27 Apr. 1917, p. 585.

Trewin, J. C. "The World of the Theatre: Friends and Acquaintances." *Illustrated London News,* 8 Feb. 1958, p. 236.

Truman, Nevill. "The Norwich Maddermarket Theatre." *Amateur Stage,* May 1929, p. 144.

Vince, H. Watson. "The British Repertory Theatres No. X: The Maddermarket Theatre, Norwich." *Theatre World,* March 1928, pp. 26–27.

Wiltshire, Norman. "Nugent Monck and the Maddermarket." *New Reading in Norwich* [Norwich Central Library Publication], No. 117 (Feb. 1978), pp. 1–4.

Wood, E. J. "An Interesting Experiment." *The Gong* [Birmingham Repertory Theatre Publication], May 1922, pp. 245–48.

Newspaper Articles

Allen, Percy. "Maddermarket Theatre, Norwich, England." *Christian Science Monitor,* 24 Dec. 1923.

Aymes, Stephen. "The Norwich Players Celebrate Their Jubilee." *Eastern Evening News* [Norwich], 18 Nov. 1960.

Cook, R. W. "The Norwich Players: A Remarkable Civic Movement." *John O'London's Weekly,* 20 May 1922.

C. V. R. "Founder Lives on in Maddermarket Tradition." *Eastern Daily Press* [Norwich], 27 Sept. 1972.

Darlington, W. A. "Decentralisation, Provinces and Suburbs." *Daily Telegraph,* 17 May 1928.

E. S. A. "The Norwich Pageant." *Spectator,* 31 July 1926.

Fletcher, Stuart. "Mussolini Makes Shaw Re-Write Play." *Daily Herald,* 12 Oct. 1938.

Fowler, Eric [Jonathan Mardle]. "The Maddermarket." *Eastern Daily Press,* [Norwich], 23 Jan. 1960.

———. "Monck and the Maddermarket." *Eastern Daily Press,* 23 Oct. 1958, p. 4fg.

G. W. B. "The Maddermarket Theatre." *Observer,* 17 May 1931.

Hobson, Harold. "The Drama in Norwich." *Christian Science Monitor,* 5 Aug. 1939.

Holbrook, David K. "In Defence of the Maddermarket." Letter. *Eastern Evening News* [Norwich], 9 May 1951, TS, pp. 1–4.

Kinder, Martin. "Early Days with the Norwich Players." *Eastern Daily Press,* 9 Dec. 1960.

———. "More Memories of the Norwich Players." *Eastern Daily Press,* 3 Feb. 1961.

"The Maddermarket Theatre." *Christian Science Monitor,* 8 Jan. 1928.

Maine, Basil. "The Norwich Players: Mr. Nugent Monck's Achievement." *Observer,* 24 June 1933.

"Many Tributes to Mr. Nugent Monck." *Eastern Daily Press,* 23 Oct. 1958, p. 6ab.

Mardle, Jonathan (pseud.).

See Fowler, Eric.

Marshall, Norman. "The Experimental Theatre: Abolishing the 'Fourth Wall.'" *Yorkshire Post* [Leeds], 8 Apr. 1930.

"Norwich Players 50 Years Old." *Eastern Daily Press,* 4 Nov. 1960.

"Obituary, Mr. Nugent Monck." *Manchester Guardian,* 23 Oct. 1958.

Orr, Christine. "Diary." *Scots Observer,* 2 Apr. 1931.

Poel, William. "An Elizabethan Playhouse: The Norwich Enterprise." *Manchester Guardian,* 1 Oct. 1921.

"Rise of the Norwich Players." *Observer,* 28 June 1936.

Stephenson, Andrew. "How Pioneer Monck Took Charge." *Eastern Daily Press,* 19 Jan. 1978.

———. "Monck at the Maddermarket." *Eastern Daily Press,* 26 Jan. 1978.

———. "Monck the Man." *Eastern Daily Press,* 2 Feb. 1978.

———. "Obituary of Mr. Nugent Monck, Shakespeare in Norwich." *The Times,* 23 Oct. 1958, p. 7c.

———. "Silver Jubilee of the Norwich Players": Three articles for the *Eastern Daily Press.* "Nugent Monck and Their Early History," 4 June 1936. "Nugent Monck and Art Triumphs," 10 June 1936. "From Drawing-Room to Banquet Hall," 19 June 1936.

———. "When the Maddermarket Didn't Move." *Eastern Daily Press,* 31 Oct. 1966.

———. "World-Wide Recognition...A Powerful Force." *Eastern Daily Press,* 7 Feb. 1958.

Tyler, George. "The Maddermarket Theatre Festival." *Yorkshire Post,* 4 Aug. 1931.

Whitworth, Geoffrey. "Where Amateurs Beat Professionals." *Daily News and Chronicle,* 7 Jan. 1931, p. 4.

Wildey, Alice. "Play's the Thing at Maddermarket." *Springfield Sunday Union* [Springfield, Mass.], 4 Aug. 1929.

Interviews

Hall, Jack. Personal Interviews. 7 Oct. 1979 and 22 Jan. 1980.

Hewett, William. Personal Interview. 3 May 1979.

Smyth, Mrs. Owen Paul (Cecily). Personal Interview. 19 Sept. 1979.

Starling, Beryl. Personal Interview. 19 Sept. 1979.

Stephensen, Andrew. Personal Interviews. 20 Dec. 1978, 25 Dec. 1978, 23 Jan. 1979.

Stephenson, Betty. Personal Interview. 23 Apr. 1979.

Wilkes, Barbara. Personal Interviews. 16 Dec. 1978, 19 Oct. 1979, 20 Jan. 1980.

BBC Radio Broadcasts

The Maddermarket Theatre, Talk by Andrew Stephenson. Portrait of a City series. BBC radio overseas broadcast. Recorded 20 Nov. 1958. Andrew Stephenson's MS.

The Maddermarket Theatre Norwich: Programme to Mark Its Golden Jubilee and the Memory of Nugent Monck with Recorded Extracts from The Merchant of Venice. Signpost from East Anglia series. 17 Nov. 1960. London, Broadcast House Recording, No. 26,625 front.

"The Scene wherein We Play In": A Programme about the Maddermarket Theatre and the Guild of the Norwich Players. Producer James McFarlan. 11 Jan. 1953. TS in Monck Collection. [Title is quote from *As You Like It,* II, vii, 137–38.]

Tribute on the Twenty-fifth Anniversary of the Maddermarket Theatre, Norwich. Midland Home Service. 23 Sept. 1948. [Reported in *EDP,* 24 Sept. 1948. No other records found.]

Other Sources

Agate, James. *Brief Chronicles.* London: Jonathan Cape, 1943.

Bablet, Denis. *Edward Gordon Craig.* Trans. Daphne Woodward. New York: Theatre Arts Books, 1966.

Banham, Reyner. "How I Learnt to Live with the Norwich Union." *The New Statesman,* 6 March 1964, pp. 372–73.

Bell, G. K. "The Year in Review. A Summary of Addresses and Reports Given at the Annual General Meeting in November 1954. Speech by the Rt. Rev. The Lord Bishop of Chichester." *Christian Drama* 2 (Spring 1955), 15–16.

Bierstadt, Edward Hale. *Dunsany the Dramatist.* Boston: Little, Brown and Co., 1920.

Board of Education, Adult Education Committee. *The Drama in Adult Education.* Paper No. 6. London: His Majesty's Stationery Office, 1926.

Bridges-Adams, William. *A Bridges-Adams Letter Book.* Ed. with Memoir Robert Speaight. London: Society for Theatre Research, 1971.

———. *The British Theatre.* British Life and Thought, No. 14. London: Longmans Green for the British Council, 1946.

———. *The Irresistible Theatre.* Vol. 1. No subsequent vols. London: Secker and Warburg, 1957.

———. "Proscenium, Forestage and O." *Drama* 62 (Autumn 1961), 24–28.

Brockett, Oscar G. *History of the Theatre.* 3rd ed. Boston: Allyn and Bacon, 1977.

———. and Robert R. Findlay. *Century of Innovation: A History of European and American Theatre and Drama Since 1870.* Englewood Cliffs, NJ.: Prentice-Hall, 1973.

Browne, Maurice. *Too Late to Lament: An Autobiography.* London: Victor Gollancz, 1955.

Buston, W. "The Norman House in Norwich and the Music House." *Country Life,* 21 Aug. 1942, pp. 360–61.

Campbell, Andrew. "Calling Southern Rhodesia: The Theatre in Education." TS prepared for radio broadcast. Norwich, Eng., County Local Studies Library, Nugent Monck Collection, n.d., pp. 1–3.

Carter, Huntly. *The New Spirit in the European Theatre, 1914–1924.* London: Ernest Benn, 1925.

Casson, Sir Lewis. "William Poel and the Modern Theatre." *The Listener,* 10 Jan. 1952, pp. 56–57.

Cheney, Sheldon. *Stage Decoration.* New York: John Day, 1928.

Child, Harold. "Revivals of English Dramatic Works 1919–1925." *Review of English Studies* 2 (Apr. 1926), 7–12.

Cook, R. W. "The Norwich Players: A Remarkable Civic Movement." *John O'London's Weekly,* 20 May 1922.

Craig, Edward. *Gordon Craig.* New York: Alfred A. Knopf, 1968.

Crosse, Gordon. *Shakespearian Playgoing, 1890–1952.* London: A. R. Mowbray & Co., 1953.

Davis, Grenda D. "The Story of a House." In *Wensum Lodge.* Norwich Education Committee. Norwich: Morris Printing Co., n.d.

Dent, Alan. *Mrs. Patrick Campbell.* London: Museum Press, 1961.

Dixon, James George. "The Canterbury Festival Plays in Production, 1928–1958." Diss. Northwestern Univ. 1977.

Dobrée, Bonamy. "The Theatre." *The Spectator,* 31 Oct. 1931, p. 567.

Dukes, Ashley. *The Scene Is Changed.* London: Winchester Publications, 1948.

Ellis, Ruth Clive. *The Shakespeare Memorial Theatre.* London: Winchester Publications, 1948.

Ellis-Fermor, Una. *"Timon of Athens." English* 1, No. 1 (1936), 64.

Elson, John. *Theatre Outside London.* London: Macmillan & Co., 1971.

Farjeon, Herbert. *The Shakespearian Scene.* London: Hutchinson & Co., 1949.

Flannery, James W. *W. B. Yeats and the Idea of a Theatre.* New Haven: Yale Univ. Press, 1976.

Granville-Barker, Harley. *Prefaces to Shakespeare.* Ed. M. St. Clare Byrne. Vols. 1–4. Princeton, N.J.: Princeton Univ. Press, Princeton Paperbacks, 1965.

The Green Room Book and Who's Who on the Stage, 1907. London: T. Sealey Clark, 1907.

Gromme, Alan, comp. *William Poel and His Stage Productions, 1880–1932.* London: William Poel Portrait Committee, 1933.

Guthrie, Sir Tyrone. *A Life in the Theatre.* New York: McGraw-Hill, 1959.

———. *Theatre Prospect.* London: Wishart & Co., 1932.

Halstead, William P. *Shakespeare as Spoken: A Collation of 5000 Acting Editions and Promptbooks of Shakespeare.* 12 Vols. Ann Arbor, Mich.: Monograph Publishing, Univ. Microfilms International, 1978–80.

Harwood, Ronald. *Sir Donald Wolfit: His Life and Work in the Unfashionable Theatre.* London: Secker and Warburg, 1971.

Heaton, Elizabeth. "Remarks on the Production of Shakespeare." *London Mercury,* Feb. 1935, pp. 398–402.

Hodges, C. Walter. *The Globe Restored: A Study of the Elizabethan Theatre.* 2nd ed. London: Oxford Univ. Press, 1968.

———. *Shakespeare's Second Globe: The Missing Monument.* London: Oxford Univ. Press, 1973.

Hogan, Robert, Richard Burnham, and Daniel P. Poteet. *The Modern Irish Drama: A Documentary History,* vol. 4, *The Rise of the Realists 1910–1915.* Dublin: Dolmen Press, 1979.

Holbrook, David. *A Play of Passion.* London: W. H. Allen, 1978.

Holloway, Joseph. *Joseph Holloway's Abbey Theatre.* Ed. Robert Hogan and Michael J. O'Neill. Carbondale: Southern Illinois Univ. Press, 1967.

———. "Collection of Newscuttings on Theatre and the Arts." National Library of Ireland MSS. 23,100–123,151.

Hone, Joseph. *W. B. Yeats, 1865–1939.* 1943; rpt. London: Macmillan & Co., 1962.

Hosley, Richard. "The Origins of the So-Called Elizabethan Multiple Stage." *The Drama Review* 12 (Winter 1968), 28–50.

Hunt, Hugh. *The Abbey: Ireland's National Theatre, 1904–1979.* Dublin: Gill and Macmillan, 1979.

———. *The Live Theatre.* London: Oxford Univ. Press, 1962.

———. "Shakespeare and the Producer." *Drama* 22 (Autumn 1951), 34–35.

Inskip, D. P. "Some English Plays and Players of 1938." *The Outspan* [South Africa], 24 March 1939, pp. 13, 15, 99, 101.

Irving, Laurence Henry Forster. *Henry Irving: The Actor and His World.* London: Faber & Faber, 1951.

Kavanagh, Peter. *The Story of the Abbey Theatre, from Its Origins in 1899 to the Present*. New York: Devin-Adair Co., 1950.

Kemp. T. C., and J. C. Trewin. *The Stratford Festival: A History of the Shakespeare Memorial Theatre* Birmingham, Eng.: Cornish Brothers, 1953.

King, T. J. *Shakespearean Staging, 1599–1642*. Cambridge, Mass.: Harvard Univ. Press, 1971.

Knight, G. Wilson. *Shakespearian Production: With Especial Reference to the Tragedies*. 3rd ed. Evanston, Ill.: Northwestern Univ. Press, 1964.

Lawrence, William John. *The Elizabethan Playhouse and Other Studies*. 2 vols. Stratford-upon-Avon: Shakespeare Head Press, 1912–13.

_____. *Pre-Restoration Stage Studies*. Cambridge, Mass.: Harvard Univ. Press, 1927.

Loewenberg, Alfred. *The Theatre of the British Isles Excluding London: A Bibliography*. London: Society for Theatre Research, 1950.

McCowan, Alec. *Young Gemini*. London: Elm Tree Press, 1979.

Mandar, Raymond, and Joe Mitchenson. *The Lost Theatres of London*. New York: Taplinger Publishing Co., 1968.

Marshall, Norman. *The Other Theatre*. London: John Lehmann, 1947.

_____. *The Producer and the Play*. 2nd ed. London: Macdonald, 1962.

_____. "The Production of Shakespeare's Plays To-day." *The Bookman*, Apr. 1932, pp. 63–64.

Moussinac, Leon. *The New Movement in the Theatre: A Survey of Recent Developments in Europe and America*. Foreword Gordon Craig. London: B. T. Batsford, 1931.

Nagler, Alois Maria. *Shakespeare's Stage*. Trans. Ralph Menheim. New Haven: Yale Univ. Press, 1958.

Nicoll, Allardyce. *English Drama 1900–1930: The Beginnings of the Modern Period*. Cambridge: At the Univ. Press, 1973.

Norfolk Drama Committee. *East Anglian Theatre: An Exhibition Devoted to the History of the Players and Playhouses of Norfolk and Suffolk, Castle Museum, Norwich, 3rd May-3rd June, 1952*. Comp. J. A. Mitchley. Norwich, Eng.: The Gallpen Press, 1952.

Orrell, John. *The Quest for Shakespeare's Globe*. Cambridge: Cambridge Univ. Press, 1983.

Peach, L. Du Garde. "I Look Around Little Theatres." *The Landmark*, Jan. 1931, pp. 29–32.

Picton, J. W. *A Great Gothic Fane: A Retrospect of Catholicity in Norwich*. Norwich, Eng.: n.p., 1913.

Playfair, Sir Nigel. *The Duenna by Richard Brinsley Sherdan, with Illustrations of the Hammersmith Production by George Sheringham*. London: Constable & Co., 1925.

_____. *Hammersmith Hoy*. London: Faber & Faber, 1930.

Poel, William. *Monthly Letters*. Selected and arranged by A. M. T[rotheway]. London: T. Werner Laurie, 1929.

_____. *Shakespeare in the Theatre*. London: Sedgwick and Jackson, 1913.

_____. *What Is Wrong with Our Stage*. London: Allen and Unwin, 1920.

Priestley, J[ohn] B[oynton]. *English Journey*. London: William Heineman and Victor Gollancz, 1934.

Purdom, C. B. *Producing Plays*. London: Dent, 1930.

Reynolds, George Fullmer. *The Staging of Elizabethan Plays: At the Red Bull Theatre, 1605–1625*. New York: MLA, 1940.

Ridge, C. Harold. *Stage Lighting*. Cambridge: W. Heffer & Sons, 1930.

Robinson, Lennox. *Ireland's Abbey Theatre: A History, 1899–1951*. London: Sedgwick and Jackson, 1951.

Ruskin, John. *The Stones of Venice*. Vol. 2. London: Smith, Elder & Co., 1853.

St. Clair Byrne, Muriel. "Stage Lighting," *The Oxford Companion to the Theatre*. Ed. Phillis Hartnoll. 3rd. ed. London: Oxford Univ. Press, 1967.

Shipp, Horace. "Theatre Art and Theatre Artists." *Artwork* 5 (Spring 1929), 60–64.

Sidnell, Michael J. *Dances of Death: The Group Theatre of London in the Thirties.* London: Faber and Faber, 1984.

Sinden, Donald. *Laughter in the Second Act.* London: Hodder & Stoughton, 1985.

―――. *A Touch of the Memoirs.* London: Hodder & Stoughton, 1982.

Speaight, Robert. *Shakespeare on the Stage: An Illustrated History of Shakespearian Performance.* London: Collins, 1973.

―――. *William Poel and the Elizabethan Revival.* London: Society for Theatre Research, 1954.

Sprague, Arthur Colby. *Shakespearean Players and Performances.* Cambridge, Mass.: Harvard Univ. Press, 1953.

Stinson, James. "Reconstructions of Elizabethan Public Playhouses." In *Studies in the Elizabethan Theatre.* Ed. Charles T. Prouty. Hamden, Conn.: The Shoe String Press, 1961, pp. 55–136.

Styan, John L. *The Shakespeare Revolution.* Cambridge: Cambridge Univ. Press, 1977.

Talbot, Godfrey. "The Leeds Civic Playhouse." *Drama,* Feb. 1931, pp. 582–86.

Trewin, John Courtenay. *The Birmingham Repertory Theatre, 1913–1963.* London: Barrie and Rockliff, 1963.

―――. *We'll Hear a Play.* London: Carroll and Nicholson, 1948.

―――. *Shakespeare on the English Stage, 1900–1964: A Survey of Productions Illustrated from the Raymond Mander and Joe Mitchenson Theatre Collection.* London: Barrie and Rockliff, 1964.

Weales, Gerald Clifford. *Religion in Modern English Drama.* Philadelphia: Univ. of Pennsylvania Press, 1961.

Whitworth, Geoffrey. "The Amateur Movement in England." *Theatre Arts Monthly,* July 1931, pp. 572–78.

Williams, Gary Jay. "Stage History of Timon of Athens." In Rolf Soellner, *"Timon of Athens: Shakespeare's Pessimistic Tragedy."* Columbus, Ohio: Ohio State Univ. Press, 1979.

Williams, Harcourt. *Old Vic Saga.* London: Winchester Publications, 1949.

Williamson, Audrey. *Theatre of Two Decades.* London: Rockliff, 1951.

Wilson, Andrew P. "Dublin Days—and Nights—II." *The Scottish Stage,* Nov. 1933, pp. 181, 184.

Yeats, W. B. "Letters to Lady Gregory, 1897–1931." Xerox copies (originals in the possession of Michael B. Yeats, 1970). Irish National Library MSS. 18,695–18,747.

Index

Plays mentioned but not discussed in the text have not been indexed. Such plays can be looked up alphabetically by title in appendices B or C, and then cross-referenced in appendix A.

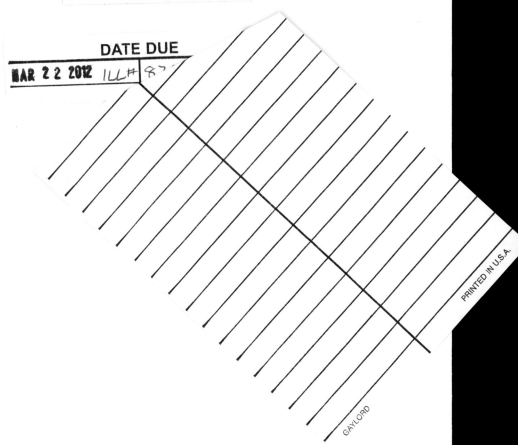